MENTAL HEALTH AND WELL-BEING INTERVENTIONS IN SPORT

Mental health within elite sport has traditionally been ignored, but recent research has shown that competitive sport can at times seriously undermine mental health and that athletes are exposed to specific stressors that hinder their mental health optimisation.

Mental Health and Well-being Interventions in Sport provides an indispensable guide for researchers and practitioners wanting to understand and implement sport-based intervention processes. This important book adopts an evidenced based approach, discussing the context of the intervention, its design and implementation, and its evaluation and legacy. With cases on depression, eating disorders, and athletic burnout, the book is designed to provide practitioners, policy makers and researchers with a cutting-edge overview of the key issues involved in this burgeoning area, while also including cases on how sport itself has been used as a method to improve mental health.

Written for newcomers and established practitioners alike, the text is an essential read for researchers and practitioners in better understanding the sport setting-based intervention processes through presenting current research, theory and practice, applicable in a variety of sports settings and contexts.

Gavin Breslin is the former Head of School of Sport and a Senior Lecturer at Ulster University, UK.

Gerard Leavey is Director of the Bamford Centre for Mental Health and Well-being at Ulster University, UK.

Routledge Psychological Interventions

Organizational Interventions for Health and Well-being
A Handbook for Evidence-Based Practice
Ed. By Karina Nielsen and Andrew Noblet

Mental Health and Well-Being Interventions in Sport
Research, Theory and Practice
Ed. By Gavin Breslin and Gerard Leavey

For more information about this series, please visit: www.routledge.com/series-title/book-series/rpi

MENTAL HEALTH AND WELL-BEING INTERVENTIONS IN SPORT

Research, Theory and Practice

Edited by
Gavin Breslin and Gerard Leavey

Routledge
Taylor & Francis Group

LONDON AND NEW YORK

First published 2019
by Routledge
2 Park Square, Milton Park, Abingdon, Oxon OX14 4RN

and by Routledge
52 Vanderbilt Avenue, New York, NY 10017

Routledge is an imprint of the Taylor & Francis Group, an informa business

British Library Cataloguing-in-Publication Data
A catalogue record for this book is available from the British Library

Library of Congress Cataloging-in-Publication Data
A catalog record has been requested for this book

ISBN: 978-1-138-50549-0 (hbk)
ISBN: 978-1-138-55171-8 (pbk)
ISBN: 978-1-315-14770-3 (ebk)

Typeset in Bembo
by Apex CoVantage, LLC

Printed and bound in Great Britain by
TJ International Ltd, Padstow, Cornwall

CONTENTS

CONTRIBUTORS

Jamie B. Barker, PhD, CPsychol, HCPC Reg, CSci. Jamie is Associate Professor of Applied Sport and Performance Psychology at Staffordshire University, UK. Jamie conducts internationally recognised research in the area of applied psychology and has an extensive range of applied practice with many groups in high performance environments (e.g., elite sport, business, military, health).

Hannah Sian Baumer, MSc Forensic Psychology and current doctoral candidate in the School of Law at Royal Holloway, University of London. Hannah researches the relationship between motivation, physical activity and wellbeing in prisons.

Jürgen Beckmann, PhD, is Professor and Chair of Sport Psychology, Department of Sport and Health Sciences, Technical University of Munich.

Gavin Breslin, PhD, is the former Head of School of Sport at Ulster University. Gavin's research and teaching interests explore the psychology of performance, mental health and wellbeing. He is a member of the Sport and Exercise Science Research Institute (SESRI), and The Bamford Centre for Mental Health and Wellbeing. He is a British Psychological Society (BPS) Chartered Sport and Exercise Psychologist, a registered practitioner of the Health Care Professions Council (HCPC), and a fellow of the Higher Education Academy. Gavin has led on policy development and has consulted with national and international athletes and teams in sport psychology. His research was instrumental in establishing the national Action Plan for Wellbeing in Sport in Northern Ireland (2018–2023).

Bradley Donohue, PhD, is a licenced psychologist and Full Professor in the Psychology Department at the University of Nevada, Las Vegas.

Marina Galante, M.S., is a clinical psychology doctoral candidate at University of Nevada, Las Vegas.

Yulia Gavrilova, M.A., is a clinical psychology doctoral candidate at University of Nevada, Las Vegas.

Tandy Jane Haughey is a lecturer in Sports Coaching and researcher in athlete mental health and wellbeing.

Diarmuid Hurley is a Doctor of Philosophy (Psychology) candidate. She has a Bachelor's degree in Psychology and Sociology and an MSc in Sport and Exercise Psychology. The focus of Diarmuid's research is the application of psychological principles in the sport and exercise domains for performance improvement, take up and maintenance of healthy behaviours and the link between sport and exercise participation and wellbeing.

Jon Jones is Partnership Development and Engagement Manager in the Faculty of Education at Edge Hill University, UK. He leads the Tackling the Blues project delivered in collaboration with Everton in the Community, which received the Most Outstanding Contribution to the Community Award at the Times Higher Education Awards in 2016.

Martin Lawlor, PhD, was the co-founder of State of Mind Ireland, a Psychiatrist, with the Health Service Executive, South Cork, Ireland and an athlete mental health advocate.

Gerard Leavey is Director of the Bamford Centre for Mental Health and Wellbeing at the University of Ulster. His work ranges from epidemiological studies on ethnic elders and refugee children to qualitative investigations of community level agencies such as sport, schools and faith based organisations and their role in the recognition and management of mental illness. Current research includes studies on young people, trust and help-seeking, mental health promotion evaluations in sport, and service use in the context of suicide in Northern Ireland.

Sarah K. Liddle, Doctor of Philosophy (Clinical Psychology) Candidate, Bachelor of Psychology (Honours). Sarah's research focuses on the prevention of mental illness and the promotion of help-seeking among adolescents in sport. With a background in both research and clinical psychology, Sarah is interested in the important relationship between mental health, physical activity and sports participation.

Rosie Meek is Head of the Law School at Royal Holloway University of London, with research expertise in sport in prisons.

Drew Neill is Student Health & Wellbeing Adviser at Ulster University.

Insa Nixdorf is Research associate at the Chair of Sport Psychology, Department of Sport and Health Sciences, Technical University of Munich.

Raphael Nixdorf is Research associate at the Chair of Sport Psychology, Department of Sport and Health Sciences, Technical University of Munich.

Helen O'Keeffe is Associate Dean in the Faculty of Education at Edge Hill University, UK. She has a PhD in Education and her research interests focus on the children and families of prisoners, mental health and wellbeing in children, qualitative studies relating to marginalised groups, community working and the role of the new professional and social justice.

Matthew Schweickle, Doctor of Philosophy (Psychology) Candidate, Bachelor of Psychology (Honours), Bachelor of Commerce (Marking). Matthew's research primarily focuses on exploring strategies to help athletes optimise their subjective experience during sport and exercise. In addition, Matthew is interested in the relationship between mental health and sport and exercise, specifically in exploring the benefits sport and exercise participation may have on mental health.

Stephen Shannon is a lecturer in sport and exercise psychology, and a researcher in mental health and wellbeing.

Andy Smith is Professor of Sport and Physical Activity in the Department of Sport and Physical Activity at Edge Hill University, UK. His research interests centre on the links between sport, education and (mental) health and leads the University's work on health and wellbeing with Everton in the Community.

Christian Swann is Senior Lecturer in Psychology, Doctor of Philosophy (Sport Psychology), BASES Accredited Sport and Exercise Scientist (Applied Psychology). Christian's research focuses on enhancing performance and wellbeing in sport and exercise. His primary interests are in the psychological states experienced during excellent performance and enjoyable exercise, the role of goal setting in exercise adherence, and the promotion of mental health and resilience through sport.

Martin J. Turner, PhD, CPsychol, HCPC Reg, CSci, Martin is a Senior Lecturer in Sport and Exercise Psychology at Staffordshire University, UK. He is a researcher, chartered consultant psychologist (BPS, HCPC Reg., CSci) and book author. He is most known for his work examining the use of Rational Emotive Behaviour Therapy (REBT) within performance settings. Martin works within elite sport (Lead Psychologist for FA England Futsal), and private and public sector organisations.

Stewart A. Vella, Doctor of Philosophy (Psychology), Dr Vella is a Senior Lecturer in the School of Psychology at the University of Wollongong. He is also a Movember Foundation Men's Health Partner. Dr Vella is a developmental sport psychologist with specific expertise in the relationships between sport participation and multiple indicators of health during childhood and adolescence. His focus is primarily on mental health. Dr Vella has over $5 million in competitive grant funding. He is currently Associate Editor at the Journal of Applied Sport Psychology.

Andrew G. Wood, BSc, MSc, MBPsS, FHEA, Andrew is a Lecturer in Sport and Exercise Psychology at Staffordshire University, UK and currently completing a PhD investigating the effects of Rational Emotive Behaviour Therapy on athletic performance. Andrew is also coming towards the end of his training as Sport and Exercise Psychologist with the British Psychological Society and is currently working as the Lead Psychologist with the England Blind Football Team.

David Woods has a Doctorate of Philosophy (Psychology), MSc in Sport and Exercise Psychology, and an MSc in Organisational Psychology. David's research explores the use of sport and exercise based interventions to benefit the mental wellbeing of people in prison.

1

GETTING STARTED

An overview

Gavin Breslin and Gerard Leavey

Introduction

Mental health has been defined as 'a state of well-being in which every individual realises his or her own potential, can cope with the normal stresses of life, can work productively and fruitfully, and is able to make a contribution to her or his community' (World Health Organization, 2014). Mental illness, in its various forms, accounts for most of the global disease burden and is enormously costly to the individual and society. It is important therefore, to develop low-cost and acceptable interventions that promote resilience and well-being.

The salutogenic aspects of sport participation, particularly through physical activity is well-established. However, paradoxically perhaps, recent evidence suggests that competitive sport may undermine mental health and that athletes are exposed to specific stressors that hinder their mental health optimisation. These stressors are: pressure to achieve success; long periods of separation from family; negative psychological sequelae following injury; alcohol and substance misuse; fear of failure and social opprobrium; relationship difficulties and interpersonal conflict; financial and employment difficulties. To date, there is a paucity of published interventions that offer guidance on how to improve the mental health of those who participate in sport. The chapters within this book describe programmes that are intended to inform the reader of how to use research, theory and integrate into practice from international experts in the field of sport psychology.

Going back to the ancient Greeks and Romans, Western societies have adopted a view of athletes as paragons of health and attendant virtues of discipline, morality, strength and beauty. Lionised, almost in the creative arts and literature, a more realistic understanding of athletes and athleticism has seldom been examined (Golden, 1998; Kyle, 2007). Traditionally, athletes have been poorly supported to manage their mental health needs and, moreover, mental health promotion within sports settings are considered as superfluous and irrelevant. Instead, like the ancient Greek gymnasia, sport club culture celebrates mental toughness and disapproval of weakness disclosure. Consequently, emotional and psychiatric problems can remain hidden, with the stigma of mental illness preventing athletes from seeking timely and appropriate help. Furthermore coaches, that is those who instruct athletes on technique, lifestyle and key decisions for success can also experience stressors and require support for managing their mental health. Our discussions with coaches suggests that all too often they strive to exude a steely projection of confidence and composure, while inwardly feeling fragile and vulnerable within a culture that demands peak performance and rewards winning. Unfortunately, athletes and coaches alike are often trapped in a culture of denial in which the mental health costs are high.

There has been a recent surge of interest in supporting the mental health and well-being of those involved in sport and their supporters (e.g., athletes, coaches, officials, parents, fans and the local community). Commendably, several psychological approaches and theoretical frameworks have been applied in attempts to tackle mental health and well-being of athletes, but theory, policy and practice in this field is still embryonic. Such approaches include, i) increasing knowledge about mental health to aid prevention and promote help seeking, ii) the development of cognitive-behavioural techniques to enhance coping (i.e., mindfulness, resilience, rational emotive behaviour therapy), and iii) the use of sport organisations to engage groups (i.e., men, those from low income areas) to promote psychosocial well-being.

What is this book about?

The development of mental health and well-being interventions in sport settings remain relatively underdeveloped and often poorly theorised (Breslin, Shannon, Haughey, Donnelly, & Leavey, 2017). This book is about applying psychology to the development of interventions to enhance mental health and well-being of those involved in participating in competitive sport (athletes, coaches). Our focus is on the design process and the content of the interventions, with an emphasis on methodological advances and what has been shown to improve awareness of mental health and well-being. Our principal goal is to help researchers and practitioners to understand better, the sport setting-based intervention processes through presenting current research, theory and practice, applicable in an interesting variety of sports settings and contexts. In doing so, the authors encourage a transition from theory to the practical aspects of conducting and evaluating mental health and well-being interventions in and through sport.

Ultimately, we intend that this book will stimulate interventions in the area of sport. More specifically, the authors of each chapter have highlighted the foundations of sport for mental health and well-being interventions. Drawing from their own activities and experience, the authors provide guidance on how to plan, design and select an appropriate programme content, and then how to implement and evaluate such interventions. The chapters of this book will support newcomers as well as established practitioners. Two sub-sections will include: i) mental health awareness programmes for athletes and coaches and ii) mental health awareness programmes for the public delivered through sport.

Section 1: Development of mental health awareness programmes for athletes, coaches and parents

In Chapter 2, *Galante, Donohue and Gavrilova* present The Optimum Performance Programme in Sport (TOPPS) to a lean sport athlete experiencing eating disorder pathology, whilst at college in the United States of America. Based on Family Centred Therapy (FCT), the authors use a unique adaptation of FCT to sport culture. They sought to examine improvements in sport performance, relationships and mental health among a vulnerable population but do so in a non-stigmatising manner and context. The authors provide recommendations for enhancing college athlete mental health and grapple with the challenges of engaging athletes in positive mental health through on-campus services.

In Chapter 3, *Insa Nixdorf, Beckmann and Raphael Nixdorf* summarise recent studies among athletes experiencing depression, burnout and chronic stress. They provide a description of how group coaching of junior elite athletes of the Bavarian Swim Association can help prevent the emergence of psychological problems. Interventions including mindfulness, cognitive-behavioural therapy and imagery were applied with positive outcomes for depression, burnout and chronic stress. The authors suggest that the diathesis-stress model once adapted can be successfully applied within sport environments to address the needs of junior elite swimmers.

In Chapter 4, *Wood, Turner and Barker,* based in England, (they) build on their ongoing work in England on Rational Emotive Behaviour Therapy (REBT) to promote psychological well-being with a Paralympic athlete. REBT offers a valuable intervention to understand and facilitate mental health in athletes. Using the ABC (DE) framework the intervention consisted of five one-to-one sessions lasting 30-minutes each. The intervention evaluation and the accompanying insightful reflections are discussed in terms of intervention effects, professional competence, the blurred boundaries between therapy and mental skills training, consultant's experience and practical guidelines for practitioners.

In Chapter 5 *Breslin, Haughey, Shannon and Neill* provide a description of their State of Mind Ireland intervention for university student athletes. This multicomponent programme delivered in partnership with students, staff and student support services was a response to the paucity of evidence based programmes designed to enhance mental health awareness of student athletes. Knowledge of mental health and intentions to offer support to peers increased for the intervention group, and remained the same for the control group. The programme with some modification is currently being integrated into university courses beyond sport to promote mental health awareness.

Views of students and a summary of ongoing theory based interventions are outlined by the authors. Chapter 6, *Liddle, Hurley, Schweickle, Swann and Vella*, present Ahead of the Game (AOTG), a multi-component mental health awareness and prevention programme that was delivered through community sports clubs in Australia. The programme includes two interventions for adolescents targeting mental health literacy and resilience, a parent mental health literacy intervention, and an intervention for coaches aimed at helping to facilitate self-determined motivation. Using a Community Based Participatory Research (CBPR) framework, AOTG was tested in organised sporting clubs at a community level. The authors provide insight into the development and delivery of the programme. Of particular interest are the online modules for adolescents and the references to evidence for the AOTG programme. Ideas for those developing programmes of this nature in the future are described.

Section 2: Engaging the wider community in mental health awareness through sport

In Section 2, we focus on how sport has been used to promote mental health awareness programmes in the community. The three chapters offer a thorough presentation of theory, research and practice intended for use among researchers in the design of community-based projects that promote mental health. In Chapter 7 *Jones, O'Keeffe and Smith* discuss the key theoretical assumptions and design principles which were used to inform the development of Tackling the Blues, a sport and education-based mental health awareness programme delivered by the official charity of Everton, the English Premier League Football Club. Tackling the Blues is delivered in schools and community settings by staff and student mentors trained in accredited mental health awareness courses. The authors reflect upon the effectiveness of the programme in its use for training undergraduate student peer mentors in programme delivery and the co-production of knowledge suitable for delivery in schools and hard-to-reach groups, mainly men in working-class communities. Particularly interesting and somewhat surprising, the programme reveals that once engaged, the appeal of the brand of a professional football club became progressively less important than other important mental health features of the programme design.

Baumer and Meek in Chapter 8 present the Cell Workout programme to engage prisoners in looking after their mental health. The authors highlight how prisons frequently fail to adopt a proactive approach to improving mental health and wellbeing through physical activity. Given the restrictive physical space associated with a cell in prison, the authors show individuals can overcome such barriers to remain active for mental health. A reflection is provided on the process of using both physiological and psychological outcome measures within a prison environment.

The theme of mental health and prisons is continued in Chapter 9 by *Woods and Breslin* in which they describe the Active Choices in Rugby Programme for prisoners. Prisons are often viewed, with much supporting evidence, as forbidden places in which attempts to undertake research have failed as often as prison breakouts! However, introducing sport and encouraging exercise in prisons may offer a partial solution to the very high levels of mental illness and suicide. In this chapter, the authors consider some of the challenges faced by the researchers. They also challenge the myths of prison environments. Of particular interest is the reflection piece that will be very informative for those about to embark on mental health in sport prison research. The authors discuss the development of the programme, efforts used to engage prisoners and the important and overlooked role and identity maintenance of the researcher during the project.

Finally, in Chapter 10, a critical reflection and the way forward for mental health in sport are presented. Specific focus will be on intervention evaluation, depth of practitioner reflections, intervention effects, professional competence, professional boundaries and practical guidelines for practitioners. Collectively, we hope you enjoy reading this textbook that emphasises the benefits of considering research, theory and practice in promoting mental health in sport. We also wish that as well as developing an appreciation for the strives made by the authors in bringing about positive changes to many people's lives, you take this information and apply it in your own practice, with an open mind that you to will reflect on your practice for the improvement of mental health in sport.

References

Golden, M. (1998). *Sport and society in ancient Greece*. Cambridge: Cambridge University Press.

Kyle, D. G. (2007). *Sport and spectacle in the ancient world*. Malden, MA and Oxford: Wiley-Blackwell.

World Health Organization. (2014). *Mental health: A state of well-being*. Geneva: World Health Organization.

SECTION 1

Development of mental health awareness programmes for athletes, coaches and parents

2

THE OPTIMUM PERFORMANCE PROGRAMME IN SPORTS

A case of bulimia nervosa in a lean sport athlete

Marina Galante, Bradley Donohue and Yulia Gavrilova

After reading this chapter you should be able to:

1　Understand how sport culture relates to the development of mental health difficulties, particularly eating disorders, in student-athletes.
2　Learn how to adapt mental health interventions to be sensitive to sport culture and engage athletes in performance programming services.
3　Understand core interventions of The Optimum Performance Programme in Sports (TOPPS) and how these interventions can be utilised to address a range of mental health concerns.
4　Appreciate the process for critically evaluating treatment programmes designed for student-athletes.

Introduction to the theme

This chapter will describe a controlled implementation of The Optimum Performance Programme in Sports (TOPPS) in a lean sport athlete demonstrating eating disorder pathology who previously rejected a campus-based psychological intervention programme. Of particular interest to the current case is the high prevalence of eating disorders in lean sports. Lean sports are characterised as sports that place high emphasis on appearance, such as figure skating, gymnastics and long distance running (Reardon & Factor, 2010; Sundgot-Borgen & Torstveit, 2010). In a sample of Australian female elite athletes, Byrne and McLean (2002) determined that 15% of lean athletes evidence either bulimia nervosa or anorexia nervosa, whereas these conditions are estimated to occur in only 2% of non-lean sport athletes and only 1% in non-athletes. More recent research has confirmed that lean sport athletes evidence higher instances of eating disorders than other sport athletes and non-athletes (Kong & Harris, 2015; Sundgot-Borgen & Torstveit, 2004, 2010; Torstveit, Rosenvinge, & Sundgot-Borgen, 2008).

Unfortunately, there are no known standardised and evidence-supported interventions designed to treat eating disorders in athlete populations specifically. This can pose substantial difficulties for athletes seeking treatment to prevent the host of negative consequences often associated with eating disorders, like malnourishment and dehydration, decreased concentration, lowered aerobic capacity, depleted energy, reproductive health difficulties and even death (Keski-Rahkonen & Mustelin, 2016; O'Brien, Whelan, Sandler, Hall, & Weinberg, 2017; Thompson & Sherman, 2007). Additionally, eating disorders in athletes may be particularly difficult to treat due to the pervasiveness of sport-related pressures to stay thin (Ferrand, Magnan, Rouveix, & Filaire, 2007). Combined with athlete tendencies to avoid treatment (Watson, 2005) and a lack of university sport psychologists employed to concurrently address mental health and sport performance optimisation (Cannole et al., 2014; Wrisberg, Withycombe, Simpson, Loberg, & Reed, 2012), validation of culturally adapted treatments for athletes who evidence eating disorders is necessary.

The present case example aims to provide an empirically supported framework for which to successfully address eating disorder pathology in collegiate athletes. Procedures for cultural adaptations, assessments by an independent assessor, and symptom improvements at post- and follow-up assessment points will be indicated. Lastly, recommendations for enhancing college campus-based psychological intervention adapted for athlete populations are discussed in light of the strong results, including methods of enhancing college campus-based psychological intervention to better fit the culture of sport.

The client

Anna presented to TOPPS as a female, collegiate athlete in a lean sport who struggled with disordered eating behaviours. Anna self-referred upon learning about the programme through a performance workshop conducted with her team. The workshop was implemented to give awareness of the services offered by TOPPS, and involved several mental skills interventions intended to improve performance on sport-specific activities. Anna sought treatment at TOPPS for binge eating and purging behaviours that interfered with her athletic performance and caused significant distress. Anna was not receiving any additional services at the time. In addition to eating pathology, Anna conveyed that she was critical of herself and evidenced negative thoughts and fears specific to re-injury; she reported having a "negative attitude" towards her sport participation, poor performance, and was unsure if she desired to continue competing. Anna desired to build a "healthy relationship with food" and improve her self-confidence related to sport and life activities.

Consistent with typical age of onset for eating disorders, Anna's struggle with dieting and compensatory behaviours began in high school. Her other teammates also dieted to stay thin, and she modelled their dieting behaviours (e.g., skipping meals, eating low calorie foods). She reported first attempting dieting solely to lose weight for improved sport performance, but this transformed into holding a negative body image. Because she had insufficient caloric intake, she had high levels of hunger and engaged in her first binge episode. This led to automatic, self-critical thoughts, feelings of guilt, and behavioural compensation by exercising excessively and eating very little the next day. These compensatory behaviours acted as negative reinforcers that minimised the anxiety associated with the idea of potential weight gain. Further, Anna also began to associate positive feelings with binge eating, like feeling hunger satisfaction (positive reinforcement). The behaviour originally developed as a method to improve sport performance, but through operant conditioning, shifted as a coping mechanism for feelings of anxiety and guilt.

Anna also reported experimenting with substances in college, occasionally using marijuana and alcohol to "have fun" with friends. Although she reported that she does not enjoy the taste of alcohol, alcohol use had positive effects in social situations (positive reinforcement) and also reduced negative effects of anxiety (negative reinforcement). Nevertheless, she reported using substances sparingly. Because she recognised negative consequences associated with alcohol use, she reported using strategies such as volunteering to act as designated driver to deter alcohol use.

Anna had struggled with disordered eating practices for four years before she attended TOPPS. Her motivation to improve her eating behaviours was influenced by a desire to be healthy. Anna desired to prevent injuries through proper nutrition; she reported a recognition that she did not need to have a certain body type to be an exceptional athlete, which improved her help-seeking behaviours and motivation to attend meetings at TOPPS.

Initial needs assessment

Baseline, 5 and 9 months post-baseline

Upon self-referral to the programme, Anna was scheduled for a 2-hour baseline assessment within one week of informed consent. A trained assessor administered a comprehensive battery of psychometrically validated assessment measures 9 days prior to intervention to establish a baseline. Anna completed the same battery of standardised tests at the completion of formal intervention (5 months post-baseline) to determine immediate treatment effects; she completed the same battery at 9 months post-baseline to assess treatment durability.

Measures included (a) a structured demographics interview to assess age, gender, ethnicity, sport, referral source, employment status, marital status and income; (b) the Structured Clinical Interview for *Diagnostic and Statistical Manual of Mental Disorders* (SCID-IV; 4th ed., text rev (First, Spitzer, Gibbon, & Williams, 2002); *DSM-IV-TR;* American Psychiatric Association [APA], 2000) to determine the presence or absence of *DSM-IV-TR* psychological disorders; (c) the Timeline Followback (TLFB; Sobell, Sobell, Klajner, Pavan, & Basian, 1986) to obtain information regarding number of days of binge drinking, number of alcoholic drinks consumed, number of legal citations, drug use; (d) the Beck Depression Inventory-II (BDI-II; Beck, Steer, & Brown, 1996) to assess mood symptoms across the past two weeks; (e) Symptom Checklist-90-Revised (SCL-90-R; Derogatis, 1994) to measure how much psychiatric symptoms distressed an individual over the past week (items rated on a scale from $0 = $ *Not At All* to $4 = $ *Extremely*); (f) Sport Interference Checklist

(SIC; Donohue, Silver, Dickens, Covassin, & Lancer, 2007) to evaluate the extent to which various factors interfere with sport performance in training, competition, and life outside of sport (items rated on a scale from 1 = *Never* to 7 = *Always*); (g) Student Athlete Relationship Instrument (SARI; Donohue, Miller, Crammer, Cross, & Covassin, 2007) to assess problems in relationship with teammates, family, coaches and peers (items rated on a scale from 1 = *Strongly Disagree* to 7 = *Strongly Agree*); (h) and the Consumer Satisfaction Questionnaire (CSQ-8; Larsen, Attkisson, Hargreaves, & Nguyen, 1979) to measure satisfaction with services received during the course of intervention (items rated on a 4-point scale). All measures have been psychometrically validated and deemed reliable and valid (Beck et al., 1996; Donohue et al., 2004; Donohue, Hill, Azrin, Cross, & Strada, 2007; Donohue, Miller et al., 2007; Donohue, Silver et al., 2007; Horowitz, Rosenberg, Baer, Ureño, & Villaseñor, 1988; Kelly et al., 2018). Likewise, various versions of the SCID are often considered the "gold standard" in diagnostic assessment (Drill, Nakash, DeFife, & Westen, 2015).

Baseline assessment results

Anna's pre-intervention results on the SCID-IV indicated that she met full DSM-IV-TR criteria for bulimia nervosa. In the past 120 days as indicated on the TLFB, Anna reported 1 day of alcohol binge drinking, 4 drinks (approximately 1 drink per month). She reported no days of drug use.

Table 2.1 displays Anna's responses to the SIC, SARI, SCL-90-R, and BDI-II measures at baseline assessment. Anna's self-reported SIC scores indicated that she

TABLE 2.1 Pre, Post, and 4-Month Follow-up Results for SIC, SARI, and SCL-90-R

Variable Assessed	Pre Assessment	4 Month Post Assessment	4 Month Follow-up	Reliable Change Index
SIC Training				
Dysfunctional Thoughts and Stress	5.50	3 (−45.45%)	2.50 (−54.55%)	6.12★
Academic Problems	3.33	1.67 (−49.85%)	2 (−39.94%)	1.77
Injury Concerns	3.67	2.33 (−36.51%)	1 (−72.75%)	3.93★
Poor Team Relationships	1	1 (0%)	1 (0%)	–
SIC Competition				
Dysfunctional Thoughts and Stress	6.25	2.75 (−56%)	3.25 (−48%)	6.67★
Academic and Adjustment Problems	1.67	1 (−40.12 %)	1.67 (0%)	–
Lack of Motivation	2.50	1 (−60%)	1 (−60%)	2.38★
Overly Confident and Critical	1	1 (0%)	1 (0%)	–
Injury Concerns	6.50	5.50 (−15.38%)	1 (−84.62%)	6.88★
Pain Intolerance	2	1 (−50%)	1 (−50%)	1.39
SARI Teammates				–
Poor Relationship and Lack of Support	1	1 (0%)	1 (0%)	

Variable Assessed	Pre Assessment	4 Month Post Assessment	4 Month Follow-up	Reliable Change Index
Pressure to Use Illicit Drugs and Being Difficult During Training	1	1 (0%)	1 (0%)	–
Not a Team Player and Too Non-Competitive	3.50	4 (+14.29%)	1 (−71.43%)	2.21★
Poor Relationships	1	1 (0%)	1 (0%)	–
Pressure to Drink Alcohol and Interfere During Competition	1	1 (0%)	1 (0%)	–
SARI Family				–
Poor Relationship and Lack of Support	1	1 (0%)	1 (0%)	
General Pressure	1	2.17 (+117%)	1 (0%)	–
Pressure to Quit or Continue Unsafely	1	1 (0%)	1 (0%)	–
Embarrassing Comments and Negative Attitude	1	1 (0%)	1 (0%)	–
SARI Coaches				–
Poor Relationship and Lack of Support	1	1 (0%)	1 (0%)	
Lack of Concern for Teamwork and Safety	1	1 (0%)	1 (0%)	–
Lack of Involvement and High Expectations	1	2.25 (+125%)	1 (0%)	–
Too Demanding	1	1 (0%)	1 (0%)	–
SARI Peers				–
Poor Relationship and Lack of Support	1	1 (0%)	1 (0%)	
Use of Recreational and Performance-enhancing Substances	1	1 (0%)	1 (0%)	–
SCL-90-R				
Somatisation	0.08 (34)	0.17 (46)	0 (30)	0.36
Obsessive-Compulsive	0.70 (42)	0.20 (33)	0 (30)	2.8★
Interpersonal Sensitivity	0.11 (31)	0 (30)	0 (30)	0.5
Depression	0.23 (31)	0 (30)	0 (30)	1.15
Anxiety	0.00 (30)	0 (30)	0 (30)	–
Hostility	0.00 (32)	0 (32)	0 (32)	–
Phobic Anxiety	0.00 (38)	0 (38)	0 (38)	–
Paranoid Ideation	0.00 (33)	0 (33)	0 (33)	–
Psychoticism	0.00 (30)	0 (30)	0 (30)	–
Global Severity Index	0.21 (30)	0.06 (30)	0 (30)	3.00★
BDI-II				
Somatic-Affective	4	0 (−100%)	2 (−50%)	1.05
Cognitive	5	3 (−40%)	2 (−60%)	2.00★
Total	9	3 (−66.67%)	4 (−55.56%)	2.00★

Note. For SIC, SARI, and BDI-II, percent change from baseline is presented in parentheses. For SCL-90-R, T-scores are presented in parentheses (Mean=50, SD=10). Percentages are reported in relation to baseline. Reliable Change Index (RCI) > 1.96 is considered significant. Significant RCIs are signified with an asterisk★.

experienced Dysfunctional Thoughts and Stress and Injury Concerns that interfered with her performance in training, competition, and life outside of sports.
Anna's scores were elevated on a number of mental health symptoms as indicated
on the SCL-90-R, including recurrent unpleasant thoughts, overeating, difficulty
making decisions and awakening in the early morning (listed in order of highest to lowest elevation). SARI subscale scores for Family, Coaches and Peers conveyed a lack of problems in these areas of relationships, suggesting these relationship
domains were functioning sufficiently in regards to her sport. BDI-II scores indicated a lack of endorsement of depressive symptoms.

Framework and intervention for delivery

The authors utilised the optimisation approach, built on the tenets of cognitive-
behavioural therapy, in which thoughts, behaviours and feelings are conceptualised
to reciprocally influence one another and sport performance; individuals receiving
services work towards optimum mental and behavioural health through cognitive
and behavioural skill acquisition (Gavrilova & Donohue, in press). An important
strength of the optimisation approach to wellness is the goal to improve cognitive
and behavioural skills beyond the absence of pathology; an athlete seeking optimisation is not required to demonstrate dysfunction to receive services (see Gavrilova,
Donohue, & Galante, 2017; Gavrilova & Donohue, in press). The goal of performance programming is to facilitate cognitive and behavioural skill development
along the optimisation continuum from non-optimal to optimal. The optimisation
approach is supported with the incorporation of significant others (e.g., coaches,
teammates, family members).

The Optimum Performance Programme in Sports, developed with support
from the National Institutes of Health to concurrently address athletes' mental
health and elevate performance on sport-related activities, actively promotes the
optimisation model of mental health as evidenced through case trials and randomised controlled trials (Chow et al., 2015; Donohue et al., 2014; Donohue et al.,
2018; Donohue, et al., 2016; Gavrilova et al., 2017; Pitts et al., 2015). The developers
of TOPPS assert that athletes are more likely to engage into optimisation services
that are sport culture-sensitive and not focused exclusively on pathology (Donohue
et al., 2013). For example, to reduce stigma associated with mental health services
in athletes (Lopez & Levy, 2013), TOPPS professionals, referred to as "performance
coaches," use non-stigmatising language, such as "intervention meetings" instead of
"treatment sessions," and employ a strength-based approach consistent with optimisation. This is particularly relevant to the treatment of eating disorders in athletes
because stigma-reducing strategies might motivate athletes to receive much needed
mental health care.

Performance programming

Anna's Performance Coach (PC) was a doctoral student with comprehensive
training in TOPPS. Anna attended all of her scheduled meetings at TOPPS. Her

supportive others (SOs) included family and friends. Each meeting lasted between 60 and 90 minutes and occurred across a 4.5-month period. Anna's intervention plan was specifically tailored to her intervention goals and baseline assessment. Intervention components were introduced cumulatively and successively; the PC implemented interventions ranked by Anna and her SOs in the order of priority and then reviewed these interventions progressively throughout treatment, but to a lesser extent relative to initial implementation.

Meeting agendas (Meetings 1–16)

Each performance meeting began with a meeting agenda intended to elicit positive expectations for the meeting and introduce planned interventions. The PC briefly described interventions and estimated times for implementation. Anna and her SOs were invited to adjust the intervention plans, including the order and duration of each agenda item, to tailor each meeting to Anna's needs. The PC also elicited positive expectations for the meeting and outlined how Anna and her SOs would contribute to the meeting. Meeting participants chose to maintain the proposed agenda items and implementation in 13 out of 16 meetings. In meetings in which implementation was changed, spontaneous life events made certain interventions more relevant to Anna than others.

Meeting conclusions (Meetings 1–15)

Each performance meeting ended with a structured meeting conclusion. The PC and Anna reviewed upcoming practice assignments for the next meeting to assure completion and understanding, and incorporated engagement strategies like proactively scheduling the next upcoming meeting, and planning the PC's attendance of practices or competitions, as desired by Anna.

Programme Orientation (Meeting 1)

The PC gave an overview of TOPPS with a structured Programme Orientation that allowed Anna to understand the structure and guidelines of the programme, while allowing the PC to assess for motivational factors. For example, Anna was motivated to attend TOPPS to cultivate "healthy" eating habits and enhance performance (Anna cited her coach as a strong motivator for performance in sport and in life). Additionally, Anna and her PC discussed SO involvement, communication guidelines, and ways in which the PC could be optimally supportive of Anna's goal achievement.

Cultural and Athletic Enlightenment (Meeting 1)

Following Programme Orientation, the first meeting also included a Cultural Enlightenment intervention and an Athletic Enlightenment intervention to address Anna's unique ethnic and sport culture. Based on the results of the Semi-Structured

Interview for Consideration of Ethnic Culture in Therapy Scale (SSIECTS; Donohue et al., 2006), Anna disagreed that her ethnic culture was a big part of her life,
but agreed that her ethnic culture was of great importance to her and that there
were many things she liked about her ethnic culture. She reported no negative
comments or arguments due to her ethnic culture, and she was unsure whether or
not she would like a professional to address her ethnic culture if she were to pursue
intervention. Alternatively, Anna agreed that her sport culture was a big part of her
life, was of great importance to her, and that there were many things she liked about
her sport culture. Although others had not said offensive things about her sport culture, she reported experiencing some arguments/problems with others due to her
sport culture. Anna felt it would be very important to consider her sport culture in
intervention meetings. Thus, performance programming was tailored to appeal to
Anna's unique sport culture.

Dynamic goals and rewards (Meetings 2–15)

The second intervention meeting involved review of assessment results to determine goal-worthy items and subscales based on elevations. Using the assessment
results, the PC and Anna collaboratively developed optimal cognitive and behavioural goals. In addition to the programmatic goals at TOPPS (i.e., regular meeting
attendance, SO involvement, completion of practice assignments, avoidance of substance use and gambling, safe sexual practices and maintenance of optimal relationships with others), Anna's goals focused on reducing stress, employing strategies to
reduce binge and purge episodes, restructuring negative thoughts to be neutral and
positive, enhancing confidence, and establishing sport-specific strategies to improve
performance. For example, to reduce binge and purge episodes, Anna set goals to
have more productive thoughts surrounding eating and body image, and to move
towards adequate nutrition. These goals included utilising strategies to recognise
triggers of bingeing and manage those triggers to limit and eliminate binge episodes by intaking 1600–1900 calories and a calcium drink (prescribed by consultation with nutritionist) each day, and engaging in appropriately portioned, regularly
scheduled meals throughout the day to reduce hunger and impulsivity to binge. To
modify negative thought patterns and increase confidence, additional goals included
challenging irrational beliefs (e.g., thought stopping and reframing), becoming more
praiseworthy of self (e.g., noting positive aspects of performance) and utilising motivational statements (e.g., "I am prepared"; Miller, 2003).

To enhance relationships, the PC and Anna worked to develop assertiveness and
communication skills. For example, Anna set a goal to be assertive when telling
sexual partners to use a condom. Goals like studying in optimal environments (e.g.,
library instead of dorm room), and utilising a planner to enhance productivity were
applied to cultivate strong academic habits. Sport-specific strategies included relaxation strategies (e.g., diaphragmatic breathing), focus statements (e.g., instructional
self-talk like "arms up") and motivational statements (e.g., I am strong) utilised at
optimal times in routines to improve activities specific to sport.

Following goal development, Anna began monitoring her progress and goal achievement on a weekly basis. Anna's SOs provided her with support (at any point during the week) and rewards (contingent on weekly goal accomplishment). For example, for support Anna's SOs passionately encouraged her and offered help in attaining sport-specific goals. Rewards included fun activities with friends (e.g., hiking) and family outings.

Anna continued to monitor her goals in the next 13 meetings. Goal monitoring was an active process engaging both Anna and the PC, in which new goals were occasionally added or existing goals revised to optimise goal accomplishment and improve outcomes. As early as in the third meeting, Anna began to show progress in accomplishing both programmatic and personal goals. For example, Anna was consistently able to avoid alcohol and drug use, and she reported improved ability to stop and restructure negative thoughts and better communication with supportive others. The seventh week of intervention marked only the second time in 4 years in which Anna was successful in avoiding both bingeing and purging behaviours in a given week. From this week forward, Anna was able to completely avoid purging behaviours throughout intervention and eliminate bingeing from meetings 11–16 (over 5 weeks). Throughout the programme, Anna maintained high goal achievement (average 90.96% achievement per meeting), with the highest achievement occurring in meetings 11–15 (average 94.62 % achievement per meeting).

Performance planning (Meeting 3)

In this athlete-driven intervention, Anna and her SOs ranked each intervention in order of importance (1=first priority, 8=last priority). The intervention plan was then tailored by the PC to echo Anna's wishes, reflecting the following order from highest to least priority: Environmental Control, Self-Control, Positive Request, Performance Timeline, Dream Job Development, Job Getting Skills, Financial Management and Goal Inspiration. The order of implementation was modified slightly in Meeting Agendas based on life events that made certain interventions more relevant than others.

Environmental control (Meetings 4, 5, and 8)

The Environmental Control (EnvCo) intervention involved altering Anna's environment so that more time was spent with goal-compatible cues and less time was spent with goal-incompatible cues. During the initial meeting, the PC explained that certain environmental cues make goal attainment more or less likely to occur. Then, Anna and her PC collaboratively developed a list of cues (i.e., people, places, situations, emotions) that facilitated Anna's goal attainment and a list of cues that inhibited her goal attainment. For example, Anna identified certain teammates who were facilitative of her study goals, while buffets and feeling stressed were identified as cues incompatible with her goals of avoiding binge and purge behaviours. Once these cues were established, Anna and her PC brainstormed strategies to spend more time with cues associated with goal attainment, and to decrease time with cues that were incompatible with goal accomplishment. Anna and the PC monitored these cues in subsequent meetings. With each future implementation of EnvCo, Anna reported improvements in study habits, eating behaviours and self-confidence.

Self-control (Meeting 5)

Self-Control (SeC) is designed to teach athletes to recognise and manage triggers (e.g., thoughts, images, feelings and behaviours) that lead to undesired, impulsive behaviours. Anna learned to identify triggers of undesired behaviours through backward chaining. Then, to effectively avoid the undesired impulsive behaviour, she utilised strategies like thought stopping, considering the negative consequences for self and others, relaxation strategies (e.g., diaphragmatic breathing), generating alternative solutions, reviewing pros and cons of these solutions and engaging in imagery for the selected alternative.

Anna chose to practice SeC for management of bingeing and purging behaviours. After a practice trial, Anna and the PC evaluated the completed steps in terms of their correctness (on a 0–100% scale), discussed what was liked about each step and what could be enhanced, and identified the most effective step. Anna then assessed the likelihood of an undesired behaviour prior to using Self-Control and immediately after. Anna reported that solution generation was the most effective step in reducing the impulsive behaviours, and the PC encouraged her to emphasise this step in subsequent trials. Anna completed all of her assigned SeC practice assignments and added generated solutions to her goal worksheet for monitoring. Anna experienced her first binge/purge-free week 2 meetings following SeC implementation.

Positive request (Meetings 6 and 7)

The Positive Request intervention improves positive communication skills that increase the likelihood of agreement with a request while preventing arguments. A series of 9 steps are followed, in which the athlete (1) makes a specific request using "please"; (2) acknowledges how it might be difficult for another person to complete the request (i.e., empathy); (3) mentions expected benefits for both self and (4) the other person; (5) offers to help the person in completing the request and (6) suggests something that can be done in exchange; (7) states appreciation for request completion; (8) provides an alternative request if the original request cannot be completed; and (9) invites the person to generate their own alternative if the original request cannot be completed.

The initial meeting of Positive Request involved modelling by the PC and role-plays by Anna to assure skill acquisition. Subsequent meetings involved review of in-vivo practice assignments. For example, Anna used Positive Request to ask her teammates to make more positive remarks and avoid making negative remarks in practice to help maintain a positive attitude. Her teammates were eager to accept her request, and Anna noted this contributed to a more positive mindset related to sport and relationships.

Reciprocity awareness (Meetings 5, 7 and 10)

The Reciprocity Awareness intervention is designed to enhance relationships by having athletes and their SOs share things they like, admire, respect or appreciate about one another. Theoretical foundations of this intervention ascertain that individuals who provide reciprocal positive reinforcement are likely to have better relationships. Reciprocity Awareness was implemented each time a new SO attended performance meetings, totalling three times throughout the course of intervention. Reciprocity Awareness includes both in-session positive exchanges and positive exchanges assigned for practice outside of TOPPS. Anna reported that Reciprocity Awareness elicited positive changes in her personal relationships, specifically with her family.

Performance timeline (Meeting 7)

The Performance Timeline is designed to enhance factors that contribute to optimum performance in sport and life situations. Each performance event is viewed on a time continuum, where performance is influenced at key time points: days, minutes and seconds before the event, the event itself, and seconds, minutes and days after the event. Anna was asked to choose a performance situation (e.g., competition) and the time point she viewed as most vital for her optimal performance. Anna identified "days before" as the most important time point, so the PC and Anna brainstormed how to optimise a number of factors (nutrition, thoughts, motivation) to enhance performance within that time point. For example, Anna used diaphragmatic breathing to reduce her stress and motivational thoughts, such as "I am prepared" and "I work hard." These strategies can be viewed as sport-specific routines for optimal performance that can be generalised to a number of performance situations in sport or life (e.g., competition, training, academic exams or presentations, job interviews, etc.).

Dream job development (Meeting 14)

The Dream Job Development (DJDev) intervention is designed to prepare athletes for their dream career. The PC and Anna discussed important aspects of the most desirable career (e.g., financial situation, benefits, travel) and generated important educational prerequisites, qualifications and people (including SOs) who could assist in achieving the dream job. Anna was successful in securing a summer position in the field of her dream career, making steps towards achieving her long-term goals.

Financial management (Meeting 15)

Financial Management (FinM) represents an ideal intervention for helping athletes learn to increase income and decrease expenses. Anna and her PC identified monthly expenses within different domains (e.g., school, living, sport-related) and monthly income from various sources. The PC calculated the difference between income and expenses; although Anna was in a financial surplus, she and her PC discussed ways to decrease expenses and increase income to optimise her financial situation. The proposed solutions were projected to yield hundreds of dollars in extra income savings. Anna and her PC then worked collaboratively to execute these money-saving and income-generating strategies.

Goal inspiration (Meeting 12)

Goal Inspiration is adapted from Consequence Review, an evidence-based intervention used to review the negative consequences of substance use and other undesired behaviours to deter participants from engaging in detrimental behaviours. Consistent with the TOPPS model, this intervention has been modified to focus on the positive consequences of achieving specific goals. Anna chose a goal-worthy area in which she desired increased motivation (i.e., adhering to her prescribed nutrition and calcium plan). Anna and her PC collaboratively brainstormed immediate and delayed positive consequences that would arise from these regular eating habits, utilising a consequence tree format. This strategy was implemented to increase Anna's motivation to abstain from binge and purge episodes, while adhering to her physician- and nutritionist-prescribed guidelines.

Last meeting generalisation (Meeting 16)

Last Meeting Generalisation was implemented and included: (1) reviewing overall progress in optimising performance in relationships, factors specific to performance, mental health, avoidance of substance use, and prevention of STIs and risk factors for HIV; (2) establishing ways Anna can maintain goal progress after TOPPS; (3) PC providing descriptive praise for effort and strategies utilised and brainstormed, and (4) exchanging was loved, admired, respected or appreciated about all persons involved in Anna's optimisation process, including the PC. Anna conveyed that her participation in TOPPS provided skills to overcome future adversities. This ends performance programming on a positive note, while incorporating relapse prevention and utilisation of TOPPS strategies in the future.

Managed care

As a college-athlete, Anna had access to numerous services and resources. Anna was not receiving any additional psychological services prior to or during the TOPPS programme. She did seek consultation with a team physician during the course of intervention who provided recommendations to Anna about safe exercise levels. Anna and her PC briefly consulted with a nutritionist to ensure that Anna was meeting adequate nutritional guidelines for her energy expenditure. Anna and the PC then worked to adhere to these guidelines and to manage the safety and health of Anna throughout her recovery.

Intervention integrity

Several strategies were employed to ensure intervention integrity. Intervention was implemented consistent with the existing FBT treatment manual (i.e., Donohue & Allen, 2011), including the use of structured agendas and standardised protocol checklists to guide intervention and measure protocol adherence; random review of session audio recordings to measure inter-rater reliability; documentation of techniques employed during sessions, the athlete's level of participation, and progress toward goal achievement, using standardised progress notes; and consumer satisfaction. The PC implementing TOPPS received ongoing clinical supervision by a licenced psychologist, including review of audio recordings and corrective feedback.

Protocol adherence

To measure intervention integrity in this study, first, the performance coach implementing TOPPS interventions calculated the adherence to standardised protocols. The overall protocol adherence over the course of 16 sessions was 88% (SD = 13%, range = 57–100%). Second, an independent rater reviewed 10% of randomly selected session audio recordings to determine the performance coach's adherence to intervention protocols. Lastly, inter-rater agreement between the performance coach and the independent rater was calculated and showed an average reliability of 86.4% (SD = 20%, range = 42–100%). The interventions in this study were implemented with high reliability (see guidelines from Bellg et al., 2004).

Consumer satisfaction and engagement ratings

Consumer satisfaction was measured by Athlete's Helpfulness Ratings on a scale of 1 through 7 (1 = *Extremely Unhelpful*; 7 = *Extremely Helpful*) and indicated that, on average, interventions were "*Extremely Helpful*." Following completion of TOPPS, Anna reported high satisfaction with the intervention, as indicated by the CSQ-8. Additionally, the PC rated Anna's Level of Engagement in each intervention component (based on attendance/promptness, participation, conduct, and home assignment completion), using a 0–100% scale (0% = *Not At All Optimal*; 100% = *Completely Optimal*). On average, Anna's level of engagement was rated at 99.75%.

5-month post-baseline assessment results

A post-intervention assessment was administered by the same assessor 6 days following Anna's completion of TOPPS. The SCID-IV re-assessment indicated that Anna met criteria for bulimia nervosa in Full Remission. Post-intervention assessment results for the SIC, SARI, SCL-90-R and BDI-II are presented in Table 2.1. Anna substantially reduced her scores on the SIC Dysfunctional Thoughts and Stress and Academic Problems subscales (greater than 40% improvements) in both training and competition domains. She additionally endorsed notable improvements on Lack of Motivation in training and showed a moderate reduction on Injury Concerns in both training and competition. The SARI results generally remained non-problematic, indicating optimal maintenance of relationships with teammates, family members, coaches and peers. On the SCL-90-R, notable improvements occurred in the Obsessive-Compulsive subscale, likely indicative of Anna's reduction in weight concerns. Interpersonal Sensitivity, Depression, Anxiety, Phobic Anxiety, Paranoid Ideation, Psychoticism and the Global Severity Index scores remained within 1–2 standard deviations below the mean. Although in the average range, Somatisation scores increased by one standard deviation, likely due to behavioural monitoring during the intervention. The BDI-II total score was reduced from 9 to 3. The TLFB results indicate that her alcohol use remained about the same low rate throughout the study. Anna did not engage in binge drinking throughout the study (see Table 2.2).

9-month post-baseline assessment

Between post and follow-up assessments, Anna came to TOPPS for a 40-minute booster meeting in which she reported some communication difficulties. Her PC reviewed the communication skills she learned at TOPPS and engaged in

TABLE 2.2 Pre, Post, and Follow-up Results for TLFB

Variable	Pre-Assessment	4 Month Post-Assessment	4 Month Follow-up Assessment
Timeline Followback	120-day period	149-day period	124-day period
Number of Drinks	4	4	8
Alcohol Days	2	3	6
Average Drinks per Day of Drinking	2	1.33	1.33
Binge Drinking Days	1	0	0
Days of Hard Drugs	0	0	0
Days of Unprotected Sex	3	3	1
Hours Worked	0	0	288
Incarcerated	0	0	0

Note. TLFB results are presented as actual occurrences of each behaviour during the respective time period.

problem-solving to generate solutions. Anna was offered additional meetings if she desired, but she felt confident in her skills and politely declined.

According to the SCID-IV results, Anna maintained full remission of her initial diagnosis of bulimia nervosa. The SIC scores continued to improve in Dysfunctional Thoughts and Stress in training (greater than 50% improvement) and Injury Concerns in both training and competition (greater than 70% improvement), and were largely maintained in Academic Problems (see Table 2.1). The SARI scores indicated absence of problems in all relationship domains, and the SCL-90-R scores indicated improvements of two standard deviations in most psychiatric dimensions. The BDI-II total score remained in the minimal range with an improvement of 55% from baseline assessment. On the TLFB, improvements were shown in binge drinking, while the number of days of alcohol consumption and the number of drinks increased. Further, as a result of the Dream Job Development intervention, Anna secured an internship position in her field of study and dramatically increased the amount of hours worked at follow-up.

Reliable change index

Reliable Change Index (RCI; Jacobson & Truax, 1991) is a metric utilised to determine if clinical change is considered significant above and beyond the standard error of measurement. The RCI considers an individual's pre- and post-test change, while also considering general measure reliability and standard error of measurement. When RCI scores are greater than 1.96, it is likely that the change in scores is reflecting true change in functioning, also referred to as meaningful change (Jacobson & Truax, 1991).

As per the Reliable Change Index, Anna evidenced significant and meaningful reductions in SIC Dysfunctional Thoughts and Stress in both training and competition, Injury Concerns in both training and competition, and Lack of Motivation affecting competition. She also evidenced significant and reliable reductions in SCL-90-R Global Severity Index and Obsessive-Compulsive symptoms, as well as significant reductions in both overall and cognitive depressive symptoms measured by the BDI-II. Anna improved her functioning with regards to SCL-90-R Somatisation, Interpersonal Sensitivity, and Depression domains, and although these subscales did not exhibit reliable change as per the RCI, these scores were not elevated at baseline and considered optimised at follow-up assessment. This finding was also true for the SIC Pain Intolerance scale in competition and the BDI-II Somatic-Affective subscale. Anna's improvement in Academic Problems in Training did not show reliable change and could have been further optimised at follow-up assessment. Reliable Change Index scores are listed in Table 2.1.

Intervention evaluation

This case study permitted an initial evaluation of the efficacy of TOPPS in treating bulimia nervosa in a lean sport athlete. Assessments conducted after formal

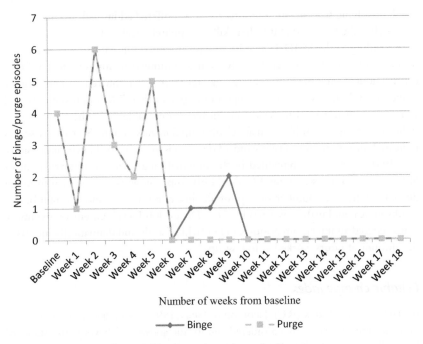

FIGURE 2.1 Binge and purge frequency throughout the Intervention

intervention revealed substantial reductions in binge-purge behaviours and full remission of eating disorder symptomatology, as well as improvements in other mental health areas, including dysfunctional thoughts, stress and obsessive-compulsive symptoms. Initiating Environmental Control and Self-Control was associated with a substantial decrease in binge/purge behaviours, as well as intrusive, negative thoughts pertaining to eating disorder symptomatology. Through continued implementation of Dynamic Goals and Rewards, Anna abstained from purging for nine consecutive weeks and reported no binge episodes for six consecutive weeks near the end of treatment (see Figure 2.1). Although not targeted with specific interventions, Anna reported reductions in worrying about injuries.

Lessons learned through self-reflection

Previous research indicates that psychological outcomes are enhanced when family members are involved with treatment planning (Sisson & Azrin, 1986). However, family involvement with interventions poses several barriers for student-athletes, like family members residing out-of-town, or conflicting schedules from SOs who are employed full or part-time. To address these barriers, PCs at TOPPS encouraged phone and FaceTime participation to involve supportive others and accommodate Anna's schedule. Anna was reluctant to involve supportive others due to time constraints and a desire for independence. The sport culture of self-reliance and self-sufficiency (e.g., Etzel, Ferrante, & Pinkney, 1991; Etzel & Watson, 2007) likely also contributed to this mindset. Although Anna was ultimately successful in attending all scheduled meetings as part of the programme, additional engagement strategies like motivational interviewing would have likely enhanced Anna's desire to involve supportive others in her performance optimisation meetings, providing additional support by which to achieve her goals.

There is also a concern of confidentiality with family-based interventions. Although meeting confidentiality is protected by state and federal laws (with the exception of harm to self and others), family members are not required to abide by the same laws as psychologists. Therefore, PCs at TOPPS introduce family members to the programme, explaining the extent of their participation and awareness of confidentiality issues. The PC in this study was also trained to avoid disclosure of information that Anna specified she desired to keep confidential from her SOs.

The optimisation model was ultimately well-suited to Anna's needs and presenting concerns. It is important to indicate that Anna initially evidenced resistance to mental health intervention. The optimisation approach and interventions tailored to sport culture appropriately engaged Anna into treatment, and allowed her to receive mental health services she otherwise may not have pursued. Engagement into services is particularly important for bulimia nervosa, as early reductions in purging behaviour consistently predict successful treatment outcome and sustained remission (Fairburn, Agras, Walsh, Wilson, & Stice, 2004; Vall & Wade, 2015).

Recommendations to clinicians and students

The present case study describes a comprehensive approach to intervention with a collegiate lean sport athlete utilising an evidence-based intervention. Although Anna was originally hesitant to seek services at TOPPS, motivating factors unique to her athletic status were integrated into intervention planning to enhance engagement and participation. TOPPS is athlete-driven, which may further enhance autonomy and motivation for change. Other evidence-supported techniques like Financial Management and Dream Job Development were utilised to manage stress and ultimately enhance performance in sport, life and mental health.

The current sport-specific adaptation of FBT has previously demonstrated improvements in student-athlete alcohol use, binge drinking, relationships, mental health, and sport-related activities in uncontrolled trials (Chow et al., 2015; Donohue et al., 2014; Gavrilova et al., 2017; Pitts et al., 2015). The present case study supports the efficacy of TOPPS in concurrently treating bulimia nervosa and elevating sport-specific activities, extending the knowledge-base and applicability of TOPPS to multiple mental health difficulties and athlete types. Leading evidence-supported treatments in bulimia nervosa show success in approximately 30–50% of patients (see Cooper & Fairburn, 2011). Therefore, TOPPS may be an efficacious treatment option for athletes demonstrating lack of motivation for eating pathology closely tied with sport-related factors. The latter contention will need to be validated in controlled research involving athletes who evidence this condition.

Many athletes demonstrate low help-seeking behaviours (Watson, 2005) and may never pursue services, potentially citing motivations similar to Anna as reasons for avoiding programming. Given that many colleges do not or cannot employ sport psychologists within athletic departments (Cannole et al., 2014; Wrisberg et al., 2012), TOPPS offers an efficacious alternative to traditional campus counselling programmes to which student-athletes are frequently referred. The TOPPS programme duration (up to 12 meetings) is typical of campus counselling centres (Barr, Rando, Krylowicz, & Winfield, 2010). Arguably the eating disorder treatment with greatest research support (Enhanced Cognitive Behaviour Therapy for Eating Disorders, CBT-E; Fairburn, Cooper, & Shafran, 2003; Fairburn, 2008) typically lasts 20 to 40 sessions depending on diagnostic severity. Thus, TOPPS may offer an additional cost-effective treatment for use on college campuses.

Utilisation of evidence-supported methods of engaging student-athletes may increase numbers of student-athletes who seek services and ultimately help provide programming to athletes who may not have received treatment otherwise. Such was the case in the present study. In instances where implementing a standardised treatment is not feasible, practitioners are encouraged to work with athletes to incorporate interventions addressing sport culture and performance programming to enhance motivation and desired treatment outcomes in this special population.

As TOPPS was originally conceptualised and validated in the United States, it would be important to consider cultural adaptations for populations in different countries, circumstances and ethnic backgrounds. For instance, TOPPS includes cultural competency interviews, such as the Semi-Structured Interview for Consideration of Ethnic Culture in Therapy Scale (Donohue et al., 2006). However, these instruments were validated in the United States. Relevant to difficulties in intervention implementation, TOPPS includes multiple intervention components requiring substantial training. The provider in this case examination completed approximately 32 hours of workshop training and weekly ongoing supervision and training from a licenced clinical psychologist for about 90 minutes a week throughout her delivery of intervention.

As universities and colleges ultimately initiate the implementation of evidence-supported and sport-specific wellness programmes for athletes, such as TOPPS, they will need to assure appropriate training, qualifications and service delivery mechanisms of providers (National Collegiate Athletic Association, 2017). Along these lines, licenced psychologists and sport performance professionals should be incorporated to work together. Within their respective professional contexts, these providers are encouraged to develop integrated programmes to assist engagement interventions shown to enhance motivation for sport-specific wellness interventions (Breslin, Shannon, Haughey, Donnelly, & Leavey, 2017). Likewise, an integrated team may assist coaches and other athletic staff in recognising signs of mental illness and making appropriate referrals via evidence-supported programmes (see Sebbens, Hassmen, Crisp, & Wensley, 2016).

Declaration of conflicting interests

The author(s) declared no potential conflicts of interest with respect to the research, authorship and/or publication of this article.

Funding

The author(s) disclosed receipt of the following financial support for the research, authorship and/or publication of this article: This research was supported by grant from the National Institute on Drug Abuse (1R01DA031828, PI Donohue).

References

American Psychiatric Association. (2000). *Diagnostic and statistical manual of mental disorders* (4th ed., text rev.) Washington, DC: American Psychiatric Association.

Barr, V., Rando, R., Krylowicz, B., & Winfield, E. (2010). *The association for university and college counseling center directors annual survey*. Retrieved from http://files.cmcglobal.com/directors_survey_2009_m.pdf

Beck, A. T., Steer, R. A., & Brown, G. K. (1996). *Manual for the beck depression inventory-II*. San Antonio, TX: The Psychological Corporation.

Bellg, A. J., Borrelli, B., Resnick, B., Hecht, J., Minicucci, D. S., Ory, M., . . . Czajkowski, S. (2004). Enhancing treatment fidelity in health behavior change studies: Best practices and recommendations from the NIH behavior change consortium. *Health Psychology, 23*(5), 443–451.

Breslin, G., Shannon, S., Haughey, T., Donnelly, P., & Leavey, G. (2017). A systematic review of interventions to increase awareness of mental health and well-being in athletes, coaches and officials. *Systematic Reviews, 6*(1), 177.

Byrne, S., & McLean, N. (2002). Elite athletes: Effects of the pressure to be thin. *Journal of Science and Medicine in Sport, 5*(2), 80–94.

Cannole, I. J., Shannon, V. R., Watson, J. C., Wrisberg, C., Etzel, E., & Schimmel, C. (2014). NCAA athletic administrators' preferred characteristics for sport psychology positions: A consumer market analysis. *The Sport Psychologist, 28*(4), 406–417.

Chow, G. M., Donohue, B., Pitts, M., Loughran, T., Schubert, K. N., Gavrilova, Y., & Diaz, E. (2015). Results of a single case controlled study of the optimum performance program in sports in a collegiate athlete. *Clinical Case Studies, 14*(3), 191–209.

Cooper, Z., & Fairburn, C. G. (2011). The evolution of "enhanced" cognitive behavior therapy for eating disorders: Learning from treatment nonresponse. *Cognitive and Behavioral Practice, 18*(3), 394–402.

Derogatis, L. R. (1994). *Symptom checklist-90-R: Administration, scoring, and procedures manual* (3rd ed.). Minneapolis, MN: National Computer Systems.

Donohue, B., & Allen D. N. (2011). *Treating adult substance abuse using Family Behavior Therapy: A step by step approach*. Hoboken, NJ: John Wiley & Sons.

Donohue, B., Chow, G. M., Pitts, M., Loughran, T., Schubert, K. N., Gavrilova, Y., & Allen, D. N. (2014). Piloting a family-supported approach to concurrently optimize mental health and sport performance in athletes. *Clinical Case Studies, 1–19.*

Donohue, B., Covassin, T., Lancer, K., Dickens, Y., Miller, Y., Hash, A., & Genet, J. (2004). Examination of psychiatric symptoms in student athletes. *Journal of General Psychology, 163,* 29–35.

Donohue, B., Gavrilova, Y., Galante, M., Gavrilova, E., Loughrana, T., Scott, J., Chow, G., Plant, C., & Allen, D. A. (2018). Controlled evaluation of an optimization approach to mental health and sport performance. *Journal of Clinical Sport Psychology, 12*, 234–267.

Donohue, B., Hill, H., Azrin, N. H., Cross, C., & Strada, M. (2007). Psychometric support for contemporaneous and retrospective youth and parent reports of adolescent marijuana use frequency in an adolescent outpatient treatment population. *Addictive Behaviors, 32*, 1787–1797.

Donohue, B., Miller, A., Crammer, L., Cross, C., & Covassin, T. (2007). A standardized method of assessing sport specific problems in the relationships of athletes with their coaches, teammates, family, and peers. *Journal of Sport Behavior, 30*, 375–397.

Donohue, B., O'Dowd, A., Plant, C. P., Phillips, C., Loughran, T. A., & Gavrilova, Y. (2016). Controlled evaluation of a method to assist recruitment of participants into treatment outcome research and engage student athletes into substance abuse intervention. *Journal of Clinical Sport Psychology, 10*, 272–288.

Donohue, B., Pitts, M., Gavrilova, Y., Ayarza, A., & Cintron, K. I. (2013). A culturally sensitive approach to treating substance abuse in athletes using evidence-supported methods. *Journal of Clinical Sport Psychology, 7*(2), 98–119.

Donohue, B., Silver, N. C., Dickens, Y., Covassin, T., & Lancer, K. (2007). Development and psychometric evaluation of the sport interference checklist. *Behavior Modification, 31*, 937–957.

Donohue, B., Strada, M. J., Rosales, R., Taylor-Caldwell, A., Hise, D., Ahman, S., . . . Laino, R. (2006). The semistructured interview for consideration of ethnic culture in therapy scale: Initial psychometric and outcome support. *Behavior Modification, 30*(6), 867–891.

Drill, R., Nakash, O., DeFife, J. A., & Westen, D. (2015). Assessment of clinical information: Comparison of the validity of a Structured Clinical Interview (the SCID) and the clinical diagnostic interview. *Journal of Nervous and Mental Disease, 203*(6), 459–462.

Etzel, E. F., Ferrante, A. P., & Pinkney, J. (1991). *Counseling college student-athletes: Issues and interventions.* Morgantown, WV: Fitness Information Technology.

Etzel, E. F., & Watson, J. C. (2007). Ethical challenges for psychological consultations in intercollegiate athletics. *Journal of Clinical Sport Psychology, 1*, 304–317.

Fairburn, C. G. (2008). *Cognitive behavior therapy and eating disorders.* New York, NY: The Guilford Press.

Fairburn, C. G., Agras, W. S., Walsh, B. T., Wilson, G. T., & Stice, E. (2004). Prediction of outcome in bulimia nervosa by early change in treatment. *American Journal of Psychiatry, 161*(12), 2322–2324.

Fairburn, C. G., Cooper, Z., & Shafran, R. (2003). Cognitive behaviour therapy for eating disorders: A "transdiagnostic" theory and treatment. *Behaviour Research and Therapy, 41*(5), 509–528.

Ferrand, C., Magnan, C., Rouveix, M., & Filaire, E. (2007). Disordered eating, perfectionism and body-esteem of elite synchronized swimmers. *European Journal of Sport Science, 7*(4), 223–230.

First, M. B., Spitzer, R. L., Gibbon, M., & Williams, J. B. (2002). *Structured clinical interview for DSM-IV-TR axis I disorders, research version, non-patient edition (SICD-I/NP).* New York, NY: Biometrics Research, New York State Psychiatric Institute.

Gavrilova, Y., & Donohue, B. (In press). Sport-specific mental health interventions in athletes: A call for optimization models sensitive to sport culture. *Journal of Sport Behavior.*

Gavrilova, Y., Donohue, B., & Galante, M. (2017). Mental health and sport performance programming with athletes who present without pathology: A case examination supporting optimization. *Clinical Case Studies, 16*(3), 234–253.

Horowitz, L. M., Rosenberg, S. E., Baer, B. A., Ureño, G., & Villaseñor, V. S. (1988). Inventory of interpersonal problems: Psychometric properties and clinical applications. *Journal of Consulting and Clinical Psychology, 56*(6), 885–892.

Jacobson, N. S., & Truax, P. (1991). Clinical significance: A statistical approach to defining meaningful change in psychotherapy research. *Journal of Consulting and Clinical Psychology, 59*(1), 12–19.

Kelly, P. J., Kyngdon, F., Ingram, I., Deane, F. P., Baker, A. L., & Osborne, B. A. (2018). The client satisfaction questionnaire-8: Psychometric properties in a cross-sectional survey of people attending residential substance abuse treatment. *Drug and Alcohol Review, 37*(1), 79–86.

Keski-Rahkonen, A., & Mustelin, L. (2016). Epidemiology of eating disorders in Europe: Prevalence, incidence, comorbidity, course, consequences, and risk factors. *Current Opinion in Psychiatry, 29*(6), 340–345.

Kong, P., & Harris, L. M. (2015). The sporting body: Body image and eating disorder symptomatology among female athletes from leanness focused and nonleanness focused sports. *The Journal of Psychology, 145*(2), 141–160.

Larsen, D. L., Attkisson, C. C., Hargreaves, W. A., & Nguyen, T. D. (1979). Assessment of client/patient satisfaction: Development of a general scale. *Evaluation and Program Planning, 2*, 197–207.

Lopez, R. L., & Levy, J. L. (2013). Student athletes' perceived barriers to preferences for seeking counseling. *Journal of College Counseling, 16*, 19–31.

Miller, A. (2003). The development and controlled evaluation of athletic mental preparation strategies in high school distance runners. *Journal of Applied Sport Psychology, 15*(4), 321–334.

National Collegiate Athletic Association. (2017, May). *Interassociation consensus document: Mental health best practices*. Retrieved from www.ncaa.org/sites/default/files/SSI_Mental HealthBestPractices_Web_20170921.pdf

O'Brien, K. M., Whelan, D. R., Sandler, D. P., Hall, J. E., & Weinberg, C. R. (2017). Predictors and long-term health outcomes of eating disorders. *PLoS One, 12*(7), e0181104.

Pitts, M., Donohue, B., Schubert, K. N., Chow, G. M., Loughran, T., & Gavrilova, Y. (2015). A systematic case examination of the optimum performance program in sports in a combat sport athlete. *Clinical Case Studies, 14*(3), 178–190.

Reardon, C. L., & Factor, R. M. (2010). Sport psychiatry: A systematic review of diagnosis and medical treatment of mental illness in athletes. *Sports Medicine, 40*(11), 961–980.

Sebbens, J., Hassmén, P., Crisp, D., & Wensley, K. (2016). Mental Health in Sport (MHS): Improving the early intervention knowledge and confidence of elite sport staff. *Frontiers in Psychology, 7*, 1–7.

Sisson, R. W., & Azrin, N. H. (1986). Family-member involvement to initiate and promote treatment of problem drinkers. *Journal of Behavior Therapy and Experimental Psychiatry, 17*, 15–21.

Sobell, M. B., Sobell, L. C., Klajner, F., Pavan, D., & Basian, E. (1986). The reliability of the timeline method of assessing normal drinker college students' recent drinking history: Utility of alcohol research. *Addictive Behaviors, 11*, 149–162.

Sundgot-Borgen, J., & Torstveit, M. K. (2004). Prevalence of eating disorders in elite athletes is higher than in the general population. *Clinical Journal of Sports Medicine, 14*, 25–32.

Sundgot-Borgen, J., & Torstveit, M. K. (2010). Aspects of disordered eating continuum in elite high-intensity sports. *Scandinavian Journal of Medicine & Science in Sports, 20*(2), 112–121.

Thompson, R. A., & Sherman, R. T. (2007). *Managing student-athletes' mental health issues*. Retrieved from www.ncaa.org/sites/default/files/2007_managing_mental_ health_0.pdf

Torstveit, M. K., Rosenvinge, J. H., & Sundgot-Borgen, J. (2008). Prevalence of eating disorders and the predictive power of risk models in female elite athletes: A controlled study. *Scandinavian Journal of Medicine & Science in Sports, 18*, 108–118.

Vall, E., & Wade, T. D. (2015). Predictors of treatment outcome in individuals with eating disorders: A systematic review and meta-analysis. *International Journal of Eating Disorders, 48*(7), 946–971.

Watson, J. C. (2005). College student-athletes' attitudes toward help-seeking behavior and expectations of counseling services. *Journal of College Student Development, 46*(4), 442–449.

Wrisberg, C., Withycombe, J., Simpson, D., Loberg, L. A., & Reed, A. (2012). NCAA division-I administrators' perceptions of the benefits of sport psychology services and possible roles for a consultant. *The Sport Psychologist, 26*, 16–28.

Further reading

The following articles provide further detail of the TOPPS programme, evidence, and associated outcomes in student-athletes.

Donohue, B., Gavrilova, Y., Galante, M., Gavrilova, E., Loughrana, T., Scott, J., . . . Allen, D. A. (2018). Controlled evaluation of an optimization approach to mental health and sport performance. *Journal of Clinical Sport Psychology, 12*, 234–267. doi.org/10.1123/jcsp.2017-0054
This study utilised controlled random assignment to intervention group methodology and demonstrated efficacy of TOPPS in reducing unprotected sex, binge drinking, and detrimental thoughts/stress, while improving relationships.

Donohue, B., Chow, G. M., Pitts, M., Loughran, T., Schubert, K. N., Gavrilova, Y., & Allen, D. N. (2015). Piloting a family-supported approach to concurrently optimize mental health and sport performance in athletes. *Clinical Case Studies, 14*(3), 1–19.
This literature reviews the innovative aspects of the TOPPS program, results from pilot data, and barriers to implementation.

Chow, G. M., Donohue, B., Pitts, M., Loughran, T., Schubert, K. N., Gavrilova, Y., & Diaz, E. (2015). Results of a single case controlled study of the optimum performance program in Sports in a collegiate athlete. *Clinical Case Studies, 14*(3), 191–209.
This article utilised multiple baseline methodology to demonstrate efficacy of TOPPS in reducing unprotected sex, binge drinking, and detrimental thoughts/stress, while improving relationships.

Pitts, M., Donohue, B., Schubert, K. N., Chow, G. M., Loughran, T., & Gavrilova, Y. (2015). A systematic case examination of the optimum performance program in sports in a combat sport athlete. *Clinical Case Studies, 14*(3), 178–190.
Authors of this study demonstrated the efficacy of TOPPS in elevating mental health and reducing substance use in a combat sport athlete.

Donohue, B., Pitts, M., Gavrilova, Y., Ayarza, A., & Cintron, K. I. (2013). A culturally sensitive approach to treating substance abuse in athletes using evidence-supported methods. *Journal of Clinical Sport Psychology, 7*(2), 98–119.
This research describes the need for athlete-specific interventions to prevent and treat substance use.

Gavrilova, Y., Donohue, B., & Galante, M. (2017). Mental health and sport performance programming with athletes who present without pathology: A case examination supporting optimization. *Clinical Case Studies, 16*(3), 1–20.
This article describes how TOPPS may be implemented with an athlete evidencing no mental health pathology who desires performance enhancement in sport and in life.

Gavrilova, Y., & Donohue, B. (In press). Sport-specific mental health interventions in athletes: A call for optimization models sensitive to sport culture. *Journal of Sport Behavior.*
This article reviews the optimization approach to mental wellness and sport performance.

3

PREVENTION OF BURNOUT AND DEPRESSION IN JUNIOR ELITE SWIMMERS

Insa Nixdorf, Jürgen Beckmann and Raphael Nixdorf

Learning objectives

After reading this chapter you should have:

1   Gained valuable background information on the importance and prevalence of depression and burnout in elite athletes.
2   Be able to distinguish between the major symptomatology of depression and burnout.
3   Understand the relations to other significant psychological variables connected to depression and burnout.
4   Critically examine prevention strategies for depression and burnout.

Introduction to the theme

Clinical disorders and mental health issues among elite athletes is a topic of increasing interest and public awareness (Schinke, Stambulova, Si, & Moore, 2017). Recent studies among athletes illustrate the severity of psychological problems such as depression and burnout. Depression can be regarded as a multisystem disorder with affective, cognitive and physiological manifestations (Insel & Charney, 2003; Lee, Jeong, Kwak, & Park, 2010). Depressive syndromes are characterised by symptoms of depressed mood, anhedonia, fatigue, feelings of guilt and suicidal ideation (DSM V, American Psychiatric Association, 2013). Burnout is mainly described as a three-dimensional syndrome in response to occupational stress, involving emotional exhaustion, cynicism and lack of professional efficacy (Maslach & Jackson, 1981; Maslach, Schaufeli, & Leiter, 2001). In sports the syndrome is referred to as athlete burnout with the three core dimensions a) physical and emotional exhaustion, b) sport devaluation and c) reduced sense of accomplishment (Raedeke & Smith, 2001).

Depending on the sample and the assessment method prevalence rates for depression appear to be at a concerning level (Gulliver, Griffiths, Mackinnon, Batterham, & Stanimirovic, 2015; Nixdorf, Frank, Hautzinger, & Beckmann, 2013; Wolanin, Hong, Marks, Panchoo, & Gross, 2016). Junior elite athletes seem to be at especially high risk (Nixdorf et al., 2013). Many correlative study designs identified sport related variables connected to elevated depression scores in elite athlete samples (e.g. injury, failure). One such variable is that athletes competing in individual sports were found to be more prone to depressive symptoms than athletes competing in team sports (Nixdorf, Frank, & Beckmann, 2016). Interestingly, athlete burnout appears to be a research topic for a longer period of time when compared to other disorders. Thus more mechanisms have been discovered regarding burnout (Eklund & DeFreese, 2015; Goodger, Gorely, Lavallee, & Harwood, 2007). Psychological factors such as personality dispositions (particularly perfectionism) or motivational aspects are being researched and discussed. These findings provide useful information for prevention strategies among elite athletes (Gustafsson, DeFreese, & Madigan, 2017). Based on this research applied sport psychology is now able to generate more specific prevention programmes in order to stabilise mental health and prevent burnout and depression. The following book chapter gives an insight into a prevention programme for burnout and depression specific to a target group of junior elite athletes competing in an individual sport discipline.

Description of the group being targeted

The group targeted in our prevention programme were junior elite swimmers. The programme was part of an applied project called "Group coaching of selected athletes of the Bavarian Swim Association", which was founded by the German Federal Institute of Sport Science (Bundesinstitut für Sportwissenschaft; BISp). The project was conducted with junior elite swimmers in order to strengthen prospectively important factors and therefore help prevent the development of psychological problems. In this matter, the prevention programme was a transfer-project developed from a research project (2014–2016), in which the goals were to identify important predictors for burnout and depression in elite athletes. Results showed that athletes in individual sports are at higher risk for depressive syndromes (Nixdorf et al., 2016). Therefore, junior elite swimmers were assumed to gain most from a preventive intervention programme.

A total of 27 female and male swimmers (aged between 12 and 16 years) participated in the applied programme. All swimmers were part of a regional, high level swim squad. Therefore, most athletes were members of the German D/C cadre squad for swimming. In order to maintain and develop their performance levels athletes endured an extensive training schedule and programme. Athletes trained approximately 8 to 9 times a week swimming between 30 and 40 kilometres (km) depending on the training phase during season. In total, most of the athletes completed 1500 km a year. In addition, athletic training was scheduled 3 times a week. Three different training facilities with locations across Munich were provided for each training group. Thus, changing locations on a regular basis was necessary. During season, athletes competed in 15 tournaments, approximately, mostly on weekends. In addition to the training obligations, all athletes attended school and had to study for their exams on a regular basis. Therefore, training had to be fitted into a tight schedule with little spare time for other hobbies and interests. Participation in the present programme was voluntary, however parental informed consent was provided.

Initial needs assessment

In line with previous research it was found that athletes in individual disciplines reported higher depression scores than athletes in team sports (Nixdorf et al., 2016). In particular, the present cohort of elite swimmers also had relatively high levels of depressive symptoms. This finding is supported by Hammond, Gialloreto, Kubas, and Davis (2013) who report a prevalence of 68% for depression in Canadian swimmers, with a strong correlation to perceived failure.

Based on the findings reported above, there is a need for improvement of athlete's mental health. However, less apparent is the question on how to improve athlete's mental health. Therefore, information on which relevant factors intervention and prevention programmes can be based on were needed, and understanding of mechanisms how depression and burnout can be developed in athletes is necessary (Frank, Nixdorf, & Beckmann, 2013). In general, both constructs (depression and burnout) can be regarded in a stress-based perspective (Frank, Nixdorf, & Beckmann, 2017).

Depression does not involve a homogeneous disease pattern. The heterogeneity of the symptoms of depressive disorders also makes it unlikely that one factor alone is responsible for the development of depression. Therefore, adopting multifactorial explanatory concepts such as vulnerability-stress models may be warranted (e.g. Alloy et al., 2006; Haffel et al., 2005; Hyde, Mezulis, & Abramson, 2008). Here, certain vulnerabilities (genetic, social or cognitive factors) in combination with a stressor (chronic or acute) can lead to depression (Lee et al., 2010). Among athletes the relation to stress is also apparent as stressors such as training loads, pressure to perform well (Nixdorf, Frank, & Beckmann, 2015) or an important competition (Hammond et al., 2013) have been associated with depressive symptoms. Frameworks to be considered in regards to athlete burnout can be based on personal factors such as the ability to efficiently cope with chronic psychological stress involved in sports (Smith, 1986), based on the conditions and environmental factors leading to autonomy and identity challenges in young athletes (Coakley, 1992), or the integration of various facets is assumed for a theoretical foundation of athlete burnout (Gustafsson, Kentta, & Hassmen, 2011).

These stress-based perspectives appear valuable, as the present sample indicated high levels of various stressors by their training schedule already. On the basis of vulnerability-stress models, various important factors (vulnerabilities and stressors) have been associated with burnout and depression. However, little evidence has shown longitudinal evidence for factors to have a prospective impact on either construct (Eklund & DeFreese, 2015; Frank et al., 2013). The beforementioned research project addressed this question and found that dysfunctional attitudes and negative coping strategies (such as resignation) act as vulnerabilities, and chronic stress as well as a lack of recovery act as stressors predicting burnout and depression among junior elite athletes across a season. Therefore, these factors appear to be important predictors and represent salient factors for prevention of mental disorders in athletes. Consequently, these factors have been the basis for the present intervention programme for junior elite swimmers. In addition, these factors served as an evaluation indicator for the assessment pre- and post-intervention.

In the present sample, the factors: coping strategies, athlete burnout, chronic stress and current state of stress and recovery were assessed. Due to the stigma and strong reservations expressed by the coaches and parents of the swimmers, an assessment of depression was resigned. Athletes' coping responses to life stressors were measured using relevant strategies from the Stressverarbeitungs-Fragebogen (SVF; Erdmann & Janke, 2008), namely resignation, flight, self-pity and positive self-instruction. The SVF focuses on dispositional coping, rather than on situational coping i.e., it indicates a temporally consistent coping style in the tested subject. The scale has good validity and reliability and was previously applied in elite athlete samples (e.g. Nixdorf et al., 2013). Chronic stress was assessed using the Screening of the Trier Inventory of Chronic Stress (TICS; Schulz, Schlotz, & Becker, 2004). The scale is designed to measure experiences of chronic stress and therefore covers the last 3 months and offers a valid and reliable scale for assessment in the general population (Schulz et al., 2004). Also for (junior) athletes, the scale was validated and normed with adequate psychometric properties (Sallen & Hoffmann, 2012). Burnout in athletes was assessed using the German version of the Athlete Burnout Questionnaire (ABQ; Raedeke & Smith, 2001; German version Ziemainz, Abu-Omar, Raedeke, & Krause, 2004). The ABQ is a valid self-report scale designed to assess the three core dimensions of athlete burnout: physical and emotional exhaustion, sport devaluation and reduced sense of accomplishment. For covering the current state of stress and recovery the Sport-Specific Acute Recovery and Stress Scale (ARSS; Hitzschke et al., 2016) was used. The scale was specifically invented and validated for covering current states of stress and recovery in athletes using 32 adjectives on a rating scale.

Furthermore, these factors were supplemented by qualitative interviews on personal goals, needs and motivation for participation in the programme. Most athletes indicated a personal need to reduce the amount of stress in their lives. In this regard, reasons for stress (stressors) mentioned mostly concerned training and school schedule, which led to difficulties in attending every obligation. Especially, time to study and time for other activities (hobbies, time with friends and family) was drastically minimised. Other important needs were based on the pressure of important events or criteria the athletes were supposed to meet, such as qualification times, personal records or championships. However, perceived pressure was also mentioned regarding school and obligations besides their main sport. Reducing stress and improving ways to cope with stressors could therefore be considered as the overall topic for all interventions delivered.

Framework and intervention for delivery

The main goal of the intervention programme was to prevent burnout and depression as consequences of extensive stress. In regard to prevention, Romano and Hage (2000) define prevention as including one or more of the following: (1) stopping a problem behaviour from ever occurring; (2) delaying the onset of a problem behaviour, especially for those at risk for the problem; (3) reducing the impact of a problem behaviour; (4) strengthening knowledge, attitudes and behaviours that promote emotional and physical well-being; and (5) promoting institutional, community, and government policies that further physical, social and emotional well-being of the larger community. This conceptualisation is consistent with Caplan (1964) who identified prevention interventions as primary, secondary and tertiary prevention, and with the alternative definition by Gordon (1983) that identified prevention interventions as universal, selected and indicated for those not at risk, at risk, and those experiencing early signs of problems. Romano and Hage (2000) also mention that although dimensions 1, 2 and 3 can be conceptualised in traditional primary, secondary and tertiary terms and refer to the individual, dimensions 4 and 5 are conceptualised within a "risk-reduction" -framework. Therefore, the present programme aimed at interventions according to primary and secondary prevention. The goal was to stabilise and strengthen the athletes in order to stop burnout and depression form occurring (point 1) and, according to Romano and Hage (2000), to strengthen knowledge, attitudes and behaviours that promote emotional and physical well-being (point 4).

As mentioned previously, depression and burnout can be addressed from a stress-based perspective. Thus, the present programme was based on a concept of improving athlete's abilities to cope with stressors and therefore enhance resilience in this regard. So, the main focus was centred on strengthening athlete's competences rather than on social or organisational factors. Thus, interventions were based on a cognitive-behavioural perspective of learning. In general, Ingram and Luxton (2005) point out that most psychological approaches rely on assumptions of dysfunctional learning as the genesis of vulnerability. Following this assumption, interventions from a cognitive-behavioural perspective seemed suitable and have been mainly applied in the programme.

In line with other cognitive-behavioural programmes on stress management (Kaluza, 2015), different approaches on stress were considered and implemented. Therefore, intervention can be focused on the stressor (instrumental management), on the cognitive beliefs (mental management) or the stress reaction (regenerative management). Many programmes consider all of these aspects in an integrated approach (Gunthner & Batra, 2012; Kaluza, 2015). For theoretical reasons however, the transactional model from Lazarus and Folkman (1987) is the most commonly applied and adapted as it relates the stressor with the stress reaction based on the personals beliefs and resources. In this perspective, the transaction between people and their external environment is central. The model assumes two appraisals of a person in regards to a potentially stressful situation. Primary appraisal evaluates whether a stressor is dangerous, positive or irrelevant. In a secondary appraisal, the person's resources (sufficient or insufficient) to deal with the stressor are analysed. If stress arises based on the appraisals, coping strategies have to be applied in order to overcome the stressful situation (Lazarus, 1991, 2006).

Illustrating the implemented programme, first considerations were due to the athlete's surrounding. Time and place of the delivered interventions were carefully chosen and evening swimming sessions were replaced with the sport psychological intervention programme. This should help minimise additional stress through the intervention meetings. In addition, as all coaches supported and scheduled the intervention dates it should help underpin the importance of the sport psychological programme for the athlete's perception.

In order to establish contact with the athletes and to introduce the prevention programme a "kick-off" meeting was arranged. The main focus was on explaining the schedule of the programme, to collect any further needs and topics of the athletes and to educate on burnout and depression in elite athletes (e.g. symptoms, aetiopathology and treatment). The intervention programme itself was divided into 3 main sections:

Section 1 "Recognize stressors, promote relaxation (long-term strategies for stress management)"

In this block of interventions, core competences were trained for stress relief and the identification of personal stressors. In addition, a goal was to establish good working conditions with the groups, which should be characterised by a collegial atmosphere during group meetings and independent transfer of the contents. As concrete interventions content from the area of mindfulness was used. Thereby, the advantage was gained that both the recognition of one's own mental processes as well as the ability to relax and self-regulate (for example in the case of focusing) are simultaneously promoted. In addition, at least one classical relaxation procedure (PMR, breathing exercises or autogenetic training) was practiced with each group.

Example of an intervention: "Picture of my week"

Background

Often the time passes by and we ask ourselves at the end of the week what we actually did for us and where we also had joy, fun and recreation. In order to plan your own everyday life a bit better and to ensure sufficient recovery, you can try the following strategy.

Execution

- Draw up a weekly schedule for the next 7 days.
- Enter your fixed dates, e.g. School, training and time to learn.
- Use a different pen (such as other colour) to recreate activities. Try to be very specific (What do you want to do, specifically with whom and how long?). Also, make sure that it is a pleasant activity for you.
- You can now mark with a "−" which activities are a burden for you during the week, and mark with a "+" which activities are recreational.
- See if you have enough rest in your week?
- Change your plan so you can plan enough restorative things during the week.

Try to follow your plan and start a new plan in 7 days. Consider your experiences from the previous week.

Goal

The goal of this strategy is to plan and schedule a week at a time, so an athlete is not overwhelmed and finds him or herself working off many obligations with time to recover (mentally and physically). The declaration of positive and negative (+ and -) to an activity helps athletes to observe their needs and to reflect on their habits. In doing so, the intervention helps identify personal stressors and resources. Its focus is therefore on an instrumental stress management (Kaluza, 2015). In addition, the planning creates a basis for implementing recreation and relaxation strategies in regards to a regenerative management (Kaluza, 2015).

Section 2 "Stress management techniques (long-term strategies for stress management)"

In the second block of interventions, various techniques and competences were developed, as planned, with the multitude of stressors of the swimmers. Coping strategies such as positive self-verbalisation and the introduced content of mindfulness were applied in stressful situations of the swimmers. Also, individual exercises were conducted as a group exercise or with the involvement of the group in order to strengthen the social structure and thus the support in the training group. Here, the implementation was also closely linked to the planned content. The essential work involved the individual implementation and transfer of the exercises to the stressors and challenges of the individual athlete.

Example of an intervention: "My mental rule of three"

Background

Especially in athletes' everyday life starting early in the morning (school, training, physiotherapy, competitions), the athletes should learn to use the little time as best as possible. Often, in addition to a full calendar of appointments, it is aggravating that our thoughts are not focusing on the current activity, but we are worrying about the future or thinking about the past. This exercise helps to focus on the here and now and on the essentials: What do I need now? What is important to do now?

Execution

Take a moment, breathe three times, and answer the following three questions (in thought or written). If you digress, that is ok. Try again and think about what is important at this moment. My mental rule of three:

1   A thought about the past: (What happened? How was that?):
2   A thought about the future: (What will come? How will that be?):
3   A thought about the current situation: (What is now? What do I need now? What is important now?):

Goal

The goal of this strategy is to focus on the here and now and to reduce distracting thoughts about the past or future by deliberately being aware of these thoughts, giving them their space and time. That way distracting thoughts or worries don't have to force themselves on an athlete at any given moment and the athlete can take control of their thoughts and focus on a current task or need.

Section 3: "Success, goals, attitudes (short-term strategies for stress management)"

In the third block, the interventions focused on the setting of goals and functional attitudes. At the same time, the goal was, above all, to work out a realistic, yet motivating assessment of one's own abilities with the individual athletes. Interventions focusing on personal values and beliefs tried to promote self-esteem, self-efficacy and self-accepting attitudes. These attitudes were additionally applied in setting personal goals.

Example of an intervention: "My own perfect companion"

Background

Each one of us has people who do a good job and people who are sometimes obstructive. For instance, they put an additional pressure on us, put high demands that are too high on us or we get the feeling that they would not believe in us. First of all, it is important that we believe in ourselves. This exercise is designed to help you support yourself, encourage yourself, motivate yourself positively and master difficult situations.

Execution

Take a moment and think about imminent difficulties. There are probably a few sentences that pop up. "This will be difficult!" or "Do not fail!". You may also remember sentences and statements from other people. Perhaps you can imagine what your father, a team colleague or your trainer would say in such a situation.

Now imagine there is a personal companion for you. A person who supports you unconditionally, who is always loyal to you and always likes you. Whatever you're doing, this companion will always stick to you and will always have your back. Now imagine what this perfect companion would say to you? What would he/she advise you, how would he/she cheer you up, and what would he/she do in your situation? Try to sketch this companion as well and as accurately as possible before your inner eye (What does he/she look like? What age is he/she? Does he/she have a comforting voice?). You can now ask him/her for advice, whenever you need him/her.

It is best to repeat this exercise a few times, so you can imagine your companion easier and quicker. You can also give him/her a name or link him/her with a symbol or small mascot (e.g., a key pendant or figure). That way he/she can always be with you in the sports bag.

Goal

The goal of this strategy is to establish a positive, supportive voice for the athletes. The imagined companion is always accessible, which can help building self-esteem and self-efficacy. This intervention can be regarded as a cognitive technique, which could be applied in cognitive-behavioural therapy and mental stress management (Kaluza, 2015; Leahy, 2017). The focus is on the athlete's attitudes and beliefs and offers a possibility to promote functional, positive beliefs and therefore reduce possible negative consequences by dysfunctional or perfectionistic attitudes (Ashby & Rice, 2002; Bianchi & Schonfeld, 2016; Madigan, Stoeber, & Passfield, 2015).

For all sections and interventions athletes were motivated to practice and try different interventions at home. In the subsequent meeting these interventions were discussed and open questions addressed. At the end of the intervention programme an overview highlighting the most valuable intervention for each participant was reviewed.

Intervention evaluation and lessons learned through self-reflection

Overall, the programme was welcomingly appreciated by participating athletes, coaches and parents. Rating of the intervention programme by the athletes was $M = 1.35$ ($SD = 0.48$) on a scale from $1 = $ *very good* to $5 = $ *bad*. In order to evaluate the implemented interventions, central markers were tested at the beginning and the end of the programme. As mentioned above the following questionnaires were assessed: the Trierer inventory for chronic stress screening, TICS (Schulz et al., 2004), relevant scales of the stress processing questionnaire, SVF (Erdmann & Janke, 2008), and the sport-specific acute recovery and stress scale (ARSS; Hitzschke et al., 2016) and the Athlete Burnout Questionnaire, ABQ (Raedeke & Smith, 2001) in its German version (Ziemainz et al., 2004).

The results in table 3.1 show a general positive trend. All variables improved on a descriptive level. Given the small sample size ($n = 11$), no statistical analyses were performed due to questionable reliability of such results.

In an anonymous evaluation at the end of the programme, the athletes rated the sessions overall as highly valuable (M = 1.35; 1 represents highest grade and 5 represents lowest grade). Especially the useful information and the comprehensive education (both rated with M = 1.47) were positively evaluated. The only difficulties were apparent with the application and practicability of the content, which received the lowest score, however they were still positively graded (M = 1.65).

Unfortunately, as in all longitudinal studies there was a loss of data due to incomplete data sets for a considerable number of participants. Only 11 athletes completed the online post-intervention measures. An "online" approach can appear as a convenient way of gathering information, however access to the internet for those participating was low. Therefore, paper and pencil face to face methods may have been preferable and should be considered in future studies. Aspects of anonymity and blinding should however be carefully considered in this regard (Brown & Fletcher, 2017).

From the reflection during the interventions, qualitative feedback and individual performance results, there remain some important aspects to be noted. A first important issue was to catch up with the daily stressors and hazards of the athlete's lives. This contributed to a diverse programme, topics and examples for upcoming interventions and eventually positively affected the athlete's motivation for participation in the programme due to a high level of autonomous regulation (Adie, Duda, & Ntoumanis, 2008; Ryan & Deci, 2000).

TABLE 3.1 Mean scores of assessed variables for intervention evaluation

	Pre-intervention		Post-intervention	
	Mean	*SD*	*Mean*	*SD*
TICS	23.55	9.50	21.00	8.53
SVF – resignation	8.90	4.30	8.36	4.37
SVF – flight	7.55	3.86	7.27	3.86
SVF – self-pity	11.00	5.00	9.82	5.00
SVF – positive self-instruction	14.18	3.54	14.64	3.83
ARSS – recovery	38.18	10.25	41.09	9.51
ARSS – stress	39.36	10.44	35.00	12.30
ABQ	19.91	7.97	19.45	8.78

Another aspect for consideration was the timing of the sessions themselves. Although already carefully considered, the intervention sessions to some degree increased the amount of the weekly obligations and were therefore counterproductive for promotion of recovery. However, based on long-term considerations, the temporary increase might be justified. For future programmes it would be valuable to consider an even closer attunement of intervention and daily programme. In this regard, training camps might offer a perfect opportunity in order to avoid additional stress. In addition, training camps offer further possibilities to practice and apply sport psychological content in practice. Further considerations are based on the results of the participating athletes. According to Brown and Fletcher (2017) the effects of psychological interventions on sport performance are moderate in general. In the present programme the overall performance of most athletes was good and in some cases even exceedingly high. This could be seen as evidence that a focus on athletes' mental health and well-being does not have to be counterproductive in terms of performance enhancement. The conclusion would be rather that promotion of mental health can be a considerable aspect not just for mental health issues but also for building a basis for sport performance. Strengthening athletes' personality, developing competencies for sports and other aspects in life, therefore offers ways to build stable and resilient athletes. This would not only be morally obligatory but might as well promote sport performance.

References

Adie, J. W., Duda, J. L., & Ntoumanis, N. (2008). Autonomy support, basic need satisfaction and the optimal functioning of adult male and female sport participants: A test of basic needs theory. *Motivation and Emotion, 32*(3), 189–199. doi:10.1007/s11031-008-9095-z

Alloy, L. B., Abramson, L. Y., Whitehouse, W. G., Hogan, M. E., Panzarella, C., & Rose, D. T. (2006). Prospective incidence of first onsets and recurrences of depression in individuals at high and low cognitive risk for depression. *Journal of Abnormal Psychology, 115*(1), 145–156. doi:10.1037/0021-843X.115.1.145

American Psychiatric Association. (2013). *Diagnostic and statistical manual of mental disorders* (5th ed.). Washington, DC: American Psychiatric Association.

Ashby, J. S., & Rice, K. G. (2002). Perfectionism, dysfunctional attitudes, and self-esteem: A structural equations analysis. *Journal of Counseling & Development, 80*(2), 197–203.

Bianchi, R., & Schonfeld, I. S. (2016). Burnout is associated with a depressive cognitive style. *Personality and Individual Differences, 100*, 1–5. doi:10.1016/j.paid.2016.01.008

Brown, D. J., & Fletcher, D. (2017). Effects of psychological and psychosocial interventions on sport performance: A meta-analysis. *Sports Medicine, 47*(1), 77–99. doi:10.1007/s40279-016-0552-7

Caplan, G. (1964). *Principles of preventive psychiatry*. New York, NY: Basic Books.

Coakley, J. (1992). Burnout among adolescent athletes – a personal failure or social-problem. *Sociology of Sport Journal, 9*(3), 271–285.

Eklund, R. C., & DeFreese, J. (2015). Athlete burnout: What we know, what we could know, and how we can find out more. *International Journal of Applied Sports Sciences, 27*(2).

Erdmann, G., & Janke, W. (2008). *Stressverarbeitungsfragebogen SVF (Handbuch): Stress, Stressverarbeitung und ihre Erfassung durch ein mehrdimensionales Testsystem*. Göttingen: Hogrefe.

Frank, R., Nixdorf, I., & Beckmann, J. (2013). Depressionen im Hochleistungssport: Präva-lenzen und psychologische Einflüsse [Depression in elite athletes: Prevalence and psy-chological factors]. *Deutsche Zeitschrift Fur Sportmedizin, 64*(11), 320–326. doi:10.5960/ dzsm.2013.088

Frank, R., Nixdorf, I., & Beckmann, J. (2017). Analyzing the relationship between depres-sion and burnout in junior elite athletes. *Journal of Clinical Sport Psychology. 11*(4), 287–303. doi: 10.1123/JCSP.2017-0008

Goodger, K., Gorely, T., Lavallee, D., & Harwood, C. (2007). Burnout in sport: A systematic review. *The Sport Psychologist, 21*, 127–151.

Gordon, R. S. (1983). An operational classification of disease prevention. *Public Health Reports, 98*(2), 107.

Gulliver, A., Griffiths, K. M., Mackinnon, A., Batterham, P. J., & Stanimirovic, R. (2015). The mental health of Australian elite athletes. *Journal of Science and Medicine in Sport, 18*(3), 255–261. doi:10.1016/j.jsams.2014.04.006

Gunthner, A., & Batra, A. (2012). Stressmanagemant als burn-out-prohylaxe [Prevention of burnout by stress management]. *Bundesgesundheitsblatt Gesundheitsforschung Gesundheitss-chutz, 55*(2), 183–189. doi:10.1007/s00103-011-1406-y

Gustafsson, H., DeFreese, J., & Madigan, D. J. (2017). Athlete burnout: Review and recommen-dations. *Current Opinion in Psychology, 16*, 109–113. doi:10.1016/j.copsyc.2017.05.002

Gustafsson, H., Kentta, G., & Hassmen, P. (2011). Athlete burnout: An integrated model and future research directions. *International Review of Sport and Exercise Psychology, 4*(1), 3–24. doi:10.1080/1750984x.2010.541927

Haffel, G. J., Abramson, L. Y., Voelz, Z. R., Metalsky, G. I., Halberstadt, L., Dykman, B. M., . . . Alloy, L. B. (2005). Negative cognitive styles, dysfunctional attitudes, and the remitted depression paradigm: A search for the elusive cognitive vulnerability to depression fac-tor among remitted depressives. *Emotion, 5*(3), 343–348. doi:10.1037/1528-3542.5.3.343

Hammond, T., Gialloreto, C., Kubas, H., & Davis, H. (2013). The prevalence of failure-based depression among elite athletes. *Clinical Journal of Sport Medicine, 23*(4), 273–277. doi:10.1097/JSM.0b013e318287b870

Hitzschke, B., Holst, T., Ferrauti, A., Meyer, T., Pfeiffer, M., & Kellmann, M. (2016). Entwick-lung des Akutmaßes zur Erfassung von Erholung und Beanspruchung im Sport. *Diagnos-tica, 62*(4), 212–226.

Hyde, J. S., Mezulis, A. H., & Abramson, L. Y. (2008). The ABCs of depression: Inte-grating affective, biological, and cognitive models to explain the emergence of the gender difference in depression. *Psychological Review, 115*(2), 291–313. doi:10.1037/0033-295X.115.2.291

Ingram, R. E., & Luxton, D. D. (2005). Vulnerability-stress models. In B. L. Hankin & J. R. Z. Abela (Eds.), *Development of psychopathology: A vulnerability-stress perspective* (pp. 32–46). Thousand Oaks, CA: Sage Publications.

Insel, T. R., & Charney, D. S. (2003). Research on major depression: Strategies and priorities. *JAMA, 289*(23), 3167–3168.

Kaluza, G. (2015). *Stressbewältigung: Trainingsmanual zur psychologischen Gesundheitsförderung.* Heidelberg: Springer-Verlag.

Lazarus, R. S. (1991). *Emotion and adaptation.* New York, NY: Oxford University Press.

Lazarus, R. S. (2006). *Stress and emotion: A new synthesis.* New York, NY: Springer Publishing Company.

Lazarus, R. S., & Folkman, S. (1987). Transactional theory and research on emotions and cop-ing. *European Journal of personality, 1*(3), 141–169.

Leahy, R. L. (2017). *Cognitive therapy techniques: A practitioner's guide.* New York, NY: The Guilford Press.

Lee, S., Jeong, J., Kwak, Y., & Park, S. K. (2010). Depression research: Where are we now? *Molecular Brain, 3,* 8. doi:10.1186/1756-6606-3-8

Madigan, D. J., Stoeber, J., & Passfield, L. (2015). Perfectionism and burnout in junior athletes: A three-month longitudinal study. *Journal of Sport & Exercise Psychology, 37*(3), 305–315. doi:10.1123/jsep.2014-0266

Maslach, C., & Jackson, S. E. (1981). The measurement of experienced burnout. *Journal of Organizational Behavior, 2*(2), 99–113.

Maslach, C., Schaufeli, W. B., & Leiter, M. P. (2001). Job burnout. *Annual Review of Psychology, 52*(1), 397–422.

Nixdorf, I., Frank, R., & Beckmann, J. (2015). An explorative study on major stressors and its connection to depression and chronic stress among German elite athletes. *Advances in Physical Education, 5*(4), 255–262. doi:10.4236/ape.2015.54030

Nixdorf, I., Frank, R., & Beckmann, J. (2016). Comparison of athletes' proneness to depressive symptoms in individual and team sports: Research on psychological mediators in junior elite athletes. *Frontiers in Psychology, 7,* 893. doi:10.3389/fpsyg.2016.00893

Nixdorf, I., Frank, R., Hautzinger, M., & Beckmann, J. (2013). Prevalence of depressive symptoms and correlating variables among German elite athletes. *Journal of Clinical Sport Psychology, 7,* 313–326.

Raedeke, T. D., & Smith, A. L. (2001). Development and preliminary validation of an athlete burnout measure. *Journal of Sport & Exercise Psychology, 23*(4), 281–306.

Romano, J. L., & Hage, S. M. (2000). Prevention and counseling psychology revitalizing commitments for the 21st century. *The Counseling Psychologist, 28*(6), 733–763.

Ryan, R. M., & Deci, E. L. (2000). Intrinsic and extrinsic motivations: Classic definitions and new directions. *Contemporary Educational Psychology, 25*(1), 54–67. doi:10.1006/ceps.1999.1020

Sallen, J., & Hoffmann, K. (2012). Spezifische Normierung des Trierer Inventars zum chronischen Stress (TICS) zur diagnostischen Anwendung im Spitzensport. *Zeitschrift für Sportpsychologie, 19*(3), 95–109. doi:10.1026/1612-5010/a000074

Schinke, R. J., Stambulova, N. B., Si, G., & Moore, Z. (2017). International society of sport psychology position stand: Athletes' mental health, performance, and development. *International Journal of Sport and Exercise Psychology,* 1–18.

Schulz, P., Schlotz, W., & Becker, P. (2004). *Trierer Inventar zum chronischen Stress.* Göttingen: Hogrefe.

Smith, R. E. (1986). Toward a cognitive-affective model of athletic burnout. *Journal of Sport Psychology, 8*(1), 36–50.

Wolanin, A., Hong, E., Marks, D., Panchoo, K., & Gross, M. (2016). Prevalence of clinically elevated depressive symptoms in college athletes and differences by gender and sport. *British Journal of Sports Medicine, 50*(3), 167–171. doi:10.1136/bjsports-2015-095756

Ziemainz, H., Abu-Omar, K., Raedeke, T., & Krause, K. (2004). Burnout im sport. *Leistungssport, 34*(6), 12–17.

Further reading

Gustafsson, H., DeFreese, J. D., & Madigan, D. (2017). Athlete burnout: Review and recommendations. *Current Opinion in Psychology, 16,* 109–113. doi:10.1016/j.copsyc.2017.05.002
Burnout is a relatively prevalent syndrome among athletes and is a significant threat to athletes' metal health. Accordingly, it is essential that sport and exercise scientists understand its aetiology. The authors give a good overview of the intensely researched topic of burnout and include recommendations too.

Nixdorf, I., Frank, R., & Beckmann, J. (2016). Comparison of athletes' proneness to depressive symptoms in individual and team sports: Research on psychological mediators in junior elite athletes. *Frontiers in Psychology*, 7, 893. doi:10.3389/fpsyg.2016.00893
Rather than just gathering descriptive variables correlating with depression in elite athletes this publication offers an underlying understanding and uncovers a psychological variable mediating the effect of individual sport athletes' higher depression scores.

Schinke, R. J., Stambulova, N. B., Si, G., & Moore, Z. (2017). International society of sport psychology position stand: Athletes' mental health, performance, and development. *International Journal of Sport and Exercise Psychology*, 1–18.
This publication offers a good overview on mental health research in sport psychology. The authors advocate a continuum from active mental illness, to sub-syndromal illness, to normal, to good mental health and to peak performance. This approach is favorable to a dichotomous classification, but further development and elaboration on this understanding is needed.

4

BOLSTERING PSYCHOLOGICAL HEALTH USING RATIONAL EMOTIVE BEHAVIOUR THERAPY

Andrew G. Wood, Martin J. Turner and Jamie B. Barker

Learning objectives

After reading this chapter you should be able to:

1   Understand the origins and central tenets of Rational Emotive Behaviour Therapy (REBT).
2   Understand the effects of irrational and rational beliefs on psychological health.
3   Outline the applications of REBT as an intervention to promote psychological health.
4   Glean professional practice insights into the application of REBT with athletes.

Introduction to REBT

"*There are three musts that hold us back, I must do well, you must treat me well, and the world must be easy*" (Epstein, 2001). In this chapter we offer an insight into the application of Rational Emotive Behaviour Therapy (REBT; Ellis, 1957) as a framework for helping athletes develop and maintain mental health. REBT is a cognitive-behavioural approach to psychotherapy based upon the premise that "people are not disturbed by things, but by the view which they take of them" (Epictetus, 1948, 55–135 A.D.). Central to REBT theory is the notion that when encountered with adversity (i.e., failure, rejection, or setbacks) those who harbour irrational beliefs will experience *unhealthy* negative emotions (UNEs; i.e., anxiety, depression, unhealthy rage) and maladaptive behaviours (e.g., avoidance, disproportionate behaviours) that hinder goal achievement (Vîslă, Flückiger, Holtforth, & David, 2016; David, Szentagotai, Eva, & Macavei, 2005). Whereas those with rational beliefs, will experience *healthy* negative emotions (HNEs; i.e., concern, sadness, healthy anger) and adaptive behaviours (problem-focussed, proportionate behaviours) that help goal achievement (Dryden & Branch, 2008). All humans to varying degrees are inherently irrational and rational, and those operating in elite sport are no exception.

Elite sport, like many performance settings, is highly demanding and athletes face various organisational, competitive, and personal stressors in the pursuit of performance excellence (Fletcher, Hanton, & Wagstaff, 2012). To compound the challenges of elite sport, the context itself may implicitly encourage irrational beliefs (Turner, 2016a). First, for some athletes, perceived self-worth is contingent on their ability to perform well and ultimately become successful (Kaplan & Flum, 2010), in turn disproportionately heightening the negative consequences of failure. For example, an athlete may perform in fear due to the belief that if they were to lose this would make them a complete failure and worthless. Athletes who are unable to accept themselves as fallible and imperfect human beings are also more susceptible to distress when encountering adversity, through harsh self-criticism and a focus upon personal inadequacies (Flett & Hewitt, 2005). Further, constant exposure to irrational language (e.g., "today is a must win game", "that was terrible today") entrenched into the sporting lexicon may further encourage an irrational approach to achievement (Turner, 2016a). Ultimately, the endorsement of irrational beliefs is detrimental to the psychological health of an athlete and hinders psychological resilience (i.e., ability to respond to adversity in a functional and adaptive manner; Dryden & Branch, 2008).

In REBT, there are four core irrational beliefs that underlie mental illness, and there are four core rational beliefs that underpin mental health (see Figure 4.1). Here, practitioners use the ABC (DE) framework (Ellis & Dryden, 1997) to dispute irrational beliefs and replace them with rational alternatives, ultimately encouraging a rational view of adversity. For example, when faced with failure (e.g., losing a game), rejection (e.g., de-selection), or poor treatment (e.g., treatment from coach or teammates), a rational view based upon the four core rational beliefs (see Figure 4.1) will lead to a healthy negative emotion and adaptive response. Considering the abundance of research documenting the efficacy of REBT within clinical and non-clinical settings (see David et al., 2005) researchers have begun to evidence the potential value of REBT to understand and promote mental health in athletes (see Turner, 2016a for a review). Although research has revealed for some individuals that irrational beliefs may harbour acute performance benefits (e.g., Wood, Barker, & Turner, 2017), evidence for the detrimental effects on psychological health is overwhelming (David et al., 2005). Most notably, irrational beliefs predict symptoms of burnout (i.e., emotional and physical exhaustion; Turner & Moore, 2015), whereas unconditional self-acceptance (a rational belief) has been associated with reduced self-blame and self-criticism (Hill, Hall, Appleton, & Kozub, 2008).

The application of clinical psychotherapeutic frameworks marks a shift in psychological interventions in sport. Using a case-example we aim to engage readers in an approach that moves beyond typical psychological-skills training as would be found with the Canon of sport psychology (Andersen, 2009), and expands the library of approaches from which sport psychologists are able to draw upon. In our chapter we discuss intervention effects, professional competence, blurred boundaries between therapy and mental skills training, consultant's experience, and professional practice guidelines.

Core Irrational Beliefs	Core Rational Beliefs
Demandingness:	**Preference**:
"I want to, and therefore I must be successful"	*"I want to, but that does not mean I must be successful"*
Awfulising:	**Anti-Awfulising**:
"It would be terrible if I did not win"	*"It would be bad, but it certainly wouldn't be terrible if I did not win"*
Self depreciation:	**Unconditional Self-acceptance**:
"Losing makes me a complete failure"	*"If I lost it does not make me a complete failure, only that I have failed this time"*
Frustration Intolerance:	**Frustration Tolerance**:
"I could not tolerate losing today"	*"Although uncomfortable, I could tolerate losing, and it is worth it to do so"*

FIGURE 4.1 Defining characteristics of irrational and rational beliefs

The Client

Sarah (pseudonym) was a 42-year-old Paralympic athlete who at the time of the intervention had made the transition to a full-time podium performance programme, training four days a week with the national team. Whilst having ambitions to represent her nation at the upcoming Paralympics Sarah had contacted a Sport Psychologist (SP; Andrew Wood) via email to seek psychological support that would help her adjust to life as a full-time professional athlete, citing a variety of personal and competitive challenges during this transition. Furthermore, it was important to consider Sarah's personal history, specifically in relation to her disability. To respect client confidentiality and anonymity we will not provide explicit detail around her physical disability or medical history. Whilst there is a dearth of research with specialised population groups such as elite athletes with a disability (Barker, Mellalieu, McCarthy, Jones, & Moran, 2013), researchers have begun to put forth important considerations for practitioners. First, athletes with a disability will experience similar (e.g., incompatible coaching style, unfair selection, expectations for medal success) and differing (e.g., inaccessible venues, lack of disability specific coaching, disability classification) stressors to able-bodied athletes (Arnold, Wagstaff, Steadman, & Pratt, 2017). Second, Paralympic athletes will also have varying psychological experiences of disability that are influenced by their history, for example acquired versus congenital (i.e., impairment present from birth). For those athletes with an acquired disability their acquisition of a physical impairment may have been gradual, or after an acute traumatic incident. To illustrate, Skordilis, Skafida, Chrysagis, and Nikitaras (2006) explain that such individuals have to deal with sudden and prolonged psychological crises alternating between acknowledging their pre-disability identity and new 'disability' identity. This can be shown in attempting super-human endeavours to portray the control, meaning, and identity they held prior to their injury. In addition, they are likely to only see themselves in a negative light, with diminished self-worth, and in some cases experience severe depression. In contrast, those with a congenital disability experience psychosocial adaptations associated with an impaired body and body image issues. Finally, researchers have also indicated that those with a physical disability are at greater risk to mental illness (e.g., depression; Fassberg et al., 2016).

Initial needs assessment

An intake interview was conducted as an appropriate means to explore Sarah's background, areas for development or concern, details of her sport, and life outside of sport, paying due care to attending to Sarah as a person and a performer (Aoyagi, Poczwardwski, Statler, Shapiro, & Cohen, 2017). No behavioural assessment strategies were implemented due to distance of Sarah's main training centre.

During the initial intake meeting with Sarah it became apparent that Sarah's history, personal events, and introduction to competitive life were inextricably linked, and were having adverse effects upon her day-to-day functioning and performances. During training camps Sarah would excessively ruminate about personal issues and found it difficult to concentrate and fully immerse herself within training. Acknowledging the detrimental effects upon her training and competition performances Sarah was angry and began to resent significant others in her personal life for not allowing her the opportunity to fulfil her potential. Subsequently, the resentment further detracted from her ability to engage within the Paralympic programme. This dislike towards others was captured within her cognitive distortions such as overgeneralising (e.g., "they must be bad people") and over-personalisation (e.g., "they must be only doing it to me"; Dryden, 2012). Sarah was also becoming overtly concerned about what others thought of her and anxious that she was not meeting others' expectations (i.e., teammates or coaching staff).

During training Sarah was easily agitated and became pent up with anger towards teammates who would un/intentionally distract her from completing her pre-performance routine. For example, she used self-talk such as "don't worry what they do" and "stop thinking about what others are doing". As purported by the ironic processing theory (Wegner, 1994), the more she demanded that others should be more considerate, the harder it became to concentrate and the more she became physically restless.

Much of her psychological unrest (e.g., anxiety, anger) was being externally attributed, and in Sarah's view her emotional disturbance (C) was directly a result of the adversity (e.g., others/events) rather than under her control. To compound the matter, the sport in which Sarah participated included minimal physical exertion, whereby success was largely attributed to psychological preparation. With the provision of full-time funding onto the performance programme Sarah was highlighted as a promising addition to the team. Nevertheless, during this transition to the senior team, she was struggling to cope (i.e., lack of concentration, easily angered, disheartened, feeling anxious) with the various personal, competitive, and organisational stressors she encountered (Fletcher, Hanton, & Mellalieu, 2006).

Based upon her use of irrational language, low levels of emotional control, and inability to cope effectively with challenges that transcended her competitive life, a REBT intervention was selected as an appropriate framework to support and develop Sarah's needs. REBT practitioners are focussed on exploring the breadth of adversities athletes may encounter, and whether their behaviours help or hinder goal achievement. Being unable to respond to situations in an adaptive or resilient manner indicates that the athlete is harbouring irrational beliefs about that give situation. In this case, it appeared Sarah held irrational beliefs that were having detrimental effects on her overall psychological health and ability to respond adaptively to the challenges she encountered. Both Sarah's personal and sporting life were extremely important to her and was eager to seek a resolution. Rather than unpicking each 'problem', the application of REBT would offer a solution that allowed Sarah to respond in a healthy adaptive manner, irrespective of the situation. Therefore, it would not just change Sarah's beliefs about one situation, but she would experience a shift towards a rational philosophy (i.e., the endorsement of rational beliefs that are supported empirically, logically, and pragmatically) that would in turn provide a pro-active approach that enhanced her psychological health and would allow her to achieve her respective goals (Turner, 2016a). A psychometric assessment of her irrational beliefs was conducted using the Shortened General Attitudes and Belief Scale (SGABS; Lindner, Kirkby, Wertheim, & Birch, 1999; see Figure 4.4). SGABS scores indicated high total irrational beliefs and irrational beliefs related to the content areas of 'demand for fairness', 'other-downing', and a 'need for approval'. It is important to state Sarah like all humans was not wholly irrational, and athletes will vary in the extent that they endorse both irrational and rational beliefs. The REBT intervention would provide a pro-active approach that not only reduced irrational beliefs but also bolstered a rational view of adversity. REBT is originally a psychotherapeutic intervention applied in clinical settings. In Sarah's case, the scope of the consultancy was not to address or treat a clinically diagnosed mental illness, but the aim was to rather use concepts and the framework of REBT (i.e., ABCDE framework) as a pro-active approach to bolster the foundations for wellbeing and effective functioning. Hence it was important for to understand and be sensitive to the somewhat blurry lines of professional competence (Roberts, Faull, & Tod, 2016). To monitor the effects of REBT and changes in Sarah's irrational beliefs measures of total irrational beliefs, demand for fairness, other-downing, and a need for approval from significant others were collected on a weekly basis. To undertake social validation of the intervention effects a semi-structured interview was conducted with Sarah to ascertain the intervention effects, successful receipt, and practitioner evaluation.

Framework and intervention for delivery

Overview of the ABC (DE) Framework Central to the practice of REBT is the situational ABC (DE) framework (see Figure 4.2), based upon the premise that people experience undesirable activating events (A; or adversity), about which they

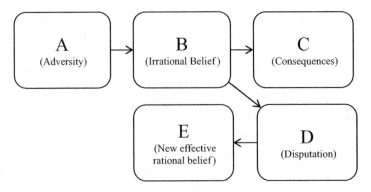

FIGURE 4.2 A schematic of the ABC(DE) framework central to the REBT process

have rational and irrational beliefs (B; David et al., 2005). These beliefs then lead to four intimately interconnected levels of cognitive, emotional, behavioural, and physiological consequences (C). To emphasise and support a rational philosophy practitioners use three main strategies to actively dispute (D) the client's irrational beliefs and replace them with more adaptive and effective rational alternatives (E). This framework helps to understand that thoughts, feelings, and actions are inter-related (David, Miclea, & Opre, 2004), therefore changes in one can lead to changes in the others. Thus, practitioners use a range of cognitive, emotional, and behavioural techniques to promote a functional and adaptive response to adversity.

Compared to other cognitive-behavioural approaches (e.g., the canon; Andersen, 2009) REBT is distinct in the following ways:

1   **Getting Better and Staying Better** – Rather than alleviating symptoms, the process of REBT targets the root cause (irrational beliefs & unhelpful behaviours Dryden & Neenan, 2015). Not only offering a sticky plaster, the application typically brings about meaningful and long-term psychological changes. (i.e., self-efficacy, enjoyment, motivation, performance Wood et al., 2017). Regular travel to national and international competitions was an inherent part of Sarah's sport. By working through the ABC(DE) framework Sarah would gain both psychological insight into her own behaviours and techniques to recognise, re-appraise, and reinforce new rational beliefs. Thus, once REBT was delivered sufficiently, Sarah would be autonomous and independent in maintaining a new rational view of adversity, and the role as a practitioner would become partially redundant.

2   **Fostering Resilience** – Instead of adopting a deficit view, REBT offers a pro-active intervention that bolsters a rational philosophy towards both participation in competitive sport and how this fits into a person's life as a whole. In turn, athletes become resilient to the acute and chronic stressors that they will inevitably encounter (Deen, Turner, & Wong, 2017). In Sarah's case the successful disputation of irrational beliefs with rational alternatives would foster a

helpful and adaptive response to stressors across all aspects of her life, and not just restricted to sport.

3 **Accepting the Circumstances** – REBT does not dispute the adversity (A) but assumes it to be true. For example, an athlete may be extremely anxious about an important competition. Rather than disputing the athletes' inference that this is an important competition (e.g., trying to convince them that it is less important), practitioners dispute (D) their irrational beliefs (B) about the adversity (A) and aims to replaces them with rational alternatives (E). Essentially, athletes will become proficient in responding functionally irrespective of the circumstances. When faced with adversity the ability to shift her mindset from the situation (i.e., uncontrollable) to her own beliefs and response (i.e., controllable) was particularly important for Sarah; as much of what she found challenging in her personal or competitive lives were unchangeable.

4 **Changing Perceptions of Negative Emotions** – REBT advocates that negative emotions prior to or after adversity are normal and vital if they are to attain their respective goals. Rather than emphasising a positive vs. negative response, focus is on *unhealthy* vs *healthy* negative emotions. In turn, this shift in perceiving negative emotions as helpful allows the athletes to then manage the situation and return to a normative or positive state in a somewhat swift fashion. The process of normalising negative emotions would help Sarah prevent the development of meta-emotions when encountering adversity (i.e., not becoming depressed about being angry, or becoming more anxious about being anxious).

REBT intervention

REBT is most effective when delivered on a one-to-one basis (Turner & Barker, 2014). Here practitioners are able to develop a strong working alliance whilst matching the pace, content, and delivery style to the client. Taking into consideration the contextual and pragmatic constraints, five one-to-one sessions and four homework tasks were delivered, each lasting for approximately forty-five minutes. The intervention was separated into an education, disputation, and reinforcement phase (see Turner & Barker, 2014 for an overview). The quality of relationship between the psychologist and the client is consistently shown as a leading factor towards successful intervention outcomes (Keegan, 2016). A collaborative and empathetic approach is particularly pertinent to REBT delivery. Elements of the REBT process required Sarah to recall challenging events (i.e., education phase) whereby the success of the disputation phases requires a willingness to let go of deeply held irrational beliefs and replace them with healthy and rational alternatives. Therefore, it was and still remains central for those using REBT to develop a strong working alliance with the client from the onset of the intervention, whether it's through varying one's likeability, credibility, or through intentional self-disclosure (i.e., helping to normalise her position; Dryden & Neenan, 2015).

Education phase

The education phase was conducted over two sessions and aimed to show Sarah that it was her beliefs (B) that determined the functionality of feelings and actions (C) rather than the adversity alone (A). To begin, Sarah was asked to detail either the most recent or a poignant situation (A) that she had recently experienced and found challenging. Athletes will typically report an account that implicitly refers to the adversity (A) or their response (C), as well offer clues to what their underlying beliefs might be. Therefore, it is up to the practitioner to pinpoint and guide the client towards unpicking the example in a strategic fashion. A poignant adversity (A) for Sarah was not being able to voice her own needs, instead having to prioritise the needs of others and feeling at the maximum capacity as to what she could deal with. Sarah then detailed the corresponding unhealthy and dysfunctional feelings (i.e., anger, guilt), thoughts (i.e., resentment towards others), physical responses (e.g., somatic symptoms), action tendencies (e.g., what she wanted to do), and behaviours (i.e., acting out or avoiding conflict). Following this, Sarah described what a functional response to the same situation would look like (e.g., "when this situation arises again how would you like to respond?"). This was important as it highlighted that a negative feeling to the situation was normal, and that a negative yet functional alternative was possible. At this point it was important to agree upon a goal that Sarah would work towards if this situation were to arise again; Sarah wanted to find the balance between prioritising her own and other's needs. After checking in with Sarah to clarify her understanding at the end of the first session, she was asked to complete an A-C diary of any challenging moments that she might experience before our next session. The Sport Psychologist (SP; first author) also asked her to ponder what she might be currently telling herself about the situation that led her to feeling and acting in this way. This was left purposefully vague so Sarah had the impetus to reflect on her own beliefs, typically a process people do not engage in. It was important to tailor the pace of the education phase to Sarah's needs because sufficient understanding of the REBT framework lays the foundation for subsequent phases. Sarah was also encouraged to voice any doubts, concerns, or questions by the SP (Dryden & Branch, 2008). Over the course of the first session Sarah was open and engaged with the intervention content (i.e., ABCDE framework) and was curious as to what would be uncovered during the next session in a week's time.

At the beginning of session two, we began by reviewing Sarah's homework task (i.e., A-C diary). This provided an opportunity to check her understanding, as well begin to discuss the beliefs that Sarah held in this given situation. Here Sarah was asked "what are you telling yourself about the situation (i.e., having to prioritise others needs over her own) that was leading to responding in this way?". Sarah's response alluded to others not respecting or understanding her needs: For example, "I would like others to consider my needs as well as their own, therefore they must, if not they are completely inconsiderate and I cannot tolerate these kinds of people". When asking clients about their underlying beliefs, it is only in exceptional cases where they will allude to their underlying beliefs straightway. Here an *inference chaining* exercise (Dryden, 1995) allowed the SP to explore the underlying irrational beliefs upon which Sarah based her inferences and evaluations of the adversity (A). This process involved asking Sarah what was bad and/or negative about this adversity (e.g., "having to support others"), where she would reply with an inference (e.g., "not being able to prioritise herself and her sport"). The SP then continuously asked the same question for each inference before eventually reaching the core irrational belief. Whilst seemingly very specific, this belief is essentially underpinned by a sense of injustice and/or unfairness. If the SP were then able to alter her irrational beliefs when Sarah faced a sense of unfairness, in the future the new rational alternatives would be both applicable and ensured she responded in a healthy and functional manner. For the remainder of the second session, the SP worked with Sarah to enhance her self-awareness and familiarity of the REBT process by working through various ABC framework for various situations that she found challenging.

Disputation phase

The disputation phase is the most important part of the REBT process. The main aim was to challenge Sarah's irrational beliefs and maladaptive behaviours and to replace them with rational alternatives. Disputing beliefs can be a challenging and sensitive process, therefore it was important to manage Sarah's expectations, as well seek her permission to continue. Initially Sarah's irrational beliefs were challenged empirically (i.e., "where is it written that others must be considerate towards you"), logically (i.e., "just because you want them to be, does that mean they have to be?"), and pragmatically (i.e., "where has this belief got you so far?"). It was apparent from Sarah's mannerisms and verbal feedback that the didactic and directive nature of the disputation phase was unexpected but that she remained open to collaboratively discuss the definitions of an irrational belief. During REBT not only as practitioners do we work to reduce irrational beliefs, but we endeavour to foster and enhance client's endorsement of rational beliefs (see Figure 4.3 for an example). Based upon Sarah's four core irrational beliefs, four new rational alternatives were established: preference, anti-awfulizing, high-frustration tolerance, and unconditional self/life/other acceptance (see Figure 4.3). The newly established rational beliefs were then subjected to an unsuccessful but similar disputation process (i.e., empirical, logical, and pragmatic arguments). This is good practice for the main reason irrational and rational beliefs are thought to exist on separate spectrums, where low levels of irrational beliefs do not signify high levels of rational beliefs (Ellis, David, & Lynn, 2010). Therefore, the unsuccessful disputation of rational beliefs reinforced the truth, logic, and helpful nature of her new rational beliefs. During the ABC(DE) framework practitioners will typically start by exploring either the adversity (A) or unhelpful negative consequences (C). Next, the helpful negative consequence and overarching goal will be outlined before the core irrational beliefs (B) are explored. Once the irrational beliefs have been agreed, the SP will dispute (D) and replace with new effective rational beliefs (E; see Figure 4.3). Not restricted to one example, the ABC(DE) framework was repeated using pertinent and challenging adversities that Sarah experienced within and outside of sport.

Adversity (A) ★1st/2nd

"Teammates actions disrupting my performance"

Irrational Beliefs (B) ★4th	**Rational Beliefs (B) ★5th**
I really want my teammates to be more considerate towards me, therefore they must be. I cannot tolerate it when they are inconsiderate, it is terrible, and makes them completely bad people.	I really want my teammates to be more considerate towards me, but that doesn't mean they have to be. Although difficult, I could tolerate it when they are inconsiderate. It is annoying but it certainly wouldn't be terrible, and it doesn't make them completely bad people.
Unhealthy Negative Consequences (C) ★ 1st/2nd	**Healthy Negative Consequences (C) ★3rd**
Inward Anger Physical Tension Agitation Verbal Aggression Loss of concentration	Slightly Annoyed. Acceptance of the situation and others. Find humour in the situation. Little resentment towards others. Able to deal with distractions and refocus on performance routines.

FIGURE 4.3 An example ABC (DE) framework formulation proforma completed with Sarah during the disputation phase

★ Indicates the order in which a practitioner will typically work through the framework.

Disputation and reinforcement phase

Continuing from the previous session, the disputation and reinforcement phase was conducted over two sessions and one homework task. Whilst the early phases of REBT can be quite formulaic within its delivery, the latter part allows the practitioner to be more flexible in the exercises (e.g., badness scale, reversal role-play), techniques (i.e., cognitive, emotive, or behavioural), and style (i.e., didactic or socratic) suited towards the clients' needs. Whilst the disputation phases may represent a turning point, there would be occasions for Sarah to test her new ability to manage adversity, as such the current phases would help reaffirm Sarah's new rational view. For example, whilst away on an international competition, one night Sarah had little to no sleep due to a teammate who was speaking loudly on the phone for long periods of time. As a result, she had become extremely angry, resenting her teammate for not allowing her to rest appropriately, perpetuating her physical frustrations and anxiety that this would now hinder her ability to perform. These examples show how Sarah was able to reflect on and consider an alternative response for the future. The following non-exhaustive techniques were used over the last two sessions to help dispute and reinforce a rational philosophy.

To target Sarah's propensity to awfulise (i.e., "it is terrible when others treat me unfairly") and gain perspective during relatively trivial moments, a technique known as a 'badness scale' was used. By rating a situation as terrible Sarah was implying that there was nothing worse in this world than being treated unfairly, thus disproportionately magnifying the consequences of being treated unfairly. First, Sarah placed numerical percentage of badness on a scale from 0–100 using a variety of life and sporting adversities. Initially, the SP offered relatively trivial examples (e.g., losing a wallet, having a cold) that were scored low on the scale. Second, the SP then offered a range of adversities that he knew would resonate with Sarah's irrational beliefs (e.g., being treated unfairly, negative judgement from coaches); expectedly these examples were placed much higher (60–100%). Following this Sarah was provided with a series of major adversities (e.g., death of a loved one) at which she suddenly came to realise that whilst being treated unfairly is bad, it certainly is not terrible. Ultimately, REBT theory proposes nothing is 100% awful and the badness scale provides a way to help athletes adjust their perspective.

To target Sarah's tendency for self and/or other downing (i.e., they are completely bad for treating me this way), we completed a 'Big I & Little I' task. Sarah was asked to draw a large I and inside it draw a variety of little I's. Here Sarah labelled each little I as an aspect of her life, the size representing its significance (i.e., family, friends, teammates). This exercise allowed Sarah to visually observe how we are unable to wholly rate people based on a single unfavourable action/outcome. We discussed famous examples in which people appear to be evil/bad people (i.e., dictators, serial killers), but in fact are not.

To further embed new rational beliefs, An Athlete Rational Resilience Credo (ARRC; Turner, 2016b) was used. A credo is defined as "a set of beliefs, which expresses a particular opinion and influences the way you live" (Dryden, 2007, p. 219). In Sarah's case, the ARRC was used to create a clear rational view that she was able to aim for and foster a rational philosophy of life. Initially, Sarah was asked to read and discuss elements of the credo. The SP then asked Sarah to personalise and re-write elements of the Credo for use whilst at home, training, or during competitions.

A behavioural technique was also used for Sarah's homework named 'In vivo desensitisation' (Froggat, 2005). Sarah was asked to seek out and approach challenging situations (e.g., facing evaluation from the coaches) rather than avoid them. Irrational beliefs are contextually sensitive and heightened in settings particularly important for the athlete (e.g., performance & family settings), and it was vital that Sarah could experientially test and challenge her old irrational beliefs, and reinforce them with rational beliefs in situations.

Intervention evaluation and lessons learned through self-reflection

Over the course of the final two sessions Sarah was making good progress and engaging with the homework tasks with utmost diligence. To illustrate the intervention

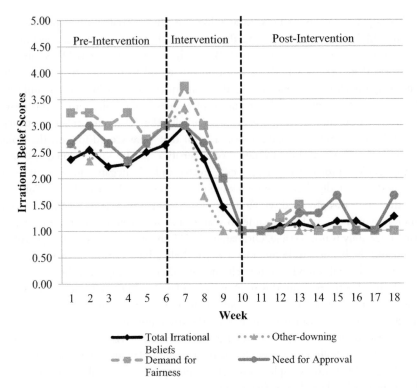

FIGURE 4.4 Meaningful and maintained reductions in irrational beliefs before and after the REBT intervention

effects and to draw together salient themes, the present section will be separated into 1) effects of REBT on Sarah's psychological resilience, 2) practitioner evaluation, and 3) lessons learned and professional practitioner insights gleaned during the consultancy process.

Healthy thoughts and feelings

The use of a questionnaire offered a practical and validated measure of Sarah's irrational beliefs. Following this, a semi-structured interview provided a useful way to explore and understand if and/or how these changes impacted her on her ability to manage and overcome the various stressors that she faced, and thus become more resilient. Sarah first indicated changes in her thoughts when experiencing challenging moments. For example, during competitive events Sarah was able to concentrate on her performances instead of becoming embroiled within an inner dialogue – denigrating others for providing a distraction. Although subtle, Sarah was showing signs of emotional responsibility even though the situation (A) did not dictate one; rather she alone was responsible for the functionality of her response. The following quote highlights this eloquently:

> *I don't get drawn into irritations on the shooting line anymore. I just ignore the nonsense going on around me, even deflecting what could be deliberate distractions and laughing them off in my head*

As a result of the intervention, Sarah noted how her perception of others had shifted. Based on the core rational belief of unconditional self/other/life acceptance Sarah did not globally condemn significant others for a single action (e.g., "they are a completely bad person because they treated me unfairly"), but instead she rated their behaviour as opposed to them as a whole (e.g., "even though they have treated me unfairly that does not mean they are a completely bad person"). Looking beyond the performance benefits, a rational view of others helped Sarah to strengthen relationships, in turn enhancing her peer interaction and the social support she was able to seek. The following quote articulates this point well:

> *My perception of others has changed, I think I look more kindly on people now. I always thought I saw the best in people, where people in the past I have thought no I don't want to talk to them they will talk my head off, I now think well actually they could with someone to talk to.*

After making a rational shift and altering her perceptions of others, Sarah was also able to brush over minor stressors and return to a normative or positive state in a somewhat swift manner. Not to mistake this for indifference towards others' actions, she rather experiences a healthy negative emotion when encountering other people's challenging behaviour. Sarah noted:

> *The intense frustration I used to experience has gone now, I might still think that's inconsiderate but it doesn't frustrate as much and I don't need five minutes in a quiet room.*

Humour and anti-awfulising

When used with sensitivity, humour can be an important component of REBT. During the latter phases of the intervention, Sarah was encouraged to reflect on her old beliefs with a wry smile and take perspective on what used to be 'awful' and 'terrible' circumstances. For example, missing the first training session of a camp may have been awful, because this reflected badly upon her professionalism. In contrast Sarah could re-appraise challenging situations by using rational self-talk:

> *I will say to myself that it isn't a catastrophe; it is just a bad day and then have a little chuckle about it. I did use the words awful and horrendous and catastrophic and it just isn't, and I have stopped using that now.*

Rational philosophy and resilience

The social validation data indicated that Sarah responded to adversity in a healthy and adaptive manner that helped rather than hindered her respective goals, thus experiencing a shift towards a rational philosophy. Irrespective of the context, a rational view ultimately leads to healthy emotions, and an adaptive response facilitates goal achievement (Dryden & Branch, 2008). The ABC(DE) framework that Sarah now understood and used as a guiding framework presented a model of optimal human functioning and resilience. Indeed, researchers have highlighted the similarities between REBT and the concept of resilience (e.g., Deen et al., 2017; Turner, 2016b). Resilience is considered a process of adapting well in the face of adversity, whereby experiencing emotional distress is a part of becoming resilient (Turner, 2016b). Further, findings support the notion that resilience is a capacity that develops over time in the context of person-environment interactions (Egeland, Carlson, & Sroufe, 1993). Essentially, resilience is becoming an important predictor of wellbeing, mental health, and performance in sport (Sarkar & Fletcher, 2014), as such REBT presents an effective means to restore, maintain, and develop an athlete's psychological health. The following quotes eloquently highlight this rational shift:

> *I feel these sessions have been incredibly helpful and I have gained tools that I will use for the rest of my life. . . . They have helped me to deal with everyday situations which would normally irritate, silly things which would get me down I don't have anymore. Yeah, I feel better in control of my emotions throughout the day, so it has helped*

Practitioner evaluation

Social validation showed that prior to the intervention showed that Sarah was concerned that the practitioner (myself) may be disinterested and would offer psychological support just by going through the motions. Nevertheless, by the end of the intervention process Sarah revealed:

> *It was obvious from the outset that Andrew was committed and friendly. I trusted him and he was incredibly enthusiastic about getting me to understand and enjoy the process of learning*

This notion was further validated using a Likert-scale from 1 (*Not at all*) to 7 (*Extremely*) whereby Sarah reported a 7, 6, and a 6 for motivation, effort, and enthusiasm in relation to the REBT intervention process. A central aim of REBT is to reduce the prevalence of irrational beliefs and replace them with rational alternatives; therefore, Sarah's endorsement of irrational beliefs were collected on a weekly basis. Using a single-case baseline design (Barker et al., 2013) Sarah reported meaningful short-term and long-term reductions in irrational beliefs between pre- and post-intervention phases (see Figure 4.4). These reductions indicated the effective application of REBT and a rational shift in the way Sarah view/perceived adverse situations.

Professional practice insights and lessons learned

As with any consultancy it was important to seek Sarah's feedback and reflect on elements of the intervention that could have been refined for future practice. First, Sarah was confused about the differentiation in healthy versus unhealthy negative emotions (HNEs vs UNEs). This was further perpetuated by varying interpretations of REBT terminology. For example, the meaning I (practitioner) draw from the word "anxious" (e.g., unhealthy negative emotion) may have been different to Sarah's definition (a normal sensation before competition). To negate pitfalls in semantics it would be important to clarify terminology and use common language throughout the REBT process. For example, when using the term 'frustration' this may represent a healthy negative emotion, whereas 'rage' indicated a unhealthy alternative. To illustrate, Lindsay, Pitt, and Owen (2014) discuss the conceptual confusions, misunderstandings, and misguided use of language that may hinder effective sport psychology practice.

Sarah also highlighted that having sessions delivered closely together allowed her to better sustain the momentum from previous sessions and apply the intersession tasks whilst the session content was still fresh within her thoughts. To outline this point Sarah noted:

> If the sessions can be bunched up together, that is better, so that you can remember what has happened each week, [and] so you can put it into practice that week then reinforce it when you sit back down. If there are three weeks between talking about it and talking about it again then you have forgotten some of the skills you were trying to learn, so it was much better being bunched up

Targeting irrational beliefs and promoting rational alternatives can be a difficult process due to the often subconscious and deeply held nature of beliefs (Dryden & Neenan, 2015). Furthermore, all humans are inherently irrational and rational beings and whilst initially the participant may report reduced irrational beliefs, it is vital to continuously reinforce rational alternatives. In turn, such a rational view becomes a habituated and automatic response when encountering various challenges. Although not used in the present case, we have developed and recommend a smartphone application that allows athletes to dispute and re-appraise challenging situations in situ; subsequently the brief and intuitive process provides the user with a set of rational beliefs for their given situation. To this end, the practitioner does not become a crutch, and athletes are provided with the autonomy to self-monitor and re-appraise challenging moments.

The present case shows the effectiveness and suitability of REBT as an intervention to bolster the psychological health of an elite athlete with a physical disability. As mentioned previously athletes with a disability will experience similar and additional stressors compared to able-bodied athletes (e.g., Arnold et al., 2017), further justifying the application of REBT as an approach to develop a rational view and psychological resilience. Nevertheless, it would be prudent to understand and/or make the following considerations. First, one should reflect on the biases and preconceptions that one may harbour regarding disability sport. Here, athletes are not defined by their disability, and shifts in terminology although subtle can clarify this point (e.g., athletes with disability, rather than disabled athletes). Second, one should find a balance between propagating autonomy, whilst making the necessary adjustments to meet their needs. Third, although in Sarah's case no amendments were made, consideration should be given to the delivery of the intervention (e.g., format, pace, resources). For example, there may exists complexities in the clients' history that will influence the athlete's willingness and/or ability to change.

The premise of REBT is simple yet powerful. The application of REBT to bolster mental health is not restricted just to elite sport, but can transcend other highly demanding settings (e.g., Healthcare, Military, Business, Emergency Services), essentially offering a framework of optimal functioning and resilience. Looking ahead, researchers are recommended to explore how irrational and/or rational beliefs are socialised, having implications for practitioners looking to foster rational environments in the pursuit of psychological health and performance.

References

Andersen, M. B. (2009). The "canon" of psychological skills training for enhancing performance. In K. F. Hays (Ed.), *Performance psychology in action: A casebook for working with athletes, performing artists, business leaders, and professionals in high-risk occupations* (pp. 11–34). Washington, DC: American Psychological Association.

Aoyagi, M. W., Poczwardowski, A., Statler, T., Shapiro, J. L., & Cohen, A. B. (2017). The performance interview guide: Recommendations for initial consultations in sport and performance psychology. *Professional Psychology: Research and Practice, 48*, 352–360.

Arnold, R., Wagstaff, C. R., Steadman, L., & Pratt, Y. (2017). The organisational stressors encountered by athletes with a disability. *Journal of Sports Sciences, 35*, 1187–1196.

Barker, J. B., Mellalieu, S. D., McCarthy, P. J., Jones, M. V., & Moran, A. (2013). A review of single-case research in sport psychology 1997–2012: Research trends and future directions. *Journal of Applied Sport Psychology, 25*, 4–32.

David, D., Miclea, M., & Opre, A. (2004). The information-processing approach to the human mind: Basics and beyond. *Journal of Clinical Psychology, 60*, 353–368. doi:10.1002/jclp.10250

David, D., Szentagotai, A., Eva, K., & Macavei, B. (2005). A synopsis of Rational-Emotive Behavior Therapy (REBT): Fundamental and applied research. *Journal of Rational-Emotive & Cognitive-Behavior Therapy, 23*, 175–221. doi:10.1007/s10942-005-0011-0

Deen, S., Turner, M. J., & Wong, R. S. (2017). The effects of REBT, and the use of credos, on irrational beliefs and resilience qualities in athletes. *The Sport Psychologist*, 1–39.

Dryden, W. (1995). *Brief rational emotive behaviour therapy*. Chichester: Wiley-Blackwell.

Dryden, W. (2007). Resilience and rationality. *Journal of Rational-Emotive & Cognitive-Behavior Therapy, 25*, 213–226. doi:10.1007/s10942-006-0050-1

Dryden, W. (2012). The "ABCs" of REBT I: A preliminary study of errors and confusions in counselling and psychotherapy textbooks. *Journal of Rational-Emotive & Cognitive-Behavior Therapy, 30*, 133–172.

Dryden, W., & Branch, R. (2008). *The fundamentals of rational emotive behaviour therapy* (2nd ed.). Chichester: John Wiley & Sons, Ltd.

Dryden, W., & Neenan, M. (2015). *Rational emotive behaviour therapy: 100 key points and techniques*. Hove: Routledge.

Egeland, B., Carlson, E., & Sroufe, L. A. (1993). Resilience as process. *Development and Psychopathology, 5*, 517–528. doi:10.1017/S0954579400006131

Ellis, A. (1957). Rational psychotherapy and individual psychology. *Journal of Individual Psychology, 13*, 38–44.

Ellis, A. (1997). Using rational emotive behavior therapy techniques to cope with disability. *Professional Psychology: Research and Practice, 28*, 17–22. doi:10.1037/0735-7028.28.1.17

Ellis, A., David, D., & Lynn, S. J. (2010). Rational and irrational beliefs: A historical and conceptual perspective. In D. David, S. J. Lynn, & A. Ellis (Eds.), *Rational and irrational beliefs in human functioning and disturbances*. Oxford: Oxford University Press.

Ellis, A., & Dryden, W. (1997). *The practice of rational emotive behavior therapy* (Vol. 43). New York, NY: Springer.

Epictetus. (1948). *The enchiridion*. Indianapolis: Bobbs-Merrill.

Epstein, R. (2001). *The prince of reason, an interview with Albert Ellis*. Retrieved May 15, 2009, from www.psychologytoday.com/articles/200101/the-prince-reason

Fässberg, M. M., Cheung, G., Canetto, S. S., Erlangsen, A., Lapierre, S., Lindner, R., . . . Duberstein, P. (2016). A systematic review of physical illness, functional disability, and suicidal behaviour among older adults. *Aging & Mental Health, 20*, 166–194.

Fletcher, D., Hanton, S., & Mellalieu, S. D. (2006). An organizational stress review: Conceptual and theoretical issues in competitive sport. In S. Hanton & S. D. Mellalieu (Eds.), *Literature reviews in sport psychology* (pp. 321–373). New York, NY: Nova Science.

Fletcher, D., Hanton, S., & Wagstaff, C. R. (2012). Performers' responses to stressors encountered in sport organisations. *Journal of Sports Sciences, 30*, 349–358.

Flett, G. L., & Hewitt, P. L. (2005). The perils of perfectionism in sports and exercise. *Current Directions in Psychological Science, 14*, 14–18.

Froggatt, W. (2005). A brief introduction to rational emotive behaviour therapy. *Journal of Rational-Emotive and Cognitive Behaviour Therapy, 3*, 1–15.

Hill, A. P., Hall, H. K., Appleton, P. R., & Kozub, S. A. (2008). Perfectionism and burnout in junior elite soccer players: The mediating influence of unconditional self-acceptance. *Psychology of Sport and Exercise, 9*, 630–644. doi:10.1016/j.psychsport.2007.09.004

Kaplan, A., & Flum, H. (2010). Achievement goal orientations and identity formation styles. *Educational Research Review, 5*, 50–67.

Keegan, R. J. (2016). *Being a sport psychologist: The intake process: Establishing a relationship, aims, expectations, and reality*. London: Palgrave Macmillan.

Lindner, H., Kirkby, R., Wertheim, E., & Birch, P. (1999). A brief assessment of irrational thinking: The shortened general attitude and belief scale. *Cognitive Therapy and Research, 23*, 651–663.

Lindsay, P., Pitt, T., & Thomas, O. (2014). Bewitched by our words: Wittgenstein, language-games, and the pictures that hold sport psychology captive. *Sport and Exercise Psychology Review, 10*, 4.

Roberts, C. M., Faull, A. L., & Tod, D. (2016). Blurred lines: Performance enhancement, common mental disorders and referral in the UK athletic population. *Frontiers in Psychology, 7*, 1067.

Sarkar, M., & Fletcher, D. (2014). Psychological resilience in sport performers: A review of stressors and protective factors. *Journal of Sports Sciences, 32,* 1419–1434.

Skordilis, E. K., Skafida, F. A., Chrysagis, N., & Nikitaras, N. (2006). Comparison of sport achievement orientation of male wheelchair basketball athletes with congenital and acquired disabilities. *Perceptual and Motor Skills, 103,* 726–732. doi:10.2466/pms.103.3.726-732

Turner, M. J. (2016a). Rational Emotive Behavior Therapy (REBT), irrational and rational beliefs, and the mental health of athletes. *Frontiers in Psychology, 7.* doi:10.3389/fpsyg.2016.01423

Turner, M. J. (2016b). Proposing a rational resilience credo for use with athletes. *Journal of Sport Psychology in Action, 7,* 170–181. doi:10.1080/21520704.2016.1236051

Turner, M. J., & Barker, J. B. (2014). Using rational emotive behavior therapy with athletes. *The Sport Psychologist, 28,* 75–90. doi:10.1123/tsp.2013-0012

Turner, M. J., & Moore, M. (2015). Irrational beliefs predict increased emotional and physical exhaustion in Gaelic football athletes. *International Journal of Sport Psychology, 47,* 187–199.

Vîslă, A., Flückiger, C., Grosse Holtforth, M., & David, D. (2016). Irrational beliefs and psychological distress: A meta-analysis. *Psychotherapy and Psychosomatics, 85,* 8–15. doi:10.1159/000441231

Wegner, D. M. (1994). Ironic processes of mental control. *Psychological Review, 101,* 34–52.

Wood, A. G., Barker, J., & Turner, M. J. (2017). Developing performance using Rational Emotive Behavior Therapy (REBT): A case study with an elite archer. *The Sport Psychologist, 31,* 78–87.

Further reading

Turner, M. J. (2016). Rational Emotive Behavior Therapy (REBT), irrational and rational beliefs, and the mental health of athletes. *Frontiers in Psychology, 7.* doi:10.3389/fpsyg.2016.01423

This article provides a review into the framework of REBT as an intervention to both understand and promote mental health in athletes.

Turner, M. J., & Barker, J. B. (2014). Using rational emotive behavior therapy with athletes. *The Sport Psychologist, 28,* 75–90. doi:10.1123/tsp.2013-0012

This article provides a detailed outline into applying REBT on a one-to-one basis to reduce irrational beliefs in athletes.

David, D., Cotet, C., Matu, S., Mogoase, C., & Stefan, S. (2017). 50 years of rational-emotive and cognitive behavioural therapy: A systematic review and meta-analysis. *Journal of Clinical Psychology, 4,* 1–15.

This article provides a contemporary review as to the effectiveness and efficacy of REBT since its conception and the proposed mechanisms of change for practitioners.

5

THE STATE OF MIND IRELAND (SOMI) PROGRAMME FOR STUDENT ATHLETES

Gavin Breslin, Tandy Jane Haughey,
Stephen Shannon, Drew Neill and Martin Lawlor

Learning objectives

After reading this chapter you should be able to:

1   Summarise the challenges faced by athletes when transitioning from school to university.
2   Describe the content of the State of Mind Ireland (SOMI) programme.
3   Be aware of the importance of theory-based programme evaluation.
4   Consider athlete recommendations when designing mental health programmes.

Introduction to the theme

Making the transition to university can be a challenging period for students. The State of Mind Ireland (SOMI) programme is a response to the paucity of programmes that are evidence and theory-based to enhance mental health awareness of student athletes (Breslin et al., 2018). The aim of this chapter is to share the process we followed in developing, recruiting, delivering, and evaluating the SOMI mental health and awareness programme to student athletes (Breslin et al., 2018). The aims of the SOMI programme were to; (1) improve student knowledge of their mental health, (2) overcome social stigma, (3) encourage engagement with others who may have mental health problems, (4) increase intentions to provide support to others, and finally (5) to increase well-being and resilience. The positive effects of the programme are described in detail elsewhere (Breslin et al., 2018) and support the programme's introduction into the Higher Education sector. This chapter will provide a detailed description of the content of the programme and the views of the athletes not published previously. Some of the lessons learned in the reflection section will provide information on how to integrate psychological theory of behaviour change into the design of a mental health awareness programme for student athletes.

Describe the client or group being targeted

One hundred and forty-two undergraduate first year student athletes who enrolled on a BSc (Honours) undergraduate sports degree were invited to take part in the SOMI programme as part of their course. Just over 70% of this cohort (n=100) attended the training (59 = male, 41 = female; mean age = 20.78; SD = 2.91). The participants represented 26 sports (see Figure 5.1), with the highest participation in soccer (21%), followed by Gaelic football (i.e., an Irish team-based sport; 16%), rugby (10%), hockey (7%), netball (5%), and golf (4%). The athletes reported low scores on assessment of knowledge and awareness of mental health and stigma, and likeliness to offer support to others who have experienced a mental health problem. These low scores supported a rationale for delivering the programme. Within the university campus, students have access to student support services for mental health. The SOMI programme was delivered as an extension to the existing service.

Initial needs assessment

Mental illness is the largest cause of ill health and disability in Northern Ireland (NI), and there are higher levels of mental illness than any other region in the United Kingdom (UK). In the 2015–16 NI Health Survey, 21% of women and

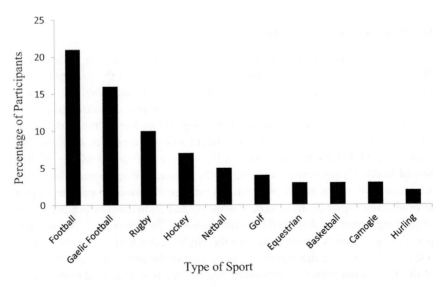

FIGURE 5.1 The top 10 sports represented in the SOMI sample

16% of men scored highly on the General Health Questionnaire (GHQ-12), suggestive of a mental health problem. Respondents in the most deprived areas were twice as likely to record a high score (27%), as those in the least deprived areas (13%). It is estimated that around 45,000 children and young people in NI have a mental health problem at any one time and that more than 20% of young people are suffering 'significant mental health problems' by the time they reach 18. With regard to suicide, 318 suicides were registered in NI during 2015 – the highest since records began in 1970. Of these, 245 (77%) were male and 132 were aged between 15 and 34 years old. Suicide rates in the most deprived areas are three times higher than in the least deprived. Furthermore, alarmingly there has been a 70% increase in the rates of anxiety and depression reported over the last 25 years, and within the UK 26% of young people have experienced suicidal thoughts. University students represent a high-risk group for the development of mental health problems (Dooley & Fitzgerald, 2013; McLafferty et al., 2017) with a need for bespoke mental health interventions (Karwig, Chambers, & Murphy, 2015). Students in Higher Education fall into the age bracket of those who are vulnerable to mental illness; three quarters of those with a mental illness first develop clinical symptoms in their mid-20s. Furthermore, a recent study of Northern Ireland students (NUS-USI, 2017) indicated that 78% of the student population had experienced 'mental health worries' in the last year, with 51% of them not seeking support for this.

Beginning university is a significant life transition period in an individual's development (Thomas, 2012), with changes to identity, the level of study, friendships, proximity of family, and financial support. With over half of young adults across the UK expected to access Higher Education by the time they are 30 (UUK, 2018), universities are facing increasing challenges regarding mental health and well-being provision. Houghton and Anderson (2017) highlight the increase of students disclosing 'mental health conditions' in recent years, without there necessarily being interventions in place to support them. While young people generally do not seek professional help for mental health problems (Gulliver et al., 2012), university students have expressed their willingness to seek help from on-campus support services (Karwig, Chambers, & Murphy, 2015). Unfortunately this is not always the case, and available support may not be valued unless students perceive themselves as being acutely at risk. NUS-USI (2017) indicate that 22% of students will seek help from friends for mental health worries, with 51% not seeking any support. The challenge is to educate students about their mental health as a preventive measure and ensure they acknowledge their mental fitness as being as an important factor as their physical health. Turner (2018) suggests that universities must deliver emotional support to students alongside their academic learning. In Breslin and McCay's (2013) survey of adults in Northern Ireland, they showed participants have a higher perceived control over their physical health compared to their mental health. In a more recent survey, Breslin et al. (2018) demonstrated that athletes with better attitudes and knowledge of mental health had a greater willingness to offer support to individuals that have a mental health problem. Both studies, when interpreted within the Theory of Planned Behaviour (Ajzen, 1985) – a psychological theory that links attitudes, social norms, and perceived control with influencing intentions to act – supports the view that providing psycho-education classes on mental health will encourage positive beliefs and behaviours for mental health promotion among young people.

A view widely supported as enhancing mental health awareness is now a prominent goal of national mental health policy in Ireland, the United Kingdom (UK), Australia, and other countries (Department of Children and Youth Affairs, 2014; Government Office for Science UK, 2008; Australian Department of Health and Ageing, 2009). In addition to the above, it has been acknowledged that there is a need to address mental health and well-being within Higher Education with the introduction of the Guidelines for Student Mental Health Policies and Procedures for Higher Education (UK Universities, 2015).

To assist in addressing some of the initial issues raised above, researchers have developed education-based programmes to enhance mental health knowledge (Chambers, Murphy, & Keeley, 2015; Gulliver, Griffiths, & Christensen, 2010; Jorm, 2012). However, there is a paucity of high quality research specific to student mental health and well-being interventions, and instead there has been an overall reliance on cross-sectional surveys as evidence. From these surveys, a significant proportion of students (more than 1 in 4) in the United Kingdom are experiencing clinically recognisable mental illness (Bewick, Gill, Mulhearn, Barkham, & Hill, 2008). An initial needs assessment within the Higher Education sector has shown that the majority of students had not received a structured mental health and well-being programme during their transition to university.

Hence, in this chapter we demonstrate that the SOMI programme has played a significant part in promoting positive mental health messages, specifically with student athletes. Three directional hypotheses were tested: (a) undergraduate student athletes who received the SOMI mental health and awareness intervention would be significantly more knowledgeable about mental health following the programme than those in the control group (not receiving the programme); (b) those who received SOMI would be significantly more likely to engage and offer support to someone with a mental health problem following the programme than those in the control group; and (c) those who received the intervention would be significantly more likely to score higher in resilience and well-being following the programme compared to those in the control group. To enhance the programme and to ensure that the learning being received was fit for purpose, qualitative views from students who received the programme were gathered and used to assist in the refinement of the programme for students who would receive the programme in the following academic year (Breslin et al., under review).

Framework and intervention for delivery

The State of Mind Ireland (SOMI) programme (Lawlor, Rae, Kelly, & Moriarty, 2015) was developed in response to the need to do more in university sport settings to enhance mental health awareness and the well-being of student athletes. SOMI (Lawlor et al., 2015) is an experiential and skill-enhancing programme that is delivered on a university campus during scheduled class time by experienced mental health and well-being tutors in partnership with students and student support services. The session uses the term mental fitness to reflect optimisation of performance through positive lifestyle to engage young people in discussion around their mental health. This is supported through experiential group learning, including: (i) a resilience case study delivered via video, (ii) examples of athletes who, despite competing in a highly masculine culture, sought help, (iii) identifying sources of support and help on campus, and (iv) inclusion of mindfulness. The main body of the programme is delivered through interactive activities centred around developing a better understanding of the area, which included group discussions of the World Health Organization's (WHO, 2010), physical activity guidelines for health, an introduction to mindfulness (Hölzel et al., 2011), and promotion of the 'Take Five' Ways to Well-Being (PHA, 2018) detailed in Table 5.1.

During the development of the SOMI programme and the initial delivery in 2016, a theoretical model was not incorporated. Retrospectively a model has been applied based on recent recommendations (Breslin et al., 2017). For example, Michie and colleagues (2016) highlighted the need for theoretical mapping in health interventions, such that the delivery techniques designed to improve the intended outcome (e.g. mental health) derive from a validated and logical psychological framework. In the case of mental health interventions, when theoretically derived constructs are concurrently practically applied and empirically measured, analyses can be designed to elicit whether the assumed theoretical processes explain changes in mental health outcomes (Hagger & Chatzisarantis, 2014). Indeed, given the Medical Research Council (MRC) outline that theory-based interventions demonstrate larger effects than interventions not underpinned by a theory (Craig et al., 2013), the present research posed an opportunity for the team to consider the application of theory to SOMI when refining the programme. We pick this up in more detail in the next section.

TABLE 5.1 The Five Ways to Well-being

1. Connect	Reach out to family, friends, colleagues, and neighbours
2. Be active	Go for a walk, run, cycle, play a game, or dance
3. Take notice	Be curious and take notice of the surrounding environment and appreciate what matters.
4. Keep learning	Try something new, rediscover old interests, set a new challenge
5. Giving	Do something nice for others, volunteer, be gentle on yourself and others.

Intervention evaluation and lessons learned through self-reflection

Four outcome measures were used to assess changes as a result of the SOMI programme. The scales were (a) The Reported and Intended Behaviour Scale (RIBS; Evans-Lacko et al., 2011) (b) The Mental Health Knowledge Schedule (MAKS) (c) The Short Warwick Edinburgh Mental Well-being Scale (SWEMWBS; Tennant et al., 2007) and (d) The Brief Resilience Scale (BRS; Smith et al., 2008). These questionnaires were combined into one survey and completed at three-time points; prior to (T1) and immediately after the training (T2) and at three months post the intervention (T3). T3 was posted to the participant's home address due to the timing of intervention delivery and end of the teaching term. For the control group, similar time points for the completion of the questionnaire were utilised: before and after a normal lecture and three-month follow up following the completion of the initial questionnaire. In addition, focus group discussions were conducted following the intervention and completion of the questionnaire. All participants were invited to take part in the focus group discussions to explore programme fidelity.

On completion of the programme it was shown that knowledge of mental health, including knowledge of mental disorders beyond that of a control group occurred (see Breslin et al., 2018). The SOMI programme also increased athlete intentions to engage and offer help/support to someone with a mental health problem. Based on these findings SOMI could be considered for inclusion in sport courses as part of the curriculum, and with some modifications it could compliment player welfare and safe guarding of athletes whilst enrolled in university.

From the focus group discussions, participants agreed that the intervention enhanced their knowledge of mental health and well-being. Participants recalled the following parts of the programme as effective: 1. Mental fitness is a less stigmatising term than Mental Health 2. The five actions for improving mental health, and 3. The video content of mental health experiences of an athlete.

In relation to mental fitness one participant said "Yeah, mental fitness appeals better, you don't feel as maybe looked at. Coming into this class, if you think 'mental health and well-being,' people think what's wrong with him? Or you know, if it's 'mental fitness' it's more general, but it's more centred, too, you know, without that name (referring to 'mental health') kind of attached."

The term "mental fitness" was used in the programme in place of "mental health" and "well-being." It was evident from the participants' views in relation to this terminology that the terms used are important in destigmatising mental health and engaging young people in messages around mental health. Participants said:

> Illnesses, kind of like you think, oh, people have illness or disorders. I think it was good the guy mentioned (referring to the trainer), what was it he said,

something like "fitness," he said there was another word for it instead of putting that label on it, "mental fitness," which was quite good.

The term "mental fitness" may have provided an adaptive approach to stressful life events, by potentially normalising distress, enhancing understanding of mental processes, reframing (improved cognitive flexibility) to enhance mastery skills, and using adversity as an opportunity to learn. Also, the term "mental fitness" may have brought new interest to a topic previously associated with stigma and avoidance of help-seeking (Byrne, 2000).

In relation to the five actions for mental health, there was a positive response from students saying: "Them five steps, it was really good, cause not only will it help you to look out for them things when it's other people, but you can go through the steps yourself so that you're not falling into that category."

When asked how the programme could be delivered in the future, participants said the programme could be delivered as it is and enjoyed the interactive component "and the way they made it interactive, like the guy got us to do that activity where they get us to try not to think of anything but listen ... that was good to get us involved, and then we kind of paid attention more maybe after that." Students commented appreciatively on specific content included in the programme, which they found impacted their learning: "The mindfulness, close your eyes, breathing, clear your mind stuff that could be used at any class like, you know, even if it is in a lecture, you can break a lecture down and do that, you know."

Students felt that although they found the setting for delivery supported them personally, they recommended that the programme be delivered in other settings, such as their sport clubs. Participants recognised that the sports club setting within university currently has little if any mental health promotion: "A workshop could be easily done with your team or your club like ... there's very little of it done."

Despite positive outcomes in knowledge, this short programme was not effective in increasing well-being or resilience. Therefore, additional sessions or utilisation of phone apps could be incorporated to enhance well-being and resilience and keep the athletes engaged. To achieve improvements in well-being or resilience, a similar optimisation approach to previous programmes that have reduced depressive symptoms and anxiety could be considered (Donohue et al., 2013, 2015; Longshore & Sachs, 2015).

The lack of theoretical application for SOMI limited our ability to determine the precise psychological and social processes of change that may explain how and why the mental health outcomes were improved (Michie et al., 2016). As such, the findings, along with the Breslin et al. (2018) study were reviewed in relation to the MRC guidelines (Craig et al., 2013) and studies (Michie, Johnston, Francis, Hardeman, & Eccles, 2008; Hagger & Chatzisarantis, 2014; Michie et al., 2016) describing theoretical application in the design and analyses of health interventions. In light of SOMI's intended outcomes (i.e. to improve intentions to offer support to those with a mental health problem, and to act for improving one's mental health), we recommend adjustment of the programme to integrate; (a) The Theory of Planned Behaviour (TPB; Ajzen, 1991) and (b) Self-Determination Theory (SDT; Ryan & Deci, 2017), as evident in Hagger and Chatzisarantis's (2014) Integrated Behaviour Change (IBC) framework, in moving forward the re-design and evaluation of the programme (Breslin et al., under review). Specifically, IBC-derived behaviour change techniques were aligned with tutor training and IBC variables which have been empirically measured and analysed through validated questionnaires (Shannon et al., under review). Having recently updated the SOMI programme to reflect theory, we recommend that future programme designers also consider the integration of theory into their programmes.

In summary, implementation of the SOMI intervention demonstrated that knowledge of mental health and intentions to offer support increased for the intervention group, compared to the control group. The findings suggest that inclusion of SOMI could be integrated into university courses to promote mental health awareness. To advance SOMI, the programme has been modified using components of an IBC framework (Hagger & Chatzisarantis, 2014), such that specific strategies designed to improve student-athlete well-being and intentions to act for one's own mental health are theoretically guided and analysed in intervention assessment (Breslin et al., under review). In pursuit of an effective programme that goes beyond awareness raising and enhances mental health, well-being, and resilience, we continue to modify SOMI for university athletes, other settings that include schools, sports clubs, locker rooms, young offender centres, workplaces, and prisons using available research, theory, and practice available.

References

Ajzen, I. (1985). From intentions to actions: A theory of planned behavior. In J. Kuhl & J. Beckmann (Eds.) *Action control: From cognition to behavior* (pp. 11–39). Berlin, Heidelberg: Springer.

Ajzen, I. (1991). The theory of planned behavior. *Organizational Behavior and Human Decision Processes, 50*(2), 179–211.

Australian Government Department of Health. (2015). Australian Government Response to Contributing Lives, Thriving Communities–Review of Mental Health Programmes and Services.

Bewick, B. M., Gill, J., Mulhearn, B., Barkham, M., & Hill, A. J. (2008). Using electronic surveying to assess psychological distress within the UK student population: A multi-site pilot investigation. *E-Journal of Applied Psychology, 4*(2), 1–5.

Breslin, G., Haughey, T., Donnelly, P., Kearney, C., & Prentice, G. (2017). Promoting mental health awareness in sport clubs. *Journal of Public Mental Health, 16*(2), 55–62.

Breslin, G., Haughey, T., O'Brien, W., Caulfield, L., Robertson, A. & Lawlor, M. (2018). Increasing athlete knowledge of mental health and intentions to seek help: The State of Mind Ireland (SOMI) pilot program. *Journal of Clinical Sport Psychology, 12*(1), 1–18.

Breslin, G., & McCay, N. (2013). Perceived control over physical and mental well-being: The effects of gender, age and social class. *Journal of Health Psychology, 18*(1), 38–45.

Breslin, G., Shannon, S., Ferguson, K., Devlin, S., Haughey, T., & Prentice, G. (2018). Predicting athletes' mental health stigma using the theory of reasoned action framework. *Journal of Clinical Sport Psychology, 12*(1), 39–56.

Breslin, G., Shannon, S., Haughey, T., Leavey, G., Sarju, N., Neill, D., & Lawlor, M. (under review). *Effect of a mental health awareness intervention among student-athletes: Testing an integrated behaviour change framework.*

Byrne, P. (2000). Stigma of mental illness and ways of diminishing it. *Advances in Psychiatric treatment, 6*(1), 65–72.

Chambers, D., Murphy, F., & Keeley, H. S. (2015). All of us? An exploration of the concept of mental health literacy based on young people's responses to fictional mental health vignettes. *Irish Journal of Psychological Medicine, 32*(1), 129–136.

Craig, P., Dieppe, P., Macintyre, S., Michie, S., Nazareth, I., & Petticrew, M. (2013). Developing and evaluating complex interventions: The new medical research council guidance. *International Journal of Nursing Studies, 50*(5), 587–592.

Department of Children and Youth Affairs. (2014). Better Outcomes, Brighter Futures: The National Policy Framework for Children and Young People 2014–2020.

Donohue, B., Chow, G. M., Pitts, M., Loughran, T., Schubert, K. N., Gavrilova, Y., & Allen, D. N. (2015). Piloting a family-supported approach to concurrently optimize mental health and sport performance in athletes. *Clinical Case Studies, 14*(3), 159–177.

Donohue, B., Pitts, M., Gavrilova, Y., Ayarza, A., & Cintron, K. I. (2013). A culturally sensitive approach to treating substance abuse in athletes using evidence-supported methods. *Journal of Clinical Sport Psychology, 7*(2), 98–119.

Dooley, B., & Fitzgerald, A. (2013). Methodology on the My World Survey (MWS): A unique window into the world of adolescents in Ireland. *Early Intervention in Psychiatry, 7*(1), 12–22.

Evans-Lacko, S., Rose, D., Little, K., Flach, C., Rhydderch, D., Henderson, C., & Thornicroft, G. (2011). Development and psychometric properties of the reported and intended behaviour scale (RIBS): A stigma-related behaviour measure. *Epidemiology and Psychiatric Sciences, 20*(3), 263–271.

Government Office for Science (2008), Foresight Mental Capital and Wellbeing Project (2008). Final Project report – Executive summary. London.

Gulliver, A., Griffiths, K. M., & Christensen, H. (2010). Perceived barriers and facilitators to mental health help-seeking in young people: A systematic review. *BMC Psychiatry, 10*(1), 113.

Gulliver, A., Griffiths, K. M., Christensen, H., Mackinnon, A., Calear, A. L., Parsons, A., . . . & Stanimirovic, R. (2012). Internet-based interventions to promote mental health help-seeking in elite athletes: An exploratory randomized controlled trial. *Journal of Medical Internet Research, 14*(3), e69.

Hagger, M. S., & Chatzisarantis, N. L. (2014). An integrated behavior change model for physical activity. *Exercise and Sport Sciences Reviews, 42*(2), 62–69.

Hölzel, B.K., Carmody, J., Vangel, M., Congleton, C., Yerramsetti, S. M., Gard, T., & Lazar, S. W. (2011). Mindfulness practice leads to increases in regional brain gray matter density. *Psychiatry Research: Neuroimaging, 191*(1), 36–43.

Houghton, A-M., & Anderson, J. (2017). *Embedding wellbeing in the curriculum.* York: The Higher Education Academy. Retrieved from www.heacademy.ac.uk/system/files/hub/download/embedding_wellbeing_in_he.pdf

Jorm, A. F. (2012). Mental health literacy: Empowering the community to take action for better mental health. *American Psychologist, 67*(3), 231.

Karwig, G., Chambers, D., & Murphy, F. (2015). Reaching out in college: Help-seeking at third level in Ireland. ReachOut Ireland.

Lawlor, M., Rae, M., Kelly, N., & Moriarty, P. (2015). State of mind Ireland: Towards a skills for life passport. Proceedings of the CRSI Conference.

Longshore, K., & Sachs, M. (2015). Mindfulness training for coaches: A mixed-method exploratory study. *Journal of Clinical Sport Psychology, 9*(2), 116–137.

McLafferty, M., Lapsley, C. R., Ennis, E., Armour, C., Murphy, S., Bunting, B. P., . . . O'Neill, S. M. (2017). Mental health, behavioural problems and treatment seeking among students commencing university in Northern Ireland. *PloS One, 12*(12), e0188785.

Michie, S., Carey, R., Johnston, M., Rothman, A., Kelly, M., Davidson, K., & de Bruin, M. (2016). From theory-inspired to theory-based interventions: Linking behaviour change techniques to their mechanisms of action. *European Health Psychologist, 18*(S), 395.

Michie, S., Johnston, M., Francis, J., Hardeman, W., & Eccles, M. (2008). From theory to intervention: Mapping theoretically derived behavioural determinants to behaviour change techniques. *Applied Psychology, 57*(4), 660–680.

National Union of Students – Union of Students Ireland (NUS-USI). (2017). *NI student wellbeing survey report.* Retrieved from http://nus-usi.org/campaigns/education-welfare/nus-usi-student-wellbeing-survey-report/

Public Health Agency. (2018). *"Take Five" steps to wellbeing.* Retrieved from www.mindingyourhead.info/take-5-steps-wellbeing

Ryan, R. M., & Deci, E. L. (2000). Self-determination theory and the facilitation of intrinsic motivation, social development, and well-being. *American Psychologist, 55*(1), 68–78.

Ryan, R. M., & Deci, E. L. (2017). *Self-determination theory: Basic psychological needs in motivation, development, and wellness.* New York, NY: Guilford Publications.

Shannon, S., Haughey, T., Leavey, G., Sarju, N., Neill, D., Lawlor, M., & Breslin, G. (under review). *Predicting student-athlete and non-athletes' intentions to self-manage mental health: A confirmatory factor and path analysis of an integrated behaviour change model.*

Smith, B. W., Dalen, J., Wiggins, K., Tooley, E., Christopher, P., & Bernard, J. (2008). The brief resilience scale: Assessing the ability to bounce back. *International Journal of Behavioral Medicine, 15*(3), 194–200.

Tennant, R., Hiller, L., Fishwick, R., Platt, S., Joseph, S., Weich, S., . . . & Stewart-Brown, S. (2007). The Warwick-Edinburgh mental well-being scale (WEMWBS): Development and UK validation. *Health and Quality of Life Outcomes, 5*(1), 63.

Thomas, L. (2012). Building student engagement and belonging in higher education at a time of change. Paul Hamlyn Foundation, 100.

Turner, C. (2018, August 7). Universities' main purpose is no longer learning, minister says as he calls for mental health focus. *The Telegraph.* Retrieved from www.telegraph.co.uk/education/2018/08/06/universities-main-purpose-no-longer-learning-minister-says-calls/

Universities UK. (2015). *Student mental wellbeing in higher education: Good practice guide.* Universities UK.

Universities UK. (2018). *Mind our futures: Starting a conversation about the support of student mental health.* Retrieved from www.universitiesuk.ac.uk/policy-and-analysis/reports/Documents/2018/minding-our-future-starting-conversation-student-mental-health.pdf

World Health Organization. (2010). *Global recommendations on physical activity for health.* Geneva, Switzerland: World Health Organization.

Further reading

The following systematic review article critically evaluates available psycho-educational programmes for athletes, coaches and officials: Breslin, G., Shannon, S., Haughey, T., Donnelly,
P., & Leavey, G. (2017). A systematic review of interventions to increase awareness of mental health and well-being in athletes, coaches and officials. *Systematic Reviews*, 6(1), 177.

Donohue, B., Gavrilova, Y., Galante, M., Gavrilova, E., Loughran, T., Scott, J., & Allen, D.
N. (2018). Controlled evaluation of an optimization approach to mental health and
sport performance. *Journal of Clinical Sport Psychology*, 1–42. This recent article articulates a mental health intervention for student-athletes which is based on an optimisation
approach for improving performance and well-being.

Sudano, L. E., Collins, G., & Miles, C. M. (2017). Reducing barriers to mental health care for
student-athletes: An integrated care model. *Families, Systems, & Health*, 35(1), 77. This article describes student-athletes service willingness alongside perceived barriers to seek help.

6

AHEAD OF THE GAME

A sports-based mental health programme for adolescent males

Sarah K. Liddle, Diarmuid Hurley, Matthew Schweickle, Christian Swann and Stewart A. Vella

Learning objectives

After reading this chapter you should be able to:

1 Understand the role that sporting clubs can play in facilitating and supporting mental health interventions.
2 Understand the relationship between sports, mental health, and adolescence.
3 Critically examine the role of formative research and community involvement in intervention development.
4 Appreciate and justify the processes required to implement a comprehensive mental health programme within a sport club.
5 Understand and describe the importance and key processes of ongoing reflection and re-evaluation during programme intervention development and implementation.

Introduction to the theme

Ahead of the Game (AOTG) is a comprehensive multi-level, multi-component programme for adolescent males delivered through community sporting clubs and organisations. The aims of the programme are to: (1) increase mental health literacy among adolescents and their social support systems; (2) increase help-seeking intentions and attitudes that facilitate help-seeking among adolescent male sport participants; and (3) increase resilience and factors which prevent the onset of mental health problems, including wellbeing and self-determined motivation. To achieve these aims, the programme includes four components, two interventions for adolescents targeting mental health literacy and resilience, a parent mental health literacy intervention, and an intervention for coaches aimed at helping them to facilitate self-determined motivation. These four distinct interventions are complemented by a messaging campaign and supplemented with online content (aheadofthegame. org.au). AOTG is primarily a mental health promotion and prevention programme that also promotes early intervention for mental illness and available support services.

Targeting mental health literacy, help-seeking, stigma, and resilience in adolescent males is important for a number of reasons. Mental disorders are recognised as one of the most prominent contributors to the global burden of disease among young people (Costello, Egger, & Angold, 2005), and they carry significant personal, social, and economic costs that can last a lifetime. Half of all mental disorders have their onset before the age of 14 years (Kessler et al., 2005), and young men and boys represent the group at highest risk of mental disorders and suicide in one third of developed countries, including Australia (Australian Institute of Health and Welfare, 2011) wherein AOTG is delivered. According to the Australian National Survey of Mental Health and Wellbeing, 14% of all adolescents aged 12 to 17 years have a mental health issue, with males (16%) showing slightly higher rates compared to females (13%) (Lawrence et al., 2015). Furthermore, suicide is the leading cause of death for Australians aged 15–44 years, with the rate among males three times the rate among females – 17.8 and 5.8 deaths per 100,000 people, respectively (Australian Bureau of Statistics, 2017).

Preventative programmes can provide protection against the onset of mental health problems. Specifically, preventative programmes aimed at adolescents can reduce and prevent the detrimental long-term impact of adolescent mental disorders which reduce the likelihood of completing school, gaining employment, and engaging as a productive member of society (Lawrence et al., 2015). Further, the need for mental health literacy among adolescents and their social support systems is substantial because a large proportion of mental disorders have their onset during adolescence (Kessler et al., 2005). This is exacerbated by the fact that most adolescents do not have the knowledge or experience to deal with the onset of mental disorders (Rickwood, Deane, Wilson, & Ciarrochi, 2005). Young people who do recognise a mental disorder are more likely to hold adaptive preferences for help-seeking (e.g. from professional sources of help; Wright, Jorm, Harris, & McGorry, 2007). However, young males have particularly negative attitudes towards mental health treatment (Gonzalez, Alegria, & Prihoda, 2005) and lack the maturity and experience to deal with mental disorders among their peers despite the fact that peers are often their first option for help-seeking (Olsson & Kennedy, 2010).

Sports participants are no less likely to experience a mental illness than the general population (Gulliver, Griffiths, Mackinnon, Batterham, & Stanimirovic, 2015). Sports participants also express additional barriers to seeking help, such as the potential impact on playing time, and being perceived as mentally weak or lacking commitment (Breslin, Shannon, Haughey, Donnelly, & Leavey, 2017; Trojian, 2016). Many sports cultures celebrate mental toughness, masculinity, and disapproval of weakness disclosure (Bauman, 2016; Doherty, Hannigan, & Campbell, 2016), potentially perpetuating the negative effects of mental illness and increasing stigma. Stigma is an important issue because it may result in problems being hidden and could prevent young people from appropriately seeking help and receiving support (Trojian, 2016). When compared to more general public health programmes, interventions that are specifically developed and tailored to the culture of sport may be particularly relevant and beneficial in the promotion of mental health and wellbeing.

It has been suggested by the United Nations (Sport for Development and Peace International Working Group, 2008), World Health Organisation (World Health Organisation, 2011), and the International Olympic Committee (IOC; Mountjoy, 2011) that sport has the potential to facilitate and promote health at a population level. In most countries, over 40% of young people participate in organised sports, with participation rates substantially higher in high income countries such as Denmark (>80%), Sweden, Canada and Australia (>60%; Tremblay et al., 2016). In Australia, the average time spent by adolescents in organised sports is over seven hours each week (Vella, Cliff, Okely, Scully, & Morley, 2013). In sum, there are several factors that contribute to the consideration of sport as a vehicle for health promotion; most notably the established health benefits, a large participation base and extended access to children and adolescents during sports participation (Geidne, Quennerstedt, & Eriksson, 2013; Kokko, 2014; Kokko, Green, & Kannas, 2013).

Describe the client or group being targeted

The AOTG programme targeted adolescent males aged 12–17 years who participated in organised sports from community grass-roots level through to elite academy level. A total of 1675 adolescent males with an average age of 14.51 participated in the programme across all implementation phases, with 283 participating in the final phase of the programme. All participating sport clubs were from a range of suburbs with ranging social-economic status from eastern New South Wales, Australia. In addition, the AOTG programme aimed to include the parents and coaches of adolescent male sport participants in distinct, complementary interventions. All interventions that comprise the AOTG programme were delivered through, and most often in conjunction with, community sporting clubs and organisations.

In line with a Community Based Participatory Research (CBPR) framework (Minkler & Wallerstein, 2003), AOTG was tested in organised sporting clubs at a community level. A community was defined as a group of sporting clubs who share the same governing body for sport, who are located close to each other within geographical boundaries defined by the governing sports association, and who compete and interact with one another on a regular (usually weekly) basis. All sporting clubs from the six most popular sporting codes for adolescent males (Soccer, Australian Rules Football, Cricket, Tennis, Basketball, Swimming) (Australian Bureau of Statistics, 2012) within the community were invited to participate.

Initial needs assessment

Consistent with a CBPR framework, development of the AOTG programme first went through a rigorous community-based needs assessment and exploration stage

(Fixsen, Naoom, Blase, Friedman, & Wallace, 2005). This stage involved extensive engagement with the extended community and consultation with key stakeholders. In total 16 focus groups were conducted with adolescent male sport participants (n = 55), 10 with their parents (n = 46) and five with coaches (n = 20). The research team also facilitated a two-day workshop in conjunction with their research partners, five national sporting organisations, and local sporting representatives to assess the feasibility of implementation approaches and potential barriers at a policy, regional, and local level.

The most salient outcomes of the initial needs assessment, which in large part dictated the AOTG programme content, were that: (1) adolescent males desired more information about mental health problems, how to recognise them, and how to provide help to their friends if they are experiencing a mental health problem (Swann et al., 2018); (2) adolescent males desired information that would help them to increase their wellbeing and prevent the onset of mental health problems (Swann et al., 2018); (3) parents of adolescent males were not adequately knowledgeable, prepared, or confident to assist children who experience a mental health problem (Brown, Deane, Vella, & Liddle, 2017; Hurley, Swann, Allen, Okely, & Vella, 2017); (4) there was significant variation in the role that coaches believed that they should play in adolescent athlete mental health, with most coaches not willing to take an active role; and, (5) coaches were interested in content regarding adolescent motivation and wellbeing, as opposed to mental health (Ferguson, Swann, Liddle, & Vella, 2018). A full description of the formative research findings is provided below.

Adolescent males

We aimed to understand adolescent males' existing knowledge, previous experience, and perceived needs regarding mental health. Additionally, their perceptions of organised sport as a vehicle for supporting mental health, and preferences for mental health interventions in sport were explored. A detailed description of the methods and results of this qualitative study can be found elsewhere (Swann et al., 2018).

Six key dimensions emerged from that initial needs assessment with adolescent males. First, they reported broadly understanding mental health as a "state of mind", with most having some experience with mental illness – either personally or through someone close to them. Adolescents also reflected that perceived masculinity was an important factor in stigmatised attitudes towards male mental health. Second, there was variation in adolescents' opinion on the relationship between sport and mental health. For some, sport was perceived as positive for mental health, especially when the primary motivation was enjoyment or fun. However, for others, sport was perceived as a negative influence on mental health, particularly when the primary motivation was performance. Third, adolescents reported that coaches could play an important role in their life, such as acting as an important avenue of support if they were struggling with a mental health problem. In addition, adolescents also reported that, in some cases, they would prefer if coaches changed their approach to focus less on winning and more on enjoyment of sport. Fourth, adolescents expressed that family is particularly important in supporting mental health through sport. However, adolescents felt that parents need to receive more information about mental health and mental illness, and that it was important that they learnt about it together. Fifth, adolescents reported a range of interests in learning about mental health. Specifically, adolescents wanted to gain knowledge around how to help a friend, and further, learn to better recognise and empathise with those who experience mental health issues. Adolescents also highlighted a desire to learn how to manage adversity, which could be used both within sport and to protect their mental health more broadly. Lastly, adolescents suggested that sport could provide an engaging environment for discussing mental health especially when compared to the school environment, further describing the utility of the group and team context in sport as a facilitator of mental health promotion. However, adolescents also reported that the success of mental health discussions within their teams may depend on how connected individuals feel to their club or team. Furthermore, adolescents expressed an interest in learning about elite athletes' mental health and also in learning about mental health from someone with lived experience of mental illness.

Parents

We aimed to investigate and understand sport parents' existing knowledge, beliefs, attitudes and perceptions of the role sport clubs play in mental health promotion and disorder prevention, and the factors that might promote or limit their participation in (and effectiveness of) mental health-focused interventions. Parents play an important role in recognising young people's mental health symptoms, providing emotional support and facilitating professional help-seeking (Mendenhall & Frauenholtz, 2015; Rickwood, Deane, & Wilson, 2007). Parents are a key source of support in adolescent sport participation (Harwood & Knight, 2015), and parent behaviour has been targeted in the youth sport environment as a mechanism to increase support and warmth and reduce conflict and pressure (Dorsch, King, Dunn, Osai, & Tulane, 2017). A detailed description of the methods and results of the qualitative study are available elsewhere (see, Hurley et al., 2017).

In summary, the majority of parents reported limited ability to recognise the presence or potential development of mental health disorders in their child. Parents' reported particular confusion about how to distinguish between possible symptoms of mental illness and "normal" male adolescent behaviours such as moodiness or oversleeping. Parents reported having insufficient knowledge about help-seeking services and treatment options and lacked the capacity and confidence to effectively communicate, support and intervene in the face of a mental health problem. These parents had favourable attitudes towards receiving education on adolescent mental health but expressed mixed views on the role of the sport club in promoting positive mental health. The sport club provided a forum for parents to talk, share advise and discuss parenting as well as look out for each other's children as a supportive community, but it was not seen as having an explicit role in mental health promotion.

Findings of the need assessment with parents suggested that the intervention should target symptom identification, provide clear guidelines and strategies on how to respond to and manage adolescent mental health disorders and how to communicate about mental health with adolescents. This would serve to ease parents' concerns about their current lack of knowledge, skills and confidence to support and protect adolescent mental health. In addition, according to the parents, interventions should build on the existing supportive social networks among sport parents, and be brief, convenient and accessible to allow for parents' reported time constraints.

Coaches

We aimed to understand coaches' existing knowledge, attitudes and beliefs regarding supporting adolescent athletes with mental health problems and the promotion of mental health and wellbeing. Additionally, coaches' preferences for coach education, including format and modality, was also explored. A detailed description of the methodology and results of the coach needs assessment has been provided elsewhere (Ferguson et al., 2018).

Coaches perceived their role as a youth sport coach to be diverse and included the promotion of athlete wellbeing. Consistent with previous research, coaches agreed that their role does include the promotion of mental health (Brown et al., 2017; Mazzer & Rickwood, 2015; Vella, Oades, & Crowe, 2011). For some coaches, this role extends to targeted actions to facilitate professional help-seeking, however, this view was not shared by all coaches. Despite the variation in the extent to which coaches described their willingness to act regarding athlete mental illness, all coaches articulated some form of role in the identification, referral and prevention of mental health problems. Notably, some coaches expressed a preference to work directly with athletes, while others preferred to notify parents. Coaches expressed a preference to receive education face-to-face, and to include practical components. These coaches preferred supplementary information to be delivered online, and for sessions to be short.

Given large discrepancies in coaches' willingness to be involved in the prevention of mental illness, we decided to build on coaches' universal belief that the promotion of wellbeing was part of their role. In particular, an intervention was designed based on self-determination theory (Ryan & Deci, 2000) that would allow coaches to: i) facilitate good quality (self-determined) motivation that would decrease the risk of mental health problems associated with the prioritisation of performance; ii) increase athlete wellbeing by increasing self-determined motivation; and, iii) lead to higher retention rates in youth sport, which have been associated with lower risk for mental health problems (Vella, Cliff, Magee, & Okely, 2015).

Framework and intervention delivery

Based on the above findings, four distinct intervention components and a supporting messaging campaign were developed to meet the needs of all stakeholders (including adolescent sport participants, their parents, coaches, clubs and regional sporting bodies), in the most feasible and engaging manner. A detailed description of the entire AOTG programme content has been reported elsewhere (Vella et al., 2018). Briefly, AOTG comprises two distinct interventions for adolescent male sports participants targeting mental health literacy and resilience, respectively. A single intervention for parents targets parental mental health literacy. Finally, a coach training programme based on self-determination theory and autonomy supportive coaching (Langan, Lonsdale, Blake, & Toner, 2015) is also included. These four interventions are supplemented by a club-based messaging campaign.

Adolescent mental health literacy: Help Out a Mate

Help Out a Mate (HOAM) is a brief 45-minute face-to-face sports-based mental health literacy intervention. The intervention is delivered by trained volunteer presenters and aims to: increase mental health literacy among adolescent males (specifically in regard to depression and anxiety); increase their skills and confidence to help a peer showing signs of a mental health problem; increase helping behaviour and supportive actions; increase appropriate help-seeking among young males at risk of mental health problems; and decrease stigmatising attitudes. The intervention was intentionally designed to be brief so that it could be presented at sports clubs to a team or group of adolescent males in or around a regularly scheduled training session. Specifically, participants are taught the HOAM action plan with regard to the provision of help to somebody else: *ask how they are; listen without judgement; ask about supportive adults; suggest sources of help;* and *check again later.* Presentation slides followed a consistent theme of a sepia-toned cartoon which had been concept-tested. Participants' confidence and intentions to help someone experiencing a mental health problem were reinforced through three brief role-plays based on the HOAM action plan.

The HOAM intervention involved the following components: (i) a description of what is mental health and mental illness; (ii) dispelling myths about mental illness; (iii) a description of depression; (iv) what is anxiety?; (v) how to provide help; and (vi) where to get reliable information. Additional resources provided to adolescents include a business card sized "Man Card", which lists key steps on how to help a friend (the HOAM Action Plan), and a list of mental health resources.

Mental health literacy refers to the knowledge, attitudes and beliefs about mental health and disorders, and the effectiveness of potential actions to benefit personal or others' mental health through symptom recognition, management and prevention (Jorm, 2012; Jorm et al., 1997). HOAM addresses these components with the content and structure developed following a review of the literature and existing programmes and materials (Black Dog Institute, 2014; Hart, Mason, Kelly, Cvetko-vski, & Jorm, 2016; Kitchener & Jorm, 2002; Ross, Hart, Jorm, Kelly, & Kitchener, 2012) and consultation with a Mental Health First Aid Trainer. Depression and anxiety are covered as these are the most common mental health problems among youth (Lawrence et al., 2015). Clarifying when signs and symptoms of depression or anxiety move from being a part of normal experience to becoming problems likely to require help-seeking is a key part of the workshop content. Other mental illnesses or the effectiveness of various treatments were not addressed due to the time limitations on the workshop. The focus was on developing the knowledge to recognise when a friend is struggling and the skills to offer support, particularly with help-seeking.

Adolescent resilience: Your Path to Success in Sport

Your Path to Success in Sport (YPTSS) is a brief 45–60-minute face-to-face work-shop supported by six internet-based (website/mobile application) modules. The primary aim of YPTSS is to increase psychological resilience: the mental processes and behaviour which promote personal assets and protect an individual from the potential negative effect of stressors (Fletcher & Sarkar, 2013). The face-to-face workshop is facilitated by trained presenters and delivered at the sports club to groups of up to 30 adolescents. The content of the workshop focuses on "expecta-tions vs reality" in the process of achieving goals (i.e., the "path to success"). This acts to identify inevitable challenges, obstacles and adversity that adolescents are likely to face in and outside of sport. The workshop then focuses on the need to build key skills through which adolescents can overcome adversity, which can be learnt via the internet-based resources.

The internet-based component of the intervention contains six modules, each of which take approximately 10–15 minutes to complete, and are designed to be completed in order. Informed by sport-based resilience literature (Fletcher & Sarkar, 2012, 2013; Galli & Gonzalez, 2015; Sarkar & Fletcher, 2014a, 2014b), the modules are: (i) problem-solving; (ii) controlling the controllables; (iii) managing your thoughts; (iv) keeping your cool; (v) playing to your strengths; and (vi) appre-ciating your team. These skills are communicated through informational videos, infographics, reflective activities and exercises to try at the end of each module. An additional recap module is also available to participants who completed the six pre-ceding modules. Upon completion of YPTSS, adolescents will have had the oppor-tunity to develop more adaptive beliefs about managing adversity and increasing their psychological resilience.

Parents

The parent intervention is a brief 60-minute face-to-face intervention with sup-plementary print and online content. The intervention aims to increase parents' knowledge and self-efficacy in dealing with mental health problems by increasing knowledge and confidence to help, reducing stigmatising attitudes and increasing engagement in actual help-seeking and support strategies. All components of mental health literacy were targeted including: 1) knowledge awareness and help-promoting positive attitudes, 2) capacity to recognise the development or signs of a mental health disorder, 3) knowledge about professional help-seeking and treatment options, 4) capacity to help and support, and finally 5) knowledge of preventive and self-help strategies.

Workshops took place at local community sport club facilities, community centres, and on a university campus and were scheduled at convenient times for parents (e.g., while son is training). Workshops were led by a member of the research team who had mental health first aid certification and experience in delivering mental health workshops. Following the workshop, parents received a pamphlet containing key information and resources from the workshop and were also directed to online resources should they require or want more information. Printed material focussed on how to tell the difference between "normal" teenage behaviour and potential warning signs of mental health problems.

The content of the parent intervention was designed to be engaging, utilising a mix of parent reflection, discussion, scenarios, presentation and some brief videos. Materials were developed and adapted from Mental Health First Aid guidelines (Fischer, Kelly, Kitchener, & Jorm, 2013; Morgan & Jorm, 2009), or used with permission from mental health organisations and parenting organisations. The content of the intervention workshop was assessed for relevance and accuracy by a Mental Health First Aid Trainer.

Coaches

The coach component of the programme was based on an existing intervention based on self-determination theory with demonstrated feasibility and acceptability with youth sport coaches (Langan et al., 2015). Using self-determination theory as a guiding framework (Ryan & Deci, 2000), the goal of the programme was to teach coaches effective strategies to support their players' basic psychological needs. These needs include autonomy (feeling self-directed and capable of making choices about one's actions), competence (feeling effective in one's interactions with the physical and social environment) and belongingness (feeling closely connected and cared for by others). In turn, the fulfilment of basic psychological needs will promote self-determined forms of motivation which we hypothesise to lead to higher rates of wellbeing and greater retention rates in sport.

Langan and colleagues' (2015) original programme involved six face-to-face training sessions delivered by a sport psychologist to each coach, on a one-to-one basis. This was adapted for the AOTG programme so that it could be feasibly delivered on a wider scale. The initial needs assessment with coaches indicated that youth sport coaches believed that some aspects of the programme could be delivered using online resources. However, they also believed that it would be important to meet with facilitators in order to ask questions and discuss specific implementation challenges. To address these concerns, a blended delivery model was designed and implemented, involving face-to-face workshops and mentoring sessions, with the addition of online self-paced tasks to facilitate continued learning. A sport psychology practitioner facilitated all workshops and mentoring sessions.

The coach intervention included two separate face-to-face workshops two hours in duration, two mentoring sessions both one hour in duration, and 11 online modules. Each online module consisted of video examples of good coaching practice and poor coaching practice, coach reflection and action planning. Videos were tailored to each participating sporting code. Mentoring sessions were facilitated by the same practitioner who facilitated the face-to-face workshops. The coach training programme followed a format that consisted of workshop 1, six online modules, mentoring session 1, workshop 2, five online modules and mentoring session 2. All online modules were completed in the prescribed order.

Intervention evaluation and lessons learned through self-reflection

The AOTG programme was implemented over three distinct phases (Vella et al., in preparation). Phase I included an initial pilot implementation which involved the collection of preliminary data on contextual variables, as well as any local adaptations within sporting clubs that were required. Phase II included programme and intervention implementation and development which involved the collection of data on the dose, reach, fidelity and cost of the programme. Phase III included the programme's full implementation which involved a robust formative evaluation of the effectiveness of the programme implementation, and the contextual information including its cost-effectiveness and possible mechanisms of change (Stetler et al., 2006). Lessons learned from each phase were used to improve the content and delivery of AOTG in subsequent phases. Changes were made in an attempt to improve resultant programme fidelity, dose delivered, dose received and cost-effectiveness. Over the course of the three phases of implementation, large and meaningful changes were made to the implementation team and the implementation model. Some of these were successful, while others were not. The culmination of the learnings over the three implementation phases are important in considering future implementation and sustainability of the AOTG programme beyond the study setting and timeframe. A full description of the implementation phases and the lessons learned is given elsewhere (Vella et al., in preparation).

The most successful implementation model was that used in the third and final phase of implementation, which led to the greatest reach, dose delivered, dose received, and was the most cost-effective. The implementation model used in this phase combined numerous key elements that were interdependent. These included:

- Full-time employment of a small group of competent and experienced implementation team members with knowledge of the organisational systems and competencies of local sporting clubs;
- Flexibility to adapt the programme processes (such as information delivery) to utilise organisational strengths and systems already existing within sporting clubs;
- Rigid around delivery and content to maximise fidelity and dose.

According to the Consolidated Framework for Implementation Research model (CFIR; Damschroder et al., 2009) there are numerous constructs that underpin successful implementation processes. One of these processes is a need for ownership of public health initiatives or interventions by community networks in the settings where they are implemented (Eckermann, Dawber, Yeatman, Quinsey, & Morris, 2014; Eckermann et al., 2014; Hawe & Potvin, 2009; Shiell, Hawe, & Gold, 2008). As such, the process of engaging key community actors is critical. Throughout the implementation of AOTG within community sporting clubs we found most value in engaging existing opinion leaders, and formally appointing internal implementation leaders as well as AOTG "champions" to enable optimal sport club community engagement, ownership and network benefits. For example, when only AOTG champions were appointed in Phases I and II, the network of influence of those champions was limited and the dose delivered was reduced because they typically held great influence over only one (or a few) teams, but had limited/no influence over other teams. As such, both opinion leaders (well-known individuals from within the club who have influence over many people) and formally appointed internal implementation leaders are necessary engagements to ensure maximum fidelity and dose of intervention within sports clubs. Often, these roles were enacted by the same person within a club, which we found to be advantageous.

The ability of the implementation team to fully execute the implementation model is important. However, meaningful benefit was derived from the process of reflection and evaluation. According to the CFIR model, reflection and evaluation is constituted by qualitative and quantitative evidence regarding the progress and success of the implementation model and its execution (Damschroder et al., 2009). Successful implementation was underpinned by both formal and informal weekly team meetings and ongoing personal debriefing focused on both the process and experience of implementation.

The most successful implementation model used was able to combine structured programme delivery to maximise the number of sessions delivered and also to ensure the fidelity or quality of delivery, while adapting recruitment and engagement strategies to leverage the strengths of each club. Indeed, where local adaptation can occur in consultation with the implementing organisation, effectiveness can be maximised. Given that some level of local adaptation may be inevitable

(Durlak & DuPre, 2008), the research team may be best served by working in conjunction with administering organisations (such as sporting clubs) to take advantage
of their implementation and organisational strengths and in maximising ownership
of health promotion strategies.

Given the heavy influence of implementation success on programme effectiveness,
no programme should be evaluated until sufficient time has been allocated to its full
implementation (Durlak & DuPre, 2008). While estimates of sufficient time alloca-
tions vary from one to three years (Fixsen et al., 2005), it is clear that implementation
improves from year to year (Durlak & DuPre, 2008). This has been the case with the
AOTG programme, where evaluation of programme effectiveness in Phases I or II
would not do justice to the true effectiveness of the programme. While decisions
regarding readiness for evaluation should be made on a case-by-case basis, the monitoring and evaluating of implementation processes can help to inform readiness for
evaluation.

Formal evaluations of some individual interventions were undertaken during the pilot phase. These evaluations showed that participation in HOAM led to
increased attitudes that promote appropriate help-seeking and reduce stigma, intentions to provide help, and knowledge about depression and anxiety (Liddle, Deane,
Batterham, & Vella, under review). Participation in the parent intervention led to
improved depression and anxiety literacy, knowledge of help-seeking options and
confidence to assist someone experiencing a mental health disorder (Hurley, Allen,
Swann, Okely, & Vella, 2018). However, given that AOTG is a multicomponent,
multi-level programme designed to target multiple stakeholders simultaneously,
effectiveness of the entire programme is of greater importance. During Phase III,
participants in clubs who implemented the AOTG programme showed increases in
wellbeing, resilience, depression and anxiety literacy, attitudes that promote help-
seeking, and intentions to seek help from formal sources such as a general practitioner or psychologist one month following participation in AOTG. Furthermore,
adolescent participants also reported greater engagement, less burnout and greater
levels of self-determined motivation at their one month follow-up (Vella et al., in
preparation).

In conclusion, there are several key factors that support the successful and cost-
effective implementation of a mental health promotion programme within organised sporting clubs. As outlined by the CFIR model, a continual process of planning,
engaging, executing, reflecting and evaluating underpins continual improvement in
implementation, as measured by fidelity, dose, reach and cost-effectiveness of health
promotion programmes. Within the organised sports clubs that participated in the
AOTG programme, the most important characteristics for successful implementation were those related to the inner setting, namely the structural characteristics, networks and communications, and readiness for implementation of the clubs
themselves. Given that implementation of health promotion programmes within
sporting clubs can be meaningfully improved over time, formative evaluation of
the implementation processes is critical in determining when the intervention is
ready for formal evaluation, dissemination and translation. At both the individual

intervention and full AOTG programme level, implementation has been shown to have meaningful benefits for adolescent male mental health. Targeting multiple stakeholders such as adolescents, parents and coaches through community sporting clubs can be an effective and engaging approach to the prevention of mental health problems and promotion of wellbeing for adolescent sport participants.

References

Australian Bureau of Statistics. (2012). *Children's participation in sport and leisure time activities 2003–2012*, 4901.0.55.001 (No. 4901.0.55.001). Canberra, ACT: Australian Bureau of Statistics.

Australian Bureau of Statistics. (2017). *Causes of death, Australia, 2016* (No. 3303.0). Canberra, ACT: Australian Bureau of Statistics.

Australian Institute of Health and Welfare. (2011). *Young Australians: Their health and wellbeing.* Canberra, ACT: Australian Institute of Health and Welfare.

Bauman, N. J. (2016). The stigma of mental health in athletes: Are mental toughness and mental health seen as contradictory in elite sport? *British Journal of Sports Medicine, 50*, 135–136. doi:10/gc95g7

Black Dog Institute. (2014). *Youth programs.* Retrieved from www.blackdoginstitute.org.au

Breslin, G., Shannon, S., Haughey, T., Donnelly, P., & Leavey, G. (2017). A systematic review of interventions to increase awareness of mental health and well-being in athletes, coaches and officials. *Systematic Reviews, 6*, 177–192. doi:10/gc95g8

Brown, M., Deane, F. P., Vella, S. A., & Liddle, S. K. (2017). Parents views of the role of sports coaches as mental health gatekeepers for adolescent males. *International Journal of Mental Health Promotion, 19*, 1–13. doi:10/gc95hf

Costello, E. J., Egger, H., & Angold, A. (2005). 10-year research update review: The epidemiology of child and adolescent psychiatric disorders: I. Methods and public health burden. *Journal of the American Academy of Child & Adolescent Psychiatry, 44*, 972–986. doi:10/fwvjfz

Damschroder, L. J., Aron, D. C., Keith, R. E., Kirsh, S. R., Alexander, J. A., & Lowery, J. C. (2009). Fostering implementation of health services research findings into practice: A consolidated framework for advancing implementation science. *Implementation Science, 4*, 1–15. doi:10/ck4bd2

Doherty, S., Hannigan, B., & Campbell, M. J. (2016). The experience of depression during the careers of elite male athletes. *Frontiers in Psychology, 7*, 1–11. doi:10/f8wgg9

Dorsch, T. E., King, M. Q., Dunn, C. R., Osai, K. V., & Tulane, S. (2017). The impact of evidence-based parent education in organized youth sport: A pilot study. *Journal of Applied Sport Psychology, 29*, 199–214. doi:10/gc95hk

Durlak, J. A., & Du Pre, E. P. (2008). Implementation matters: A review of research on the influence of implementation on program outcomes and the factors affecting implementation. *American Journal of Community Psychology, 41*, 327–350. doi:10/gqg

Eckermann, S., Dawber, J., Yeatman, H., Quinsey, K., & Morris, D. (2014). Evaluating return on investment in a school based health promotion and prevention program: The investment multiplier for the Stephanie Alexander kitchen garden national program. *Social Science & Medicine, 114*, 103–112. doi:10/f597t2

Ferguson, H., Swann, C., Liddle, S. K., & Vella, S. A. (2018). Investigating youth sports coaches' perceptions of their role in adolescent mental health. *Journal of Applied Sport Psychology*, in press, 1–16. doi:10.1080/10413200.2018.1466839

Fischer, J. A., Kelly, C. M., Kitchener, B. A., & Jorm, A. F. (2013). Development of guidelines for adults on how to communicate with adolescents about mental health problems and other sensitive topics: A Delphi study. *SAGE Open, 3*, 1–15. doi:10/gc95hj

Fixsen, D. L., Naoom, S. F., Blase, K. A., Friedman, R. M., & Wallace, F. (2005). *Implementation research: A synthesis of the literature.* Tampa, FL: University of South Florida.

Fletcher, D., & Sarkar, M. (2012). A grounded theory of psychological resilience in Olympic champions. *Psychology of Sport and Exercise, 13,* 669–678. doi:10/bcg4

Fletcher, D., & Sarkar, M. (2013). Psychological resilience. *European Psychologist, 18,* 12–23. doi:10/bwr7

Galli, N., & Gonzalez, S. P. (2015). Psychological resilience in sport: A review of the literature and implications for research and practice. *International Journal of Sport and Exercise Psychology, 13,* 243–257. doi:10/bcg5

Geidne, S., Quennerstedt, M., & Eriksson, C. (2013). The youth sports club as a health-promoting setting: An integrative review of research. *Scandinavian Journal of Public Health, 41,* 269–283. doi:0.1177/1403494812473204

Gonzalez, J. M., Alegria, M., & Prihoda, T. J. (2005). How do attitudes toward mental health treatment vary by age, gender, and ethnicity/race in young adults? *Journal of Community Psychology, 33,* 611–629. doi:10/d8hbbg

Gulliver, A., Griffiths, K. M., Mackinnon, A., Batterham, P. J., & Stanimirovic, R. (2015). The mental health of Australian elite athletes. *Journal of Science and Medicine in Sport, 18,* 255–261. doi:10/gc95hq

Hart, L. M., Mason, R. J., Kelly, C. M., Cvetkovski, S., & Jorm, A. F. (2016). "teen Mental Health First Aid": A description of the program and an initial evaluation. *International Journal of Mental Health Systems, 10,* 1–18. doi:10/gc95g9

Harwood, C. G., & Knight, C. J. (2015). Parenting in youth sport: A position paper on parenting expertise. *Psychology of Sport and Exercise, 16,* 24–35. doi:10/gc95hm

Hawe, P., & Potvin, L. (2009). What is population health intervention research? *Canadian Journal of Public Health, 100,* 8–14. doi:10.17269/cjph.100.1748

Hurley, D., Allen, M. S., Swann, C., Okely, A. D., & Vella, S. A. (2018). The development, pilot, and process evaluation of a parent mental health literacy intervention through community sports clubs. *Journal of Child and Family Studies,* 1–12. doi:10/gdjx3g

Hurley, D., Swann, C., Allen, M. S., Okely, A. D., & Vella, S. A. (2017). The role of community sports clubs in adolescent mental health: The perspectives of adolescent males' parents. *Qualitative Research in Sport, Exercise and Health, 9,* 372–388. doi:10/gc95hn

Jorm, A. F. (2012). Mental health literacy: Empowering the community to take action for better mental health. *American Psychologist, 67,* 231–243. doi:10/fbjbqw

Jorm, A. F., Korten, A. E., Jacomb, P. A., Christensen, H., Rodgers, B., & Pollitt, P. (1997). Mental health literacy: A survey of the public's ability to recognise mental disorders and their beliefs about the effectiveness of treatment. *Medical Journal Australia, 166*(4), 182–186.

Kessler, R. C., Berglund, P., Demler, O., Jin, R., Merikangas, K. R., & Walters, E. E. (2005). Lifetime prevalence and age-of-onset distributions of DSM-IV disorders in the national comorbidity survey replication. *Archives of General Psychiatry, 62,* 593–602. doi:10/b3b2pv

Kitchener, B. A., & Jorm, A. F. (2002). Mental health first aid training for the public: Evaluation of effects on knowledge, attitudes and helping behavior. *BMC Psychiatry, 2,* 1–6. doi:10/cfd9rh

Kokko, S. (2014). Sports clubs as settings for health promotion: Fundamentals and an overview to research. *Scandinavian Journal of Public Health, 42,* 60–65. doi:10/f6rjvc

Kokko, S., Green, L. W., & Kannas, L. (2013). A review of settings-based health promotion with applications to sports clubs. *Health Promotion International, 29,* 494–509. doi:10/f6q6rk

Langan, E., Lonsdale, C., Blake, C., & Toner, J. (2015). Testing the effects of a self-determination theory-based intervention with youth Gaelic football coaches on athlete motivation and burnout. *Sport Psychologist, 29*(4), 293–301.

Lawrence, D., Johnson, S., Hafekost, J., Boterhoven de Haan, K., Sawyer, M. G., Ainley, J., & Zubrick, S. R. (2015). *The mental health of children and adolescents: Report on the second Australian child and adolescent survey of mental health and wellbeing.* Canberra, ACT: Department of Health.

Liddle, S. K., Deane, F. P., Batterham, M., & Vella, S. A. (under review). *A brief sports-based mental health literacy program for adolescent males: A cluster-randomised controlled trial.*

Mazzer, K. R., & Rickwood, D. J. (2015). Mental health in sport: Coaches' views of their role and efficacy in supporting young people's mental health. *International Journal of Health Promotion and Education, 53,* 102–113. doi:10/gc95hc

Mendenhall, A. N., & Frauenholtz, S. (2015). Predictors of mental health literacy among parents of youth diagnosed with mood disorders. *Child & Family Social Work, 20,* 300–309. doi:10/f7ksk4

Minkler, M., & Wallerstein, N. (2003). Part one: Introduction to community-based participatory research. In *Community-based participatory research for health* (pp. 5–24). San Francisco, CA: Jossey-Bass.

Morgan, A. J., & Jorm, A. F. (2009). Self-help strategies that are helpful for sub-threshold depression: A Delphi consensus study. *Journal of Affective Disorders, 115,* 196–200. doi:10/cbhzgb

Mountjoy, M. (2011). Health and fitness of young people: What is the role of sport? *British Journal of Sports Medicine, 45,* 837–838. doi:10/fc8kx7

Olsson, D. P., & Kennedy, M. G. (2010). Mental health literacy among young people in a small US town: Recognition of disorders and hypothetical helping responses. *Early Intervention in Psychiatry, 4,* 291–298. doi:10.1111/j.1751-7893.2010.00196.x

Rickwood, D. J., Deane, F. P., & Wilson, C. J. (2007). When and how do young people seek professional help for mental health problems? *Medical Journal of Australia, 187,* S35–S39.

Rickwood, D. J., Deane, F. P., Wilson, C. J., & Ciarrochi, J. (2005). Young people's help-seeking for mental health problems. *Australian E-Journal for the Advancement of Mental Health, 4,* 218–251. doi:10/bnftsx

Ross, A. M., Hart, L. M., Jorm, A. F., Kelly, C. M., & Kitchener, B. A. (2012). Development of key messages for adolescents on providing basic mental health first aid to peers: A Delphi consensus study. *Early Intervention in Psychiatry, 6,* 229–238. doi:10/fxw2kc

Ryan, R. M., & Deci, E. L. (2000). Self-determination theory and the facilitation of intrinsic motivation, social development, and well-being. *American Psychologist, 55*(1), 68–78. doi:10/c48g8h

Sarkar, M., & Fletcher, D. (2014a). Ordinary magic, extraordinary performance: Psychological resilience and thriving in high achievers. *Sport, Exercise, and Performance Psychology, 3,* 46–60. doi:10/gc95hh

Sarkar, M., & Fletcher, D. (2014b). Psychological resilience in sport performers: A review of stressors and protective factors. *Journal of Sports Sciences, 32,* 1419–1434. doi:10/bchc

Shiell, A., Hawe, P., & Gold, L. (2008). Complex interventions or complex systems? Implications for health economic evaluation. *British Medical Journal, 336,* 1281–1283. doi:10/dw2kvm

Sport for Development and Peace International Working Group. (2008). *Harnessing the power of sport for development and peace: Recommendations to governments.* Geneva: United Nations.

Stetler, C. B., Legro, M. W., Wallace, C. M., Bowman, C., Guihan, M., Hagedorn, H., . . . Smith, J. L. (2006). The role of formative evaluation in implementation research and the QUERI experience. *Journal of General Internal Medicine, 21*(Suppl 2), S1–S8.

Swann, C., Telenta, J., Draper, G., Liddle, S. K., Fogarty, A., Hurley, D., & Vella, S. A. (2018). Youth sport as a context for supporting mental health: Adolescent male perspectives. *Psychology of Sport and Exercise, 35,* 55–64. doi:10/gc5922

Tremblay, M. S., Barnes, J. D., González, S. A., Katzmarzyk, P. T., Onywera, V. O., Reilly, J. J., . . . Global Matrix 2. 0 Research Team. (2016). Global matrix 2.0: Report card grades on the physical activity of children and youth comparing 38 countries. *Journal of Physical Activity and Health, 13,* S343–S366.

Trojian, T. (2016). Depression is under-recognised in the sport setting: Time for primary care sports medicine to be proactive and screen widely for depression symptoms. *British Journal of Sports Medicine, 50,* 137–139. doi:10/gc95hb

Vella, S. A., Cliff, D. P., Magee, C. A., & Okely, A. D. (2015). Associations between sports participation and psychological difficulties during childhood: A two-year follow up. *Journal of Science and Medicine in Sport, 18*(3), 304–309. doi:10/gc95hv

Vella, S. A., Cliff, D. P., Okely, A. D., Scully, M. L., & Morley, B. C. (2013). Associations between sports participation, adiposity and obesity-related health behaviors in Australian adolescents. *International Journal of Behavioural Nutrition and Physical Activity, 10,* 113. doi:10/bqr8

Vella, S. A., Lonsdale, C., Eckermann, S., Fogarty, A., Deane, F. P., Swann, C., . . . Telenta, J. (in preparation). *Formative evaluation of the implementation of a sports-based mental health program for adolescent males: Ahead of the game.*

Vella, S. A., Oades, L., & Crowe, T. (2011). The role of the coach in facilitating positive youth development: Moving from theory to practice. *Journal of Applied Sport Psychology, 23,* 33–48. doi:10/cmbw92

Vella, S. A., Swann, C., Batterham, M., Boydell, K. M., Eckermann, S., Fogarty, A., . . . Miller, A. (2018). Ahead of the game protocol: A multi-component, community sport-based program targeting prevention, promotion and early intervention for mental health among adolescent males. *BMC Public Health, 18,* 1–12. doi:10/gc95hg

World Health Organisation. (2011). *Promoting sport and enhancing health in European Union countries: A policy content analysis to support action.* Copenhagen: World Health Organization, Regional Office for Europe.

Wright, A., Jorm, A. F., Harris, M. G., & McGorry, P. D. (2007). What's in a name? Is accurate recognition and labelling of mental disorders by young people associated with better help-seeking and treatment preferences? *Social Psychiatry and Psychiatric Epidemiology, 42,* 244–250. doi:10/bp9w85

Further reading

Swann, C., Telenta, J., Draper, G., Liddle, S. K., Fogarty, A., Hurley, D., & Vella, S. A. (2018). Youth sport as a context for supporting mental health: Adolescent male perspectives. *Psychology of Sport and Exercise, 35,* 55–64. doi:10.1016/j.psychsport.2017.11.008

This article thoroughly describes the methodology of research using focus groups and describes the process of qualitative data analysis. It describes important insights into the potential role of sport as a vehicle for mental health promotion as perceived by Australian adolescent males.

Vella, S. A., Swann, C., Batterham, M., Boydell, K. M., Eckermann, S., Fogarty, A., . . . Miller, A. (2018). Ahead of the game protocol: A multi-component, community sport-based program targeting prevention, promotion and early intervention for mental health among adolescent males. *BMC Public Health, 18*(390), 1–12.

This article provides a thorough explanation of the intervention and research protocol of the Ahead of the Game programme, and will expand in detail on the description provided in this chapter.

Hurley, D., Swann, C., Allen, M. S., Okely, A. D., & Vella, S. A. (2017). The role of community sports clubs in adolescent mental health: The perspectives of adolescent males' parents. *Qualitative Research in Sport, Exercise and Health, 9*(3), 372–388.

Through qualitative evaluation, this article provides important insights into the role that the sporting context could play in the promotion of mental health and prevention of mental illness, as perceived by parents. It will additionally describe what parents currently know and wish to know regarding adolescent mental health in order to support their children.

Hurley, D., Allen, M. S., Swann, C., Okely, A. D., & Vella, S. A. (2018). The development, pilot, and process evaluation of a parent mental health literacy intervention through community sports clubs. *Journal of Child and Family Studies*, 1–12.

This article would provide additional explanation of the development of the Parent intervention of Ahead of the Game, including appropriate research design and analytical procedures to evaluate the intervention.

7

TACKLING THE BLUES

A sport and education-based mental health programme for children and young people

Jon Jones, Helen O'Keeffe and Andy Smith

Learning objectives

After reading this chapter you should be able to:

* Understand the relationship between mental health, education and social inequality.
* Critically examine the features of a sport and education programme which addresses mental health awareness in children and young people.
* Appreciate and justify the benefits of using quantitative and qualitative methods with children and young people in mental health programmes.
* Summarise the benefits of deploying a realist evaluation approach to understanding school-based mental health programmes.

Introduction to the theme

Writing in 2014, the House of Commons Health Committee (2014, p. 11) noted that, by comparison to other groups, there is a 'lack of reliable data about the state of children's and young people's mental health' in England and elsewhere in the United Kingdom (UK). They added that:

> The shortfall of information in this area is not confined to data on the prevalence of mental health problems amongst children and young people, but extends into information about service provision as well, including levels of demand, access and expenditure.
>
> *(House of Commons Health Committee, 2014, p. 13)*

This was regarded as particularly problematic in policy terms for, not only does the absence of prevalence data make it difficult to estimate accurately the scale of mental illness among children and young people (CYP), it also limits the degree to which more adequate and cost-effective policy and health care services can be developed to tackle mental illness and promote good mental health, and better inform decisions about access to services and their use (House of Commons Health Committee, 2014). In a review of the health of CYP in the UK published three years later, the Royal Colleges of Paediatrics and Child Health (RCPH) similarly argued that the 'lack of data on children and young people's mental health is a gap that urgently needs action, given evidence of increasing concerns about our children's mental health across all countries' (RCPH, 2017, p. 9). They added that the 326 CYP whom they consulted as part of their review identified mental health as a major source of concern, particularly in relation to self-esteem and self-confidence, the lack of support available to them in primary and secondary schools, the length of waiting times to access mental health services and lack of clarity about who they should turn to for advice and support (RCPH, 2017). In this regard, the CYP recommended that 'mental health education should be specifically taught from primary school onwards so that they could be more confident and better prepared to cope with the challenges of mental health in adolescence and adulthood' (RCPH, 2017, p. 8).

Notwithstanding the lack of reliable data on the mental health of CYP, evidence suggests that many mental illnesses are chronic and often begin early in life, and that CYP from more deprived backgrounds have worse health and wellbeing than those in higher socio-economic groups – a trend which has worsened since 2012 (RCPH, 2017). It is estimated that around 1 in 10 of 5–16-year-olds experience a clinically diagnosable mental illness; half of all adult mental illnesses (excluding dementia) are first experienced by age 14; and approximately 75 per cent of mental illnesses experienced by adults were first present by the age of 18 (Department of Health [DH], 2015; Public Health England [PHE], 2016; RCPH, 2017). National data also indicate that six-in-ten looked after children have some form of emotional or mental illness and up to three-quarters of CYP with mental illness are not in contact with appropriate mental health services (PHE, 2016). In this regard, particular criticism has been paid to the perceived inadequacy of mental health services – known in the UK as Child and Adolescent Mental Health Services (CAMHS) – and their failure to adequately address rising mental illness in CYP. Consequently, attention is increasingly centred on the potential of other settings – such as schools – to act as important contexts for prevention and early intervention work in relation to mental health and wellbeing (Cane & Oland, 2015; PHE, 2015; Sharpe, Ford, Lereya, Owen, Viner, & Wolpert, 2016).

In this chapter, we will discuss the initial design and development of an ongoing sport and education-based mental health programme – *Tackling the Blues* (TtB) – which was introduced in January 2015 for primary and secondary school-aged CYP who are experiencing, or are at risk of developing mental illness. More specifically, we examine (i) how participants were identified, recruited and engaged; (ii) features of the selected theoretical framework (i.e. realist evaluation) which underpinned the programme; (iii) the lessons learned from using the brand of a professional football club to engage CYP and the training and use of university student peer mentors; and (iv) the inevitable limitations of the programme imposed by the various inequalities which beset the participants' lives.

Group targeted

In school year 2015/16, the target client group of TtB were 6–16-year-olds attending 14 junior (primary) schools, secondary schools in three areas of north-west England (Liverpool, Sefton and Lancashire). These areas include some of the most deprived local authorities nationally, where approximately 10 per cent of CYP have a diagnosed mental illness (PHE, 2017). For example, according to the 2015 Indices of Multiple Deprivation, Liverpool is the fourth most deprived local authority in England, with 32 per cent of CYP living in poverty and where mental illness is significantly higher than the national average (Department for Communities and Local Government [DCLG], 2015). Data from PHE (2017) also indicate the significant health problems experienced by CYP who lived in the target areas where TtB was delivered in 2015/16:

- Liverpool is ranked third lowest in England for child wellbeing (based on the child wellbeing index);
- 513 CYP in Liverpool were admitted to hospital for mental health conditions or self-harm;
- CYP in Merseyside are in the worst 25th percentile for obesity, not in education, employment or training (NEET), low academic achievement (gaining fewer than 5 A★- C GCSEs) and looked after in care;
- Lancashire is in the top 25th percentile nationally for the number of 15-year-olds who have been bullied recently;
- Sefton is in the top 25th percentile for children under 15 providing unpaid care and for children under 15 who have parents in alcohol treatment.

While structurally similar, the junior, primary and secondary schools which the participants attended and which engaged in TtB varied in their socio-demographic profiles. The IMD rank of the nine junior and primary schools (pupils aged 2–11) ranged from 22,861 (the least deprived) to 737 (the most deprived) with an average rank of 7,531. The average proportion of pupils eligible for free school meals (FSM, a common proxy school-level measure of deprivation) was 31.2 per cent (range 11.2 to 54.7), and the number of pupils attending the schools ranged from 184 to 393. In the five secondary schools (pupils aged 11–18), the average IMD rank was 11,212 (range 2,379 to 22,861) and the proportion of pupils eligible for FSM ranged from 6.3 to 37.2 per cent, with an average of 23.1 per cent. The number of pupils attending the schools ranged from 720 to 1,653.

The target group of participants who engaged in TtB included CYP who were identified by their school as having a diagnosed mental illness (identified by their use of services such as CAMHS), or as displaying behaviours or symptoms which

TABLE 7.1 Mental health risk factors identified by schools (based on PHE, 2016)

Child	Family	School
Behavioural disorders (e.g. ADHD)	Family disharmony or break–up	Bullying
Low self-esteem	Parent or parents with a mental illness	Discrimination
Physical illness	Parental criminality or alcohol and/or drug abuse	Deviant peer influences
Difficult temperament	Death and loss	Breakdown in or lack of positive friendships
Communication difficulties		Poor pupil–teacher relationship

are associated with poor mental health and which might lead to the diagnosis of mental illness if the pupil was accessing specialist mental health services (PHE, 2016). A number of risk factors associated with poor mental health or the existence of a mental illness were identified by the school, and are summarised in Table 7.1.

Initial needs assessment

Once identified, recruited to and engaged in the programme, the participants' mental health needs and current status were assessed using a variety of methods. A mixed-methods approach incorporating KIDSCREEN-27 questionnaires (Ravens-Sieberer et al., 2014) to provide a baseline assessment of quality of life (QoL) and wellbeing, and focus groups and write and draw techniques to help examine mental health awareness. These methods were also used regularly throughout the programme as part of a realist evaluation framework (explained in more detail later) to help us understand what worked, for whom, in what circumstances, in what respects, over what durations, with what outcomes, and why (Pawson, 2006, 2013; Pawson & Tilley, 1997).

KIDSCREEN questionnaires

The KIDSCREEN-27 version was selected for use on TtB. KIDSCREEN questionnaires have been developed by European paediatric researchers working across 13 different countries for use in epidemiologic public health surveys, clinical intervention studies and research projects, helping standardise QoL measurements in CYP aged 8–18-years-old (Ravens-Sieberer et al., 2014). There are three versions of the questionnaire: KIDSCREEN-52, KIDSCREEN-27 and KIDSCREEN-10, each of which are based on 'the definition of QoL as a multidimensional construct covering physical, emotional, mental, social, and behavioral components of well-being and functioning as perceived by patients and/or other individuals' (Ravens-Sieberer et al., 2014, p. 792). It has been shown to be a reliable, valid, culturally sensitive and conceptually/linguistically appropriate measure in many countries including England (see Ravens-Sieberer et al., 2014).

KIDSCREEN-27 has five dimensions: Physical Wellbeing; Psychological Wellbeing; Autonomy and Parents; Peers and Social Support; and School Environment. A global score is derived from responses given to questions answered on 5-point Likert type scales assessing the frequency or intensity of particular behaviours. Although it is said to take around 10 minutes to complete (Ravens-Sieberer et al., 2014), in practice our participants took up to 30 minutes to complete the questionnaires which were distributed to CYP on a face-to-face basis in a school classroom prior to engaging in the programme and then after 12 school weeks of delivery. Intended as a screening (during the initial needs assessment), monitoring and evaluation tool (Ravens-Sieberer et al., 2014), KIDSCREEN-27 helped us to assess changes in subjective health and wellbeing during this period within and between schools. The results of the questionnaire also enabled us to help contextualise the responses given in the supplementary focus groups held with participants.

Focus groups

During the baseline assessments, focus groups were used with participants in each school to help identify key features of the mental health of individuals and the group, and at various times throughout the delivery of TtB to explore their experiences of the programme and any changes in their subjective health and wellbeing. All focus groups involved participants who were already known to each other from TtB and, in that regard, had experienced some 'particular concrete situation' (Merton & Kendall, 1946, 541) (i.e. had engaged in TtB and had a diagnosed or potentially diagnosable mental illness) which meant they also consisted of 'groups in the sociological sense of having a common identity or continuing unity, shared norms, and goals' (Merton, 1987, p. 555). Useful for unearthing reasons for crucial choices on the programme (Pawson & Tilley, 1997), the focus groups provided participants with an opportunity to discuss a range of topics and stimulate interaction amongst group members (Morgan, 2010). In particular, participants were encouraged to share and compare relevant thoughts, actions and experiences (Morgan, 2006) and these included, *inter alia*, their understanding and experiences of mental health and wellbeing, their experiences of TtB, their social relationships with significant others (e.g. parents, friends, teachers and programme mentors) inside and outside of the programme, and other risks to their mental health (e.g. loneliness, social media use, bullying). This was particularly important not only to the initial needs assessment, but especially to follow-up focus groups in which we sought to understand the participants' experiences of the on-going development and delivery of TtB. Thus, maximising participants' engagement in the sharing and comparing of thoughts and experiences during the course of the focus groups was essential because:

> When the participants are mutually interested in the discussion, their conversation often takes the form of sharing and comparing thoughts about the topic. That is, they share their experiences and thoughts, while also comparing their own contributions to what others have said. This process of sharing and comparing is especially useful for hearing and understanding a range of responses on a research topic. The best focus groups thus not only provide data on *what* the participants think but also explicit insights into *why* they think the way they do.
>
> *(Morgan, 2006, p. 123; emphases in the original)*

To generate further data on what the participants thought and felt about their mental health and TtB more broadly, and why this was so, we also incorporated a series of write-and-draw techniques into our research.

Write, draw, show and tell techniques

As part of the educational workshop activities and focus groups, participants were encouraged to supplement their answers to questions with a series of write, draw, show and tell (WDST) techniques to help maximise their engagement in, and enhance our learning from, the process. Driessnack (2006) advocates the use of this type of child-centred research technique, suggesting that the act of drawing helps take the focus away from the adult researcher, reduce the power imbalances involved, and instead provide a way for CYP to share their lived experiences of the topics in hand in their own terms. More recently, Noonan, Boddy, Fairclough, and Knowles (2016) have claimed that in contrast to traditional (and hitherto dominant) write and draw approaches, the WDST method encourages children 'to articulate their own meaning embedded within their drawing' (Noonan et al., 2016, p. 3), assists in the formation of individual narrative commentary, and 'provides children with alternative ways of expression and enables a deeper exploration of children's thoughts and perceptions by not limiting children to verbal communication' (Noonan et al., 2016, p. 4).

During educational workshop activities delivered as part of TtB, participants were encouraged to engage in WDST via art and drawing activities to reveal their understanding of mental health topics, for example emotions, feelings, coping and anxiety, their thoughts about the TtB sessions in which they had been involved, and the importance of social relationships during and outside of TtB sessions. This technique not only helped provide an assessment of the participants' knowledge and understanding of mental health which could then be tracked throughout their involvement in the programme, but it also proved to be successful in making sense of the experiences recalled in ways that might not have been possible if focus groups had been the sole method used. The WDST approach also emphasised to participants that understanding their lifeworlds, from their perspective and experiences (Noonan et al., 2016), was of central importance to maximising the effectiveness of the programme.

Framework and intervention for delivery

TtB is a prevention and early intervention programme delivered in partnership by Edge Hill University and Everton in the Community (the official charity of Everton Football Club) between October and July (i.e. during a normal whole school year). Since its launch, TtB has engaged 392 young people (204 males; 188 females) weekly in primary schools, secondary schools and community groups through a range of interactive and engaging activities intended to tackle experiences of mental illness and promote good mental health.

Like many public health and education programmes (Moore et al., 2014; Pawson, 2006; Pawson & Tilley, 1997; Wong, Greenhalgh, Westhorp, & Pawson, 2012), the intention of TtB was to contribute towards the improvement of health and education of a particular population (school-aged CYP) or 'at-risk' group (those with a diagnosed/diagnosable mental illness). More specifically, TtB was intended to contribute to improvements in mental health awareness among CYP and improve understanding of the complex aetiologies, risk factors and mechanisms of managing experience of mental illness.

From the outset, we were acutely aware that introducing TtB into diverse and complex environments such as schools would present many challenges, and that the delivery of the programme was likely to result in the production of many outcomes, some intended, others unintended and unpredictable. The production of such unintended outcomes, it should be noted, is the *normal* result of (often very) large numbers of people acting in ways which may or may not have been anticipated (Elias, 1978). Thus, it is unlikely that the programme could be equally effective (if at all) in achieving the intended aims for all participants in all schools given, for example, the complex interactions between pupils' individual and family circumstances, experience of school and their engagement in the programme.

In light of these observations and experience of previous practice, we sought to combine our focus on outcomes with a concern to undertake a process evaluation of the programme within the framework of realist evaluation, which is a form of theory-driven evaluation (see Pawson, 2006, 2013; Pawson & Tilley, 1997). As Wong et al. (2012, p. 95) have noted, because

> realist approaches acknowledge and accommodate the messiness of real-world interventions, and because they ask different questions (not just 'whether' but 'how' and 'for whom'), they can inform the tailoring of interventions and policy for particular purposes (such as for particular kinds of learning), particular target groups and particular sets of circumstances.

Realist evaluation is thus centrally concerned with developing and refining theoretical explanations of programme effectiveness by focusing on a key proposition: 'what is it about a programme that works for whom, in what circumstances, in what respects, over which duration . . . and why' (Pawson, 2013, p. 15)? These are known as programme *conditionalities*, or caveats, which focus attention on the *necessary conditions* (i.e. participation is a necessary condition to obtain any of a programme's supposed benefits) and *sufficient conditions* (those under which potential programme impacts might be achieved) which help explain programme effectiveness (Pawson, 2006, 2013; Pawson & Tilley, 1997). The concern with understanding the necessary and sufficient conditions of a programme such as TtB reflects the focus of realist evaluation on *programme mechanisms* (i.e. the people) and *families of mechanisms* (i.e. the processes, experiences and relationships formed) which helps make programmes work, and it reflects how these can be explained theoretically. More specifically, enabling participants to make different choices (expressing previous experiences, beliefs, attitudes) and use choice-related behaviours (or 'reasoning') and/or the resources (e.g. information, skills, material resources, support) available to them in particular contexts are what constitutes the mechanisms that make programmes more likely to work and produce the desired outcomes (Coalter, 2007, 2016; Pawson, 2006, 2013). A consideration of these issues helps realist evaluators to understand whether the original programme theory (i.e. how the programme was originally assumed to work) was met by the actualities of the programme mechanisms (Pawson, 2013), and how the outcomes produced can be explained.

Since explaining the context-mechanism-outcome configuration of programmes is central to any realist approach to theory-based evaluation (Pawson, 2006, 2013; Pawson & Tilley, 1997), it was essential that TtB was designed and delivered in ways that accounted for the inevitable contextual variations (e.g. in pupils' mental health needs and knowledge, school arrangements, pre-existing relationships) encountered in schools, rather than adopting a one-size-fits-all approach. Since the school setting is frequently identified as an important context for the promotion of emotional and social competence (Barry, Clarke, Jenkins, & Patel, 2013) where the social interactions between CYP, teachers and other professionals are crucial, TtB was designed to take into account the nature of these pre-existing relationships which shape much of the time participants spend whilst at school. We also sought to develop an in-depth understanding of the characteristics of the specific groups of CYP regarded by schools as benefitting from the programme, especially their values, preferences, motivations and mental health challenges that they encountered (Morgan, Young, Smith, & Lubans, 2016). These were in turn considered in relation to teachers' background knowledge of pupils' needs and engagement, existing curricular content on (mental) health and wellbeing, availability of resources and leadership commitment to the aims of the programme (Askell-Williams, Dix, Lawson, & Slee, 2013), all of which varied across schools.

Other features of our formative evaluation work included the co-development of a series of mental health-themed sporting and education-based activities which were tailored to personal and group needs – within and between schools – on the basis of the findings of the initial needs assessment. These were constructed using the school setting and values of the participants to determine what themes would best address their particular mental health needs (e.g. depression, anxiety, self-harm) (Askell-Williams et al., 2013) before the programme was delivered, but also throughout its delivery in response to extensive feedback from participants, facilitators and key stakeholders. As well as the types of activities to be delivered, we also explored the participants' and stakeholders' preferences for other features of the programme, including the setting, mode of delivery, duration of activity and the 'dose' of activity. We also sought to use the brand of Everton Football Club as a 'hook' to engage participants via the design and recruitment strategy of TtB. In particular, the Everton brand was used: (i) to help deliver activities at the football club stadium and training ground: (ii) as a basis for enabling participants to name and design the programme; (iii) and to encourage the recruitment and retention of volunteer university student mentors by providing them with Everton in the Community and TtB branded kit and equipment.

The recruitment of student mentors was particularly important and central to the design and delivery of TtB for, as Pawson (2004) has noted, the development of positive mentoring relationships (in our case, between university and school students) can be critical for maximising the effectiveness of programmes. While the impact of mentoring relationships is of course conditional and circumstantial (rather than a given) (Pawson, 2004), we deliberately sought to recruit a mix of male and female student mentors (or 'coaches', as they were sometimes seen as by the participants) who would deliver the activities in an empathetic manner, that is, with a sensitivity towards, and with an appreciation of, the diverse mental health needs of CYP, and with appropriate resources to support themselves and the participants. They were also encouraged to develop relationships with participants which were perceived to be less hierarchical and authoritarian than those which are common in many school-based pupil-teacher relationships, whilst retaining an important degree of respect, trust and mutual understanding (Pawson, 2004). These types of non-authoritarian and supportive relationships were considered crucial to facilitating engagement in the programme generally, and generating informal discussion about mental health and illness in particular.

To help build mentors' confidence in facilitating and supporting discussion around mental health, they were each required to undertake a variety of training courses related to mental health. These included the two-day Mental Health First Aid (MHFA) course, the one-day MHFA Schools and Colleges programme, and the safeTALK suicide alertness training programme. These were also complemented by a suite of sports coaching, education and safeguarding training to assist with the practical delivery of other elements of the programme.

Informed by the theoretical premises and assumptions of our realist evaluation approach, and the lessons learned from its formative development, TtB was delivered as a 'plus-sport' programme, where sporting activities which acted as a 'fly paper' to recruit participants were supplemented by other non-sporting activities (such as education workshops) through which much of the developmental work and learning took place (Coalter, 2007). The programme incorporated a mixture of one-hour long sport, physical activity and education-based mental health awareness activities delivered to 6–16-year-olds in curricular or extra-curricular time between October and July of the school year. To encourage programme acceptability by the participants, TtB used engaging activities and games from the outset that, where appropriate, were different to their traditional school lessons.

The classroom-based educational workshop sessions (including the WDST methods noted earlier) were used to encourage CYP to talk informally about mental health, establish their understanding of the aetiology and risk factors for mental illness, and how conditions associated with mental illness can be managed effectively. Some activities, including 'emoji bingo', where children and young people choose emojis related to feelings and emotions they have experienced during that week, were developed in response to the ways in which CYP interacted with others on a daily basis and as a non-threatening means of discussing the importance of emotions and feelings to mental health. The sporting activities provided in all sessions, self-selected or designed by the participants, were intended to be perceived as 'fun' and based on their values and preferences and developed their understanding of the related education theme on mental health. The developmental potential of these activities – which were deliberately responsive and sensitive to the changing nature of participants' needs and experiences – was greatly facilitated by the length (i.e. school year long) of the project, which was an important prerequisite for developing long-term opportunities for establishing trust and rapport with the same mentors allocated to their school (Pawson, 2004).

Intervention evaluation and lessons learned through self-reflection

As we noted earlier, TtB is an on-going programme which at the time of writing was nearing the end of its second year of delivery. The first year of delivery was supported by 12 months external funding received from a local Clinical Commissioning Group and the involvement of a young carers group, though in the second year the programme was delivered without external funding by Edge Hill University and EitC only. In November 2016, the impact of TtB was recognised at the national Times Higher Education Awards having been successful in the Outstanding Contribution to the Local Community category, and it is on some of the lessons learned from the project delivery in this period that we shall focus here.

The brand of professional football: a necessary but insufficient condition

At the outset of the project we, like several others before us, felt that the brand and attraction of a professional football club would be important to the recruitment of participants to the programme and to its effectiveness (see Hunt et al., 2014; Parnell, Stratton, Drust, & Richardson, 2013). In practice, the appeal of working in collaboration with a local Premier League football club (and, to a much lesser extent, a university) was most attractive to the head teachers and senior leaders of schools rather than to the CYP. It became clear that engagement in the programme represented an important marketing opportunity for schools and also an opportunity to communicate their external engagement to parents, guardians and pupils, a feature which has become increasingly established in the commercial and marketing operations of schools (Ball, 2012, 2013) and in subjects such as physical education (PE) and sport (Evans & Davies, 2014; Smith, 2015; Williams & Macdonald, 2015). It also provided an important opportunity to engage in externally provided, and above all cost free, opportunities to promote pupil engagement in physical activity related activities which were expected to make a positive contribution to pupils' health, education and wellbeing and other school-level outcomes (PHE, 2015, 2016). This, together with the very real pressures on school budgets, resources, staff workload, pupil standards, curriculum activity and league table performance (Ball, 2012, 2013), proved very favourable in securing consent to work with schools in our target areas.

While initially powerful, the appeal of the brand of a professional football club became progressively less important for pupils and diminished considerably in the course of the first few months of delivery. During this time, other more important features of the programme design became much more significant. Central among these were: (i) the non-threatening, non-authoritarian relationships established between the mentors and mentees; (ii) the emphasis placed on fun, enjoyment and choice, especially in relation to the selection and ownership of activities; (iii) the familiarity established between project staff, mentors and pupils via consistent and regular contact in each of the schools; (iv) the use of real world examples of others (including sportspeople and high-profile celebrities) as a starting point for personalised discussions about mental health and illness which were of most relevance to individual pupils; and (v) the use of modern technologies (such as mobile phones and emojis) and WDST techniques to express thoughts, feelings and emotions which underpinned experiences of mental illness. We shall focus on one of these – the relationships between mentors and mentees – next, but it was clear that despite the claimed effectiveness of leveraging the brand of professional football (or other sports) clubs, in our experience this was a necessary but insufficient condition for engaging pupils and their schools in TtB.

Relationships between mentors and their mentees

We noted earlier that attractiveness factors, such as the qualities of the peer leader or mentor, the activity setting and the relationships with other participants, often encourage people to remain engaged in programmes such as TtB and that these cannot be separated from the physical components of programmes, particularly when promoting mental health awareness topics (Fox, 2000). Of particular importance to the success of TtB has been the investment of time and resources in fostering positive, supportive and mutually respectful relationships between the programme lead, mentors and mentees. The decision to recruit and prioritise the work of student mentors was driven by a concern with reducing the potential status differentials between CYP and adults which characterises traditional relationships in schools. As shown in many mentoring programmes (Pawson, 2004), downplaying the status distinctions between themselves and adults such as teachers enabled the mentors to be perceived by the mentees as being more similar, relevant and simply 'like them'. Bridging the status gap with CYP was critical for engaging them in the various activities provided and especially in discussions about personal circumstances, experiences of mental health, social relationships and other concerns – all crucially from the perspective of the CYP themselves, rather than adult-interpretations of the circumstances described.

One of the outcomes of reducing the status distinctions between the mentor and mentee was the emergence and development of affective, emotional bonds between the two groups (Pawson, 2004). This was an important ingredient in encouraging pupils to continue attending TtB and engaging with the activities delivered, though this was by no means guaranteed. Indeed, it is well established that 'the success of mentoring turns minutely on the mentee's appetite for change' (Pawson, 2004, p. 4) which is to a large extent mediated by the mentee's level of identification with their present status. This 'reference group affiliation' provided an important insight into 'determining whether, how and in what respects they might be persuaded or helped to change' (Pawson, 2004, p. 5) their thoughts and actions in relation to mental health and illness. The degree to which participants engaged in TtB was (especially for males) connected to their social identities, loyalties and ties (Pawson, 2004), and also to their association with the identities of the mentors. Indeed, the social identities of the student mentors, like those of the mentees, were located along a continuum between, at the one end, an active role model encouraging pupils to 'do as I do' and, at the other end, a more passively oriented mentor whose own status was not 'conceived as a goal for the protégé, but rather as an available resource' (Pawson, 2004, p. 5) to access, use and learn from as needed. Neither were privileged, and it appeared that a mixture of these approaches – and the many variants in between – were important to stimulating desired behavioural change among the participants.

Being realistic: social inequalities and programme effectiveness

All programmes have certain limitations and have only degrees of effectiveness. The reasons for this are many and diverse, some of which may be known, others of which may be more difficult to determine. Some of the clues to these can be understood by applying the principles of realist evaluation articulated here and elsewhere (Pawson, 2006, 2013; Pawson & Tilley, 1997), throughout all stages of programme design, delivery and evaluation; others might be gleaned from an understanding of the broader social contexts in which programmes like TtB are delivered. In our case, it is important to remind ourselves that TtB continues to be delivered in a context of rising mental illness among CYP living in areas of significant socio-economic deprivation, where there is a significant unmet demand for mental health services which is being exacerbated by real-terms reductions in funding and an unsupportive public health and sport policy context (Smith, Jones, Houghton, & Duffell, 2016).

The launch of TtB in 2015 coincided with the publication in the same year of *Future in Mind: Promoting, Protecting and Improving Our Children and Young People's Mental Health and Wellbeing* (DH, 2015), which was released by the Children and Young People's Mental Health and Wellbeing Taskforce. *Future in Mind* made a whole series of recommendations, including in relation to: the structural complexity which characterises service delivery and policy making; the need for care pathways delivered by joined up approaches to services for all CYP; sustaining a culture of continuous evidence based service improvements and sound investment strategies; and, of particular relevance here, the need to build resilience, promote good mental health and adopt prevention and early intervention strategies during childhood (DH, 2015). While not new, the emphasis in *Future in Mind* on prevention and early intervention during childhood was crucial because what happens to children makes a profound difference on their childhood and later mental health, and this varies by social circumstance, with mental health becoming progressively worse and with incidence of mental illness increasing as one descends the social ladder. Many of the participants in TtB were recruited from some of the types of disadvantaged and deprived communities where mental illness is especially prevalent, where it is experienced in family contexts characterised by clusters of adverse experiences which threaten mental health (Marmot, 2010, 2015) and where the scale of material inequality has a fundamental impact on the quality of social relationships (Dorling, 2018; Wilkinson & Pickett, 2010, 2017). The experience of these kinds of inequalities in early childhood is significant for, as Marmot (2015, p. 121) has noted, they have

> a powerful effect on health and disease in adult life. . . . The long-term effects of early exposure and the accumulation of advantage and disadvantage through life, whereby childhood experiences determine education, employment, income and, more generally, empowerment in adult life, are responsible for determining inequalities in health.

Since the first symptoms of mental illness often present in childhood (as witnessed in our participants) and can contribute to the perpetuation of cycles of inequality through generations, the emphasis on prevention and early intervention in programmes such as TtB may assist the management and improvement of lifetime public mental health, reduce the costs associated with and help prevent mental illness, as well as enhance the capacity of people to parent so that their children also have reduced risk of mental illness and disadvantage (HMG/DH, 2011; Marmot, 2010, 2015). However, as in many other countries and particularly during times of austerity, policy decisions that lead to reductions in investments in mental health services which focus on prevention and treatment (especially during childhood) is often something of a false economy, and may do more to increase than decrease the costs of mental health care and associated service costs. These policy decisions have also been shown to widen income and wealth inequalities in many countries around the world, with the result that the larger the income differences in a society are the higher the prevalence of many health and social problems that tend to occur most frequently lower down the social ladder (Wilkinson & Pickett, 2010, 2017). Considering the costs to individuals, communities and whole societies of inequality, it would be churlish to conclude individual programmes such as TtB will have a significant impact on breaking down deeply entrenched patterns of social inequality experienced by those in the communities it serves. This conclusion may appear rather defeatist, and is certainly not one which is likely to appeal to even the most open-minded of policy makers or funders, but it is a realistic one and certainly one that is fundamental to understanding the potential effectiveness of programmes such as TtB. As we have attempted to show in this chapter, there is, however, much potential in using approaches like realist evaluation to better understand the degree to which sports-based programmes, such as TtB, can contribute meaningfully to collective efforts intended to improve the mental health of children and young people.

References

Askell-Williams, H., Dix, K., Lawson, M., & Slee, P. (2013). Quality of implementation of a school mental health initiative and changes over time in student's social and emotional competence. *School Effectiveness and School Improvement, 24*, 357–381.

Ball, S. (2012). *Global education inc: New policy networks and the neoliberal imaginary*. London: Routledge.

Ball, S. (2013). *The education debate* (2nd ed.). Bristol: Policy Press.

Barry, M., Clarke, A. M., Jenkins, R., & Patel, V. (2013). A systematic review of effectiveness of mental health promotion interventions for young people in low and middle income countries. *BMC Public Health, 13*, 835–854.

Cane, E., & Oland, L. (2015). Evaluating the outcomes and implementation of a TaMHS (Targeting Mental Health in Schools) project in four West Midlands (UK) schools using activity theory. *Educational Psychology in Practice, 31*, 1–20.

Coalter, F. (2007). *A wider social role for sport*. London: Routledge.

Coalter, F. (2016). Youth and sport-for-change programmes: What can you expect? In K. Green & A. Smith (Eds.), *The Routledge handbook of youth sport*. London: Routledge.

Department for Communities and Local Government. (2015). *English indices of deprivation*. London: Department for Communities and Local Government.

Department of Health (DH). (2015). *Future in mind: Promoting, protecting and improving our children and young people's mental health and wellbeing*. London: Department of Health.

Dorling, D. (2018). *Do we need economic inequality?* Bristol: Policy Press.

Driessnack, M. (2006). Draw-and-tell conversations with children about fear. *Qualitative Health Research, 16*, 1414–1435.

Elias, N. (1978). *What is sociology?* London: Hutchinson.

Evans, J., & Davies, B. (2014). Physical education PLC: Neoliberalism, curriculum and governance: New directions for PESP research. *Sport, Education and Society, 19*, 869–884.

Fox, K. (2000). The influence of exercise on self-perceptions and self-esteem. In S. J. H. Biddle, K. R. Fox, & S. H. Boucher (Eds.), *Physical activity and psychological well-being* (pp. 89–117). London: Routledge.

Her Majesty's Government/Department of Health (HMG/DH). (2011). *No health without mental health: A cross-government mental health outcomes strategy for people of all ages.* London: HMG/DH.

House of Commons Health Committee. (2014). *Children's and adolescents' mental health and CAMHS.* London: Stationary Office.

Hunt, K., Gray, C., Maclean, A., Smillie, S., Bunn, C., & Wyke, S. (2014). Do weight management programmes delivered at professional football clubs attract and engage high risk men? *BMC Public Health, 28,* 690–701.

Marmot, M. (2010). *Fair society healthy lives (The Marmot Review): Strategic review of health inequalities in England post 2010.* London: Marmot Review.

Marmot, M. (2015). *The health gap: The challenge of an unequal world.* London: Bloomsbury.

Merton, R. K. (1987). Focussed interviews and focus groups: Continuities and discontinuities. *Public Opinion Quarterly, 51,* 550–566.

Merton, R. K., & Kendall, P. L. (1946). The focussed interview. *American Journal of Sociology, 51,* 541–557.

Moore, G., Audrey, A., Barker, M., Bond, L., Bonnell, C., Cooper, C., . . . Baird, J. (2014). Process evaluation in complex public health intervention studies: The need for guidance. *Journal of Epidemiology and Community Health, 68,* 101–102.

Morgan, D. L. (2006). Focus group. In V. Jupp (Ed.), *The Sage dictionary of social research methods* (pp. 121–123). Thousand Oaks, CA: Sage Publications.

Morgan, D. L. (2010). Reconsidering the role of interaction in analysing and reporting focus groups. *Qualitative Health Research, 20,* 718–722.

Morgan, P., Young, M., Smith, J., & Lubans, D. (2016). Targeted health behavior interventions promoting physical activity: A conceptual model. *Exercise Sport Science Review, 44,* 71–80.

Noonan, R., Boddy, L., Fairclough, S., & Knowles, Z. (2016). Write, draw, show, and tell: A child-centred dual methodology to explore perceptions of out-of-school physical activity, *BMC Public Health, 16,* 326.

Parnell, D., Stratton, G., Drust, B., & Richardson, D. (2013). Football in the community schemes: Exploring the effectiveness of an intervention in promoting healthful behaviour change. *Soccer & Society, 14,* 35–51.

Pawson, R. (2004). *Mentoring relationships: An explanatory review.* Leeds: University of Leeds.

Pawson, R. (2006). *Evidence-based policy: A realist perspective.* London: Sage Publications.

Pawson, R. (2013). *The science of evaluation.* London: Sage Publications.

Pawson, R., & Tilley, N. (1997). *Realistic evaluation.* London: Sage Publications.

Public Health England (PHE). (2015). *Promoting children and young people's emotional health and wellbeing: A whole school and college approach.* London: Public Health England.

Public Health England (PHE). (2016). *The mental health of children and young people in England.* London: Public Health England.

Public Health England (PHE) (2017). *Children's and young people's mental health and wellbeing profiling tool.* London: Public Health England.

Ravens-Sieberer, U., Herdman, M., Devine, J., Otto, C., Bullinger, M., Rose, M., & Klasen, F. (2014). The European KIDSCREEN approach to measure quality of life and well-being in children: Development, current application, and future advances. *Quality of Life Research, 23,* 791–803.

Royal Colleges of Paediatrics and Child Health (RCPH). (2017). *State of child health report 2017.* London: Royal Colleges of Paediatrics and Child Health.

Sharpe, H., Ford, T., Lereya, S., Owen, C., Viner, R., & Wolpert, M. (2016). Survey of schools' work with child and adolescent mental health across England: A system in need of support. *Child and Adolescent Mental Health, 21,* 148–153.

Smith, A. (2015). Primary school physical education and sports coaches: Evidence from a study of school sport partnerships in north-west England. *Sport, Education and Society, 20,* 872–888.

Smith, A., Jones, J., Houghton, L., & Duffell, T. (2016). A political spectator sport or policy priority? A review of sport, physical activity and public mental health policy. *International Journal of Sport Policy and Politics, 8,* 593–607.

Wilkinson, R., & Pickett, K. (2010). *The spirit level: Why equality is better for everyone.* London: Penguin.

Wilkinson, R., & Pickett, K. (2017). The enemy between us: The psychological and social costs of inequality. *European Journal of Social Psychology, 47,* 11–24.

Williams, B., & Macdonald, D. (2015). Explaining outsourcing in health, sport and physical education. *Sport, Education and Society, 20,* 57–72.

Wong, G., Greenhalgh, T., Westhorp, G., & Pawson, R. (2012). Realist methods in medical education research: What are they and what can they contribute? *Medical Education, 46,* 89–96.

Further reading

Noonan, R., Boddy, L., Fairclough, S., & Knowles, Z. (2016). Write, draw, show, and tell: A child-centred dual methodology to explore perceptions of out-of-school physical activity. *BMC Public Health, 16,* 326.
This article outlines the write, draw, show and tell method which can be effective in generating data on mental health and illness among children and young people.

Ravens-Sieberer, U., Herdman, M., Devine, J., Otto, C., Bullinger, M., Rose, M., & Klasen, F. (2014). The European KIDSCREEN approach to measure quality of life and well-being in children: Development, current application, and future advances. *Quality of Life Research, 23,* 791–803.
This article outlines the development of the KIDSCREEN questionnaire which can be used to examine subjective health and wellbeing in children and young people.

Wilkinson, R., & Pickett, K. (2017). The enemy between us: The psychological and social costs of inequality. *European Journal of Social Psychology, 47,* 11–24.
This article explores the links between income inequality and various social and health problems which need to be considered in any evaluation of programmes intended to address mental health and illness.

SECTION 2

Engaging the wider community in mental health awareness through sport

8

MOTIVATING PRISONERS TO EXERCISE

An evaluation of the Cell Workout Workshops

Hannah Sian Baumer and Rosie Meek

Learning objectives

After reading this chapter you should be able to:

1   Understand the principles of Self-Determination Theory and how these can be applied to support prisoners' exercise motivation and well-being.
2   Critically examine sports-based interventions in a prison setting.
3   Summarise the mental health needs of prisoners and understand what is needed to support these.

Introduction to the theme

This chapter presents an evaluation and observation of the Cell Workout Workshops, an innovative prison-based physical activity intervention for prisoners run by ex-prisoner, L. J. Flanders, inside a Category B adult male prison in the UK.

The mental well-being of offenders is of concern from the moment they encounter the criminal justice system, often presenting with a range of extensive health and social problems (Stewart, 2008), with far greater prevalence than reflected in the general population (Lester, Hamilton-Kirkwood, & Jones, 2003; Senior & Shaw, 2007). Moreover, releasing offenders into the community without engaging them in any health rehabilitation processes during their incarceration has worsening effects on their physical and mental well-being (De Viggiani, 2007; Fazel & Danesh, 2002; Gatherer, Moller, & Hayton, 2005). Prisons are fast becoming a holding place for individuals with a wide range of mental and emotional disorders that the prison service is not currently equipped to deal with, and in responding to this prominent contemporary public health matter, it is argued that those with responsibility for prisons regimes need greater support to facilitate health rehabilitation through the treatment of offenders' physical and psychological needs. The prison setting, all too often, fails to adopt a proactive approach to improving health (Gatherer, Enggist, & Moller, 2014; Jakab, 2014), and efforts to introduce 'health promoting prisons' by the World Health Organisation in 1995 have fallen short (WHO, 1995; Woodall, 2016).

Alternative strategies to promote prisoners' well-being are clearly required, and research demonstrates that sport and exercise can play a key role in this. Researchers have established the benefits of sport in prisons on rehabilitation and health behavioural change (Buckaloo, Krug, & Nelson, 2009; Nelson, Specian, Tracy, & DeMello, 2006), particularly in promoting desistance, positive social relationships, identity transformation and education and employment opportunities (Meek, 2014). The relevance of the research discussed in this chapter lies in its potential to expand a currently limited field of academic research by promoting the use of sport and exercise to improve physical and mental well-being in the prison setting.

Description of the group being targeted

Those participating in the Cell Workout Workshops were serving a prison sentence at a category B local male prison. The Service Specification for Physical Education (for application in prisons), published by the National Offender Management Service (NOMS), specifies that, where reasonably permitted, prisoners over the age of 21 should be allowed to participate in an average of one hours' worth of physical education (PE) a week (NOMS, 2011). In contrast, the recommended weekly level of physical activity from the Department of Health (DoH) is 150 minutes of moderate intensity activity (DoH, 2011), whilst healthcare campaigns increasingly focus on 'lifestyle exercise' – the incorporation of exercise into one's daily routine, with guidelines measuring the recommended amount of physical activity as 10,000 steps per day (Spilner & Robertson, 2000). These figures and recommendations are contentious in the context of prisons when offenders are spending much of their day in their cells, unable to maintain an active lifestyle and accrue physical activity through alternative means.

At present, there are approximately 120 male prisons across all categories in England and Wales, with a male prisoner population of 82,181 as of 3 November 2017 (Ministry of Justice, 2017). The most recent annual report released by Her Majesty's Chief Inspector of Prisons included findings from inspections of 34 establishments covering adult male prisons and young offender institutions holding young adult men, as well as a survey of 6,362 male prisoners. This report revealed that the number of these male prisons that provided a *good* or *reasonably good* amount of purposeful activity was just 44%, although this is an increase of 20% from the previous year. Perhaps of greater concern is that just 2 of the 11 local prisons included in the report were rated as providing reasonably good amounts of purposeful activity, with the remaining nine local prisons rated as either not sufficiently good or poor in terms of purposeful activity provision (HM Majesty's Chief Inspector of Prisons, 2016). However, despite this increase and the inspectorate's expectation that prisoners would be unlocked for 10 hours a day, only 14% of male prisoners surveyed report this to be the case, and of greater concern is that just 16% of those surveyed spend less than two hours out of their cell on a weekday. One way of meeting the recommended physical activity guidelines is through prison gym use. An average of 31% of prisoners use the gym three times or more a week, and 46% go outside for exercise three or more times a week.[1] According to Condon, Hek, and Harris (2008), these exercise participation figures may be higher than they would be for these individuals if they were not in prison, however, there are considerable problems with the variability of access, with prisoners across all categories of prisons finding that their access to the gym is infrequent or non-existent, with no apparent reasons for the variation.

Leon & Norstrom's physical activity pyramid (1995) suggests that a complete exercise programme essential to receiving preventative health benefits should aim to encourage active daily lifestyles alongside recreational, resistance and leisurely forms of structured physical activity. However, an exercise prescription that reflects the preference of each individual whilst spanning such a variety of physical activity types is just not possible within the current confines and restrictions of the prison environment. Injuries are a strong influence on maintenance or dropout rates of physical activity in the community (Sallis et al., 1990), and injured prisoners may suffer even further, as those who are injured in the community generally report more time spent walking as a form of exercise (Hofstetter et al., 1991), whereas opportunities for walking are limited for prisoners. Although remedial gym sessions are available for people referred by the prison healthcare team, these are limited in frequency and duration; depending on the injury and related exercise intensity they may not provide sufficient time and resource as an alternative to walking. Taking these factors into account, the challenge that prisons face is the provision of a varied physical activity programme delivered with limited time and resources.

Structural barriers to exercise engagement in prisons are evident. It is widely known that difficulties in recruiting and retaining staff has led to a forced change in regime across some UK prisons which sees prisoners behind their cell doors for much of the day (Independent Monitoring Board, 2013). However, reasons for the varying levels of participation in physical activity across prisons are more diverse than this and include cultural and individual barriers. Researchers, therefore, must look to identify the attitudes and beliefs surrounding such barriers so that they can be transformed to increase prisoners' motivation to engage in physical activity, and in turn, promote healthy lifestyle behaviours.

Initial needs assessment

Due to the constraints of the prison regime the amount of contact time available with participants during the two-week Cell Workout Workshops was limited. There was only one opportunity for a brief individual consultation at the outset of the workshops which was used to obtain physiological measurements and answer any questions, the remaining contact time between the trainer and the participants was delivered in time-limited group sessions. Consequently, providing sufficient support to cater for individual needs whilst maximising impact by engaging a sizeable group of prisoners in each workshop was not possible. Therefore, it was decided that a formal individual needs assessment was not appropriate, and instead the design of the workshops was informed by academic literature on the specific healthcare needs of the prison population and a review of prison-based physical activity interventions.

Prisoners' health needs

Mental health, substance misuse and communicable diseases have been identified as the three most prevalent healthcare issues in UK prisons (Watson, Stimpson, & Hostick, 2004), with over 70% of prisoners in England and Wales suffering from two or more mental health problems (Social Exclusion Unit, 2002). A recent investigation by the Prisons and Probation Ombudsman (PPO) discovered that nearly one in five prisoners diagnosed with a mental health problem had not received any care from a mental health professional (PPO, 2016), whilst the high attrition rates for those who do engage in psychological and related therapies in prison can cause major difficulties (McGuire, 2008; Stewart, 2008).

In addition to these complications, there are many more prisoners living with mental health issues that remain undiagnosed, as well as prisoners who, although perhaps without a clinical disorder, nevertheless are vulnerable to mental illness due to overcrowding, violence, inadequate health services, isolation and a lack of purposeful activity (Durcan & Zwemstra, 2014). Thus, a comprehensive approach to improving psychological well-being is needed to engage the diverse prisoner population and support the existing provision of mental health services in prisons.

Introducing sport and exercise programmes into prisons as a means of improving psychological well-being creates an opportunity to address unmet needs as well as supporting existing healthcare pathways. Despite claims to the contrary, people from so-called 'hard to reach' socially and economically deprived communities, similar to the backgrounds of many prisoners, respond very well when encouraged to engage in leisure-time physical activity of at least moderate intensity, with long-term adherence amongst sedentary individuals from such communities (Lowther, Mutrie, & Scott, 2002), and interest in participating in sport and physical activity of all kinds is often high in prisons (Buckaloo et al., 2009; Meek & Lewis, 2012). Additionally, it could be argued that sport and exercise has a broader reach than more traditional means of prison-based psychological interventions such as pharmacology or psychotherapy, as there are likely to be high numbers of prisoners with mental health illnesses who remain undiagnosed and therefore do not seek or qualify for treatment, whereas inclusion in physical activity should aim to be all-inclusive. Furthermore, the experience of incarceration is likely to have a negative psychological impact on all prisoners to some extent, and formal psychological treatment is not always necessary. Sport and exercise can provide an informal means of support to promote well-being on a larger scale and perhaps ease the pressure on existing prison-based healthcare providers.

Previous research into the mental health needs of service users in a high secure setting[2] led to the development of the domains of need model (Glorney et al., 2010) which, given the prevalence of poor psychological well-being in the general prisoner population, was considered a suitable reference point for the development of the Cell Workout Workshops.

The domains of need model identifies eight domains: Therapeutic Engagement, Risk Reduction, Education, Occupational, Mental Health Recovery, Management and Promotion of Physical Healthcare, Diversity and Spirituality, and Care Pathway Management. Although the Cell Workout Workshops aim to improve prisoners' mental well-being, they are not formal psychological interventions, and as such, the domains of risk reduction, mental health recovery and care pathway management were not explicitly considered in their development. However, needs across the remaining five domains have been addressed along with their sub-needs and proposed interventions, as outlined in Table 8.1.

It can often be the case in forensic settings that academia and practice act in relative isolation. Conducting empirical research can be problematic in forensic

TABLE 8.1 Domains of need, sub-needs and proposed interventions considered in the development in the workshops, as outlined in Glorney et al.'s (2010) domains of need model

Domain of need	Sub-need(s)	Intervention(s)
Therapeutic Engagement	• Develop relationships with others • Enhance treatment engagement	• Group psycho-educational work • Motivational work • Contact with family
Education	• Improve mental/ physical health and risk awareness • Language, literacy, numeracy skills	• Educational groups/ courses • Discussion groups
Occupational	• Achieve a balanced lifestyle • Develop interpersonal skills • Promote social inclusion	• Provide opportunities for inclusion • Assess and provide means to develop independent functioning • Facilitate roles of responsibility
Management and promotion of physical healthcare	• Address physical health problems • Promote physical health	• Medical screening/ consultation • Health information and discussion • Sports activities
Diversity and spirituality	• Recognise, understand and support needs within and beyond the prison	• Work with families • Facilitate cultural practice needs and (external) support

settings due to constraints around accessibility, whilst practitioners are often guided by experience rather than academic scholarship. However, it is imperative that these two groups can inform one another to create a more comprehensive understanding of 'what works' in prisons, and this is particularly true of a field such as sport and exercise which has received relatively little attention to date. In recognition of this, the workshops' development also drew on good practice and experience across the various practitioners and organisations in community settings that use sport and exercise for rehabilitation by engaging those at risk of offending in healthy behaviours and alternatives to crime. In 2016 the UK umbrella organisation, the National Alliance of Sport for Desistance from Crime (NASDC), consulted with 69 organisations across England and Wales delivering sports interventions and a further 202 service users across the criminal justice system in order to develop their own 'theory of change', a sector-wide framework to support the development of effective programmes using sports and physical activity to promote desistance from crime (NASDC, 2016). The framework outlines five measurable outcomes which were taken into consideration in the development of the Cell Workout Workshops as a means of highlighting their importance in the justice system, namely: a better use of time (thus promoting desistance from crime); pathways into education/employment; physical and mental well-being; individual development; and social and community development.

Promoting diversity

If the workshops are to be considered an effective means of increasing well-being in the context of prisons, then it is crucial that the chosen sample reflect the diverse nature of the prisoner population. The prison in which the workshops are delivered is divided into six wings which accommodate prisoners based on several factors including sentence length and vulnerability. To promote participation from a diverse range of prisoners five wings were given the opportunity to engage in the workshops. These wings included prisoners who were on remand (awaiting sentencing), convicted, engaged in integrated drug treatment services (IDTS), vulnerable, employed, unemployed and those on the resettlement unit designed to prepare prisoners for release. The workshops were promoted on the wings using posters and word of mouth, with the only criteria for application being English literacy at a basic level which was crucial for engagement in the workshops' theory sessions, although limited literacy support was provided when requested.

Sport and exercise interventions in prisons tend to favour participation from those who are responsibly behaved and well-disciplined, with selection criteria often including consideration of the prisoners' current level within the Incentives and Earned Privileges (IEP) scheme.[3] The Prison Reform Trust recognise that rewards for good behaviour should be distinct from the support and information prisoners need to prepare for resettlement, and selection and engagement with only those who are most compliant undermines the principles of the scheme

(Prison Reform Trust, 2014). The Cell Workout Workshops are not a leisure activity; they have been designed to promote well-being in a population who are most at need, and as such participation should not be viewed as a luxury only afforded to those whose behaviour conforms to the expectations of the prison. Arguably, such an intervention is likely to have the greatest impact on those who are *not* conforming and therefore need additional support to engage them in their sentence planning.

The broad demographic of those participating in the workshops mean that the exercises must be adaptable to suit a range of abilities whilst also addressing the pertinent issue of accessibility within prisons. As such, the workshops focused on body weight training exercises designed for safe and effective use in a prison cell. The premise of this approach to exercise is that it can be adapted to suit individuals of any age, ability or fitness level, and importantly, that it can be performed inside a prison cell without the need for any equipment.

Key outcome variables

An examination of the relationship between motivation, fitness and health is crucial in maximising mental well-being from sport and exercise participation (Power, Ullrich-French, Steele, Daratha, & Bindler, 2011), and to align with HM Prison and Probation Service's (HMPPS) priority to reduce reoffending, prison-based programmes such as the Cell Workout Workshops must promote long-term behavioural change in its participants. Therefore, to measure the potential long-term impact of the workshops, participants' level of motivation to engage in physical activity is considered as a key outcome variable, alongside measures of psychological well-being and physical fitness. The relationship between these variables to promote behavioural change is discussed in greater detail in the following section.

Framework and intervention for delivery

Researchers are becoming increasingly aware of the importance of applying theoretical frameworks to inform the development of sport and exercise interventions, and recommendations have been made to incorporate a theory of change approach into the Medical Research Councils' framework for complex interventions (De Silva et al., 2014). Meek and Lewis' (2014) review of a sports initiative for young men in prison highlights the need for future initiatives to draw upon behaviour change theories to assist in our understanding of the specific role that sport has to play in sport-based interventions with prison populations. This is supported by Woods, Breslin & Hassan's (2017) review which proposes that testing behaviour change theories within the design and evaluation of interventions leads to a clearer understanding of what works and why, facilitating the development of practical guidelines for prisons to use in sport and exercise service provisions that explicitly target psychological well-being.

Self-determination theory

The measures used to evaluate the Cell Workout Workshops are underpinned by Self-Determination Theory (SDT; Deci & Ryan, 1985a), a clear and testable theory of behavioural change that has been used in previous physical activity research (Chatzisarantis, Hagger, Biddle, & Karageorghis, 2002; Daley & Duda, 2006; Power et al., 2011; Ullrich-French & Cox, 2009; Wang, Chatzisarantis, Spray, & Biddle, 2002). Self-Determination Theory proposes that internal motivation can predict behaviour regardless of self-efficacy, unlike more traditional behaviour change theories such as Social Cognitive Theory (Bandura, 1986) and the Transtheoretical Model of Behaviour (TTM; Prochaska & Clemente, 1983), which place self-efficacy at the heart of behavioural change. According to Chatzisarantis, Biddle, and Meek (1997), cognitive theories such as the TTM analyse behaviours in terms of cognitive representations of desired outcomes, whilst failing to recognise the conditions within which these desires are formed and the significant impact this has on the strength of intentions. In response to this, SDT identifies three innate psychological needs that influence the strength of intentions when behavioural desires are formed: competence (Harter, 1978; White, 1963); relatedness (Baumeister & Leary, 1995; Reis et al., 2000) and autonomy (deCharms, 1968; Deci, 1975). These basic psychological needs are central to SDT, proposing that satisfaction of these needs is a requirement for self-motivation, social functioning and well-being. The application of SDT to promote long-term adherence to exercise behaviours is centred on the basic needs of autonomy and relatedness.

Most healthy behaviours are extrinsically motivated, that is, we engage in them because they are instrumental in achieving desired outcomes, such as increasing fitness, rather than out of pure enjoyment or because we find them inherently satisfying. To explain how an initially extrinsically motivated behaviour can become more autonomous, Deci and Ryan's (1985b) sub-theory of Organismic Integration Theory (OIT) proposes a self-determination continuum consisting of four sub-types of extrinsic motivation: external regulation, introjection, identification and integration. External regulation of exercise behaviours is characterised by processes such as compliance or rewards, such as joining in a PE class to avoid punishment from a teacher. If support for autonomy and relatedness are provided, then motivations to exercise become more internalised and move across the continuum to a higher quality of motivation, resulting in enhanced performance, persistence and creativity.

Support for the application of Self-Determination Theory in the context of sport and exercise in prisons is provided by NASDC's (2016) theory of change which includes three key elements reflecting the basic psychological needs of competence, autonomy and relatedness, respectively: being adaptable to needs; encouraging ownership and promoting choice; and using relatable coaches. Thus, the Cell Workout Workshops apply SDT alongside the domains of need as a comprehensive framework to promote prisoners' well-being and engagement by promoting internalisation of motivations to exercise through support of the three basic psychological needs in relation to exercise.

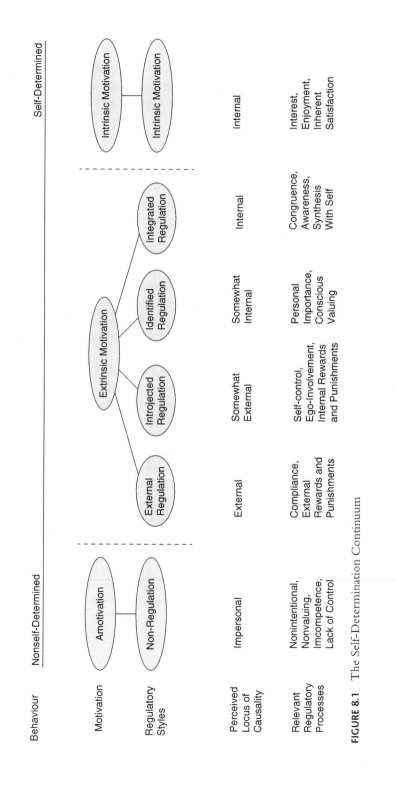

FIGURE 8.1 The Self-Determination Continuum

The workshop content

The Cell Workout Workshops were delivered by a qualified personal trainer and ex-prisoner Lewis Flanders (L.J.). Whilst serving his prison sentence, and in response to a lack of gym access, L.J. wrote a book based on safe and effective body weight exercises which can be performed in a prison cell. L.J.'s book, 'Cell Workout' (Flanders, 2016) is available in prison libraries across the UK. The primary aim of the book was to improve the health and well-being of inmates through exercise, education and self-achievement.

A total of ten workshops were delivered inside the prison, each workshop running for two consecutive weeks with 15 prisoners attending a three-hour morning and a one hour 45 minute afternoon session from Monday to Friday. There is a fortnightly lockdown of all cells due to staff training, so each cohort attended nine days' worth of sessions across the duration of the workshop. The morning sessions were exercise based and aimed to introduce the principles of cell workouts as outlined in the book, whilst the afternoon sessions were theory-based and focused on topics such as goal setting and nutrition. The workshops culminated in a graduation day centred around an awards ceremony with a certificate of achievement, a chance to reflect on experiences of the workshop, and an opportunity for participants to lead their own workout.

The workshops were advertised on posters in five different wings across the prison. The poster explained what the workshops offered in terms of an 'Intense Cell Workout bodyweight training session' and 'Group discussions including self-achievement'. The poster also highlighted that the workshops were available to 'All ages, abilities and fitness levels'. Participation requirements included English literacy at key stage 2, a positive reference from a wing officer and to be available to participate in all sessions. It was also made clear that all those accepted onto the course would be required to undertake a health check and gym induction prior to commencement. A total of 86 prisoners expressed an interest in participating in the first workshop. Wing officers reviewed these applications and excluded applications from prisoners who had caused trouble in recent weeks, and highlighted any prisoners who they felt would engage positively. Prisoners on each wing had an opportunity to apply for at least two workshops, and those who were unsuccessful in their initial application were given priority to participate in the following workshop, providing it was being delivered on their wing.

Workouts

The first Monday of the workshop was used to gather participants' physiological data in assigned individual slots referred to as full body health MOTs, where data was recorded across 10 measures including resting heart rate, body weight, lung capacity and body fat. In line with the domain of *management and promotion of physical healthcare* from the domains of need model, these sessions included a consultation with L.J. to discuss physical fitness and general well-being prior to the start of the workshops, answering any specific queries and providing advice on how to achieve health goals. The first time the participants met as a group was on the morning of the second day of the workshop where they all participated in a physical workout. The workouts lasted for 40 minutes and were based on the body weight exercises outlined in the Cell Workout book including aerobic exercises such as running on the spot and strength building exercises such as press-ups. Each 40-minute session focused on a muscle group, including chest, back, arms, legs and abdominals. To support participants' sense of autonomy and competence there was an emphasis on choice with regards to the intensity and style of the workouts, and so each exercise was demonstrated with both a beginners' and an advanced option. For example, conventional press-ups with just toes and hands meeting the floor were offered as the advanced version, whilst the beginners' version encouraged the individual to bring their knees into contact with floor for additional support. Exercises were performed for 30 seconds in total with 15 seconds' rest. Flanders (2016) provides more details on the exercises and guidance on how they are performed.

Initially, the morning workouts were led by the trainer, allowing attendees to become familiar with the principles of the exercises in the book and to build on their fitness and strength. As the workshop progressed and the attendees' competence grew there was a shift of responsibility to the participants as they were encouraged to think of their own exercise routines. To address occupational needs to develop interpersonal skills and promote social inclusion the final group session on the second Friday of the workshop consisted of a series of five-minute group workouts led by each of the participants individually, thus promoting independent functioning across the whole group.

The latter part of the first morning session began with L.J. telling his own story, explaining how and why his personal experience of prison inspired him to write the Cell Workout book and eventually devise these workshops, highlighting barriers encountered and how these were managed. This introduced the participants to the key themes of motivation and resilience which were highlighted throughout the workshop, as well as created a genuine sense of relatedness between the trainer and the participants, which was central to their continued engagement.

Upon commencing the workshop each participant was given a copy of the Cell Workout book which formed the focus of the late-morning sessions. The book introduces the reader to static body weight exercises, high-intensity interval training (HIIT) and relaxation techniques. Each exercise performed in the morning workout was studied in-depth, helping to develop a better understanding of how they can be performed safely and effectively, as well as how they can be utilised to improve both mental and physical well-being. This included highlighting the differences between active versus passive stretching and aerobic versus anaerobic training to identify when these are most useful, explaining the importance of balancing exercise intensity and duration in different measures depending on the desired outcome, and teaching basic relaxation techniques to promote positive thoughts and boost energy levels. Providing participants with this level of detail promoted competence and enabled them to engage in autonomous exercise, whether this be in their cell, the landing or the prison gym.

Soft skills sessions

The workshops' afternoon sessions were an opportunity to address the needs of therapeutic engagement and education in greater depth. These theory-based sessions include group discussions, motivational work and talks from organisations running educational courses in the prison. The first week's sessions addressed behavioural change and how to achieve it, exploring the difference between a fixed and growth mindset, the importance of setting manageable SMART (specific, measurable, agreed, realistic and time-based: Doran, 1981) targets, the Theory of Change, motivation and the power of resilience. Participants were encouraged to set themselves a target or targets at the start of the workshop which they were asked to write down and either share with the group or with a chosen 'supporter', either in or outside the prison. Although it was stipulated that the targets should be measurable and achievable they did not have to relate to exercise, for example they might be to smoke one less cigarette a day (at this point the prison smoking ban in England and Wales had not come into force), or to write to an estranged friend or family member. The session on resilience encouraged participants to identify any potential barriers to achieving their targets and how they might go about managing these, and in the final session of the workshop everyone revisited their targets and were invited to share their progress, either with the group or their supporter. By introducing the idea of setting personal, achievable targets that can be measured and shared with significant others, these sessions aimed to help prisoners identify the aspects of their lives which they have control over, supporting a sense of autonomy and competence which is often lacking in the prison environment.

The second week's afternoon sessions aligned with existing educational programmes within the prison including the Prisoners' Education Trust's 'Fit for Release' report, focusing on how sports-based learning can help prisoners engage in education, gain employment and desist from crime (Meek & Champion, 2012); two organisations looking to improve healthy eating inside prisons; and the Centre for Entrepreneurs Ltd., promoting the role of entrepreneurship in breaking the cycle of offending (centreforentrepreneurs.org). Participants were encouraged to engage with these organisations and programmes to seek opportunities for further education and employment opportunities following completion of the workshop.

'Supporters' day

To promote therapeutic engagement further and to support spiritual needs it was considered crucial to engage individuals from outside of the prison who were close to the participants. As well as encouraging prisoners to identify a 'supporter' with whom to share their goals and achievements, a 'supporters' day' was also held on the day of the final workshop session. Unfortunately, due to time and resource constraints, not all participants were able to take part in this family day; instead the trainer chose a selection of participants who he felt would benefit most from participating. These included those who improved most on their measures of well-being, those who engaged most with the workshops and those who saw the greatest increase in their fitness. The supporters' day provided the prisoners with an opportunity to demonstrate what they had learnt to friends and family by delivering a short workout to their fellow participants. This also provided a valuable opportunity to gather data from friends and family about their thoughts and perspectives on the workshops, along with contact details to increase the chances of obtaining follow-up data post-release, which is notoriously difficult to obtain.

Intervention evaluation and lessons learned through self-reflection

The present evaluation adopted a mixed-methods design across physiological and psychological variables to identify any changes in participants' exercise motivation, fitness levels or physical and emotional well-being, whilst seeking to provide tangible explanations for these changes.

The life of a prisoner differs dramatically from those on the 'outside'; many experience mental health problems which are often undiagnosed, and the isolation, risk and uncertainty which they continuously experience is likely to have an ongoing impact on their well-being. Therefore, psychological or behaviour measures which are appropriate for the general population, or even the clinical population, may not be suitable for those in prison and it is important to consider the construct validity of any measure being used on prisoners.

A recent systematic review of the impact of sport-based interventions on the psychological well-being of people in prison by Woods et al. (2017) proposed that future research of this kind should make clear and balanced choices in relation to measurement scales, using a broad range of robust measures focusing on both increases in well-being and decreases in ill-being, with a specific definition of psychological well-being as well as utilisation of pre-post designs and follow-up data. In response to Woods et al.'s (2017) timely review, the present research employed a broad range of qualitative and quantitative measures at three time points with a focus on increasing well-being, as well as considering decreases in ill-being.

Health outcome measures

Physiological data across 11 variables was collected through full body health MOTs with as many participants as possible at two time points: the first Monday of the workshops (start: $n = 89$) and the second Thursday (end: $n = 78$). Eight of the measures saw significantly positive changes from the start to the end, namely, body weight ($Z = -1.932, p < .053$), body fat percentage ($Z = -3.832, p < .000$), basal metabolic rate ($Z = -2.183, p < .029$), bone density ($Z = -2.250, p < .024$), water level percentage ($Z = -2.351, p < .019$), muscle mass ($Z = -2.881, p < .004$) and lung capacity ($Z = 6.654$, p < .000), whilst the remaining three (heart rate, pulse rate and blood oxygen) moved in a positive direction.

All psychological measures were reviewed for suitability on the prison population, and questions were rephrased if possible, or removed if they were deemed entirely unsuitable. Surveys were completed by prisoners prior to beginning the workshop (start: $n = 105$), on the final day of the workshop (end: $n = 70$) and again at between two to six months following completion of the workshop (follow up: $n = 34$). Due to the nature of the prison environment and the frequency with which prisoners can move within and between prisons, obtaining follow-up data can be particularly challenging, and studies often fail to provide any longitudinal data at all (Woods et al., 2017). However, in light of the potential adverse effect caused by a lack of purposeful activities to engage with following prison-based interventions (as demonstrated by Leberman, 2007) it is crucial to obtain as much follow-up data as possible, and the present evaluation managed to obtain data from all 34 participants who remained in the prison 10 months following the start of the first workshop.

To avoid ambiguity, the surveys provide a clear definition of exercise at the outset, followed by a visual-analogue stages of change ladder as developed by Beiner and Abrams (1991), measuring participants' motivation to engage in physical activity. The stages of change, as developed by Prochaska and DiClemente (1983), are of relevance in relation to increasing motivation to exercise through the principles of Self-Determination Theory by helping to identify the type of regulatory style required. Readiness to exercise increased significantly for participants from the start to the end of the workshops ($Z = -5.648$, $p < 0.000$), and was still significantly higher at follow up compared to the start ($Z = -3.559$, $p < 0.000$), suggesting that engagement with exercise was being maintained to some extent.

Previous research has highlighted the importance of clearly defining what is meant by 'well-being' when reviewing sport-based interventions in prison (Woods et al., 2017), whilst Pollard and Lee (2003) emphasise the importance of assessing more than one domain of well-being. In response to this, prisoners' well-being was measured in terms of their health-related quality of life (HRQL) using a revised version of the Medical Outcomes Survey Short Form-36 (MOS SF-36) questionnaire (Ware & Sherbourne, 1992) outlining five domains of well-being[4]: physical functioning, general health, social functioning, emotional well-being and vitality. Physical and social functioning outcomes remained consistently high with median scores of 100 at all three time points: the maximum score possible. Measures of vitality, emotional well-being and general health increased significantly from the start to the end of the workshops ($Z = -3.426$, $p = 0.001$; $Z = -5.230$, $p = 0.001$; and $Z = -5.936$, $p = 0.001$, respectively), and general health continued to increase significantly at follow up compared with the end ($Z = -2.584$, $p = 0.010$). Unfortunately, follow-up measures in the other two domains were not as positive, in fact, vitality and emotional well-being had both significantly *decreased* at follow up compared with the end of the workshops ($Z = -4.215$, $p < 0.000$; and $Z = -4.468$, $p < 0.000$, respectively).

The three basic psychological needs were assessed using a scale adapted for use in relation to exercise (Basic Psychological Needs in Exercise Scale; BPNES; Vlachopoulos & Michailidou, 2006). Measures of competence, relatedness and autonomy had all increased significantly from the start to the end of the workshops ($Z = -3.135, p = 0.002; Z = -3.634, p < 0.000;$ and $Z = -3.796, p < 0.000$, respectively). Relatedness and competence remained significantly higher at follow than at the start ($Z = -3.044, p = 0.002;$ and $Z = -3.177, p = 0.001$, respectively). Perceived autonomy support was also measured at the end of the workshops using The Sport Climate Questionnaire, revealing a mean score of 6.85 out of a maximum 7. However, measures of autonomy on the BPNES had begun to decrease at follow up and were lower than they had been at the start, although this was not significant.

Analysis of qualitative responses provided in the end and follow-up surveys as well as interviews with 15 participants revealed tremendously positive outcomes. There was an overwhelming sense that the workshops and L.J.'s story had 'reignited' something within participants, encouraging them to use their time proactively. Participants who did not exercise prior to the workshops had grown in competence, and many reported that they were now engaging in exercise on the wing or getting to the gym when possible, whilst those who were already regular exercisers had relished the opportunity to learn more about exercise and nutrition. Just over a third of participants had signed up to or were already engaged in an educational course within the prison as a direct result of participating in the workshops, either because it had motivated them to do so or provided them with information they had not previously known about. The importance of a supportive environment which promotes autonomy to increase motivation for exercise is recognised throughout the literature (Andrews & Andrews, 2003; Meek and Lewis, 2012, 2014; Biddle, Fox, Boutcher, & Faulkner, 2000; Sloan, Gough & Conner, 2010), and two of the key themes in prisoners' discourse about the workshops were relatedness and comradery; L.J.'s position as an ex-prisoner and the element of relatedness that this provided became crucial in the promotion of prisoners' motivations to engage in the workouts as well as the soft skills sessions, and participants were able to exercise and engage positively and freely with other prisoners in the workshops in a way which can be tough in other areas of the prison where they are often negotiating risk.

The decrease in follow-up measures of emotional well-being, vitality and autonomy for exercise are reflective of the impact that can be had when a positive intervention such as this is complete, and prisoners are then left without any purposeful activity to engage in. With more time and resource, the workshops would seek to employ serving prisoners to act as supporters within the prison, engaging with participants of the workshops following completion, providing them with new exercise and nutrition plans, delivering regular group workouts and acting as a figure of relatedness.

The present evaluation has highlighted the importance of continued support and engagement with prisoners following an intervention such as this one, as well as the potential for sport and exercise-based interventions to engage prisoners in other healthy behaviours such as education and employment. Evaluations of prison-based interventions such as the Cell Workout Workshops in the form of natural experiments are crucial in informing the prison service about 'what works' in relation to motivating prisoners to engage in healthy behaviours, particularly given the current lack of sports-based interventions to support prisoners' well-being.

Notes

1 Figures exclude open prisons
2 A high secure setting is a hospital that detains individuals under the Mental Health Act 1983 as amended in 2007 (c. 20) who are deemed to require treatment in conditions of high security due to dangerous, violent or criminal propensities as outlined by the National Health Service Act, 2006 (c. 41)
3 The IEP scheme is a tool used by prison management to incentivise conforming behaviour by offering prisoners the chance to earn benefits such as increased gym access in exchange for responsible behaviour. The scheme consists of three levels; basic, standard and enhanced.
4 Domains measuring role limitations due to physical and emotional problems and bodily pain were removed as they referred to engaging in daily activities which were not applicable to all prisoners.

References

Andrews, J. P., & Andrews, G. J. (2003). Life in a secure unit: The rehabilitation of young people through the use of sport. *Social Science & Medicine, 56*, 531–550.

Bandura, A. (1986). *Social foundations of thought and action: A social cognitive theory.* Englewood Cliffs, NJ: Prentice-Hall.

Baumeister, R., & Leary, M. R. (1995). The need to belong: Desire for interpersonal attachments as a fundamental human motivation. *Psychological Bulletin, 117*, 497–529.

Beiner, L., & Abrams, D. B. (1991). The contemplation ladder: Validation of a measure of readiness to consider smoking cessation. *Health Psychology, 10*, 360–365.

Biddle, S. J. H., Fox, K. R., Boutcher, S. H., & Faulkner, G. (2000). The way forward for physical activity and the promotion of psychological well-being. In S. J. H. Biddle, K. R. Fox, & S. H. Boutcher (Eds.), *Physical activity and psychological well-being* (pp. 154–168). London: Routledge.

Buckaloo, B. J., Krug, K. S., & Nelson, K. B. (2009). Exercise and the low-security inmate: Changes in depression, stress, and anxiety. *The Prison Journal, 89*(3), 328–343.

Chatzisarantis, N. L. D., Biddle, S. J. H., & Meek, G. A. (1997). A self-determination theory approach to the study of intentions and the intention-behaviour relationship in children's physical activity. *British Journal of Health Psychology, 2*, 343–360.

Chatzisarantis, N. L. D., Hagger, M. S., Biddle, S. J. H., & Karageorghis, C. (2002). The cognitive processes by which perceived locus of causality predicts participation in physical activity. *Journal of Health Psychology, 7*, 685–699.

Condon, L., Hek, G., & Harris, F. (2008). Choosing health in prison: Prisoners' views on making healthy choices in English prisons. *Health Education Journal, 67*(3), 155–166. doi:10.1177/0017896908094633

Daley, A. J., & Duda, J. L. (2006). Self-determination, stage of readiness to change for exercise, and frequency of physical activity in young people. *European Journal of Sport Science, 6*(4), 231–243. https://doi.org/10.1080/17461390601012637

deCharms, R. (1968). *Personal causation.* New York, NY: Academic Press.

Deci, E. L. (1975). *Intrinsic motivation.* New York, NY: Plenum.

Deci, E. L., & Ryan, R. M. (1985a). *Intrinsic motivation and self-determination in human behavior.* New York, NY: Plenum.

Deci, E. L., & Ryan, R. M. (1985b). The general causality orientations scale: Self-determination in personality. *Journal of Research in Personality, 19,* 109–134. doi:10.1016/0092-6566(85)90023-6

Department of Health. (2011). *Physical activity guidelines for adults (19–64 years).* Retrieved from www.gov.uk/government/uploads/system/uploads/attachment_data/file/213740/dh_128145.pdf

De Silva, M. J., Breuer, E., Lee, L., Asher, L., Chowdhary, N., Lund, C., & Patel, V. (2014). Theory of change: A theory-driven approach to enhance the medical research council's framework for complex interventions. *Trials, 15,* 267. doi:10.1186/1745-6215-15-267

de Viggiani, N. (2007). Unhealthy prisons: Exploring structural determinants of prison health. *Sociology of Health & Illness, 29,* 115–135.

Doran, G. T. (1981). There's a S. M. A. R. T. way to write a management's goals and objectives. Management Review: AMA Forum, 70(11), 35–36.

Durcan, G., & Zwemstra, J. C. (2014). Mental health in prison. In World Health Organisation (Ed.), *Prisons and health* (pp. 87–85). Copenhagen: World Health Organisation.

Fazel, S., & Danesh, J. (2002). Serious mental disorder in 23000 prisoners: A systematic review of 62 surveys. *The Lancet, 359*(9306), 545–550.

Flanders, L. J. (2016). *Cell workout.* England: Hodder & Stoughton.

Gatherer, A., Enggist, S., & Moller, L. (2014). The essential about prisons and health. In S. Enggist, L. Moller, G. Galea et al. (Eds.), *Prisons and health* (pp. 1–5). Copenhagen: World Health Organization.

Gatherer, A., Moller, L., & Hayton, P. (2005). The world health organization European health in prisons project after 10 years: Persistent barriers and achievements. *American Journal of Public Health, 95*(10), 1696–1700.

Glorney, E., Perkins, D., Adshead, G., McGauley, G., Murray, K., Noak, J., & Sichau, G. (2010). Domains of need in a high secure hospital setting: A model for streamlining care and reducing length of stay. *International Journal of Forensic Mental Health, 9*(2), 138–148.

Harter, S. (1978). Effectance motivation reconsidered: Toward a developmental model. *Human Development, 1,* 661–669.

Her Majesty's Chief Inspector of Prisons. (2016). *HM chief inspector of prisons for England and Wales annual report 2015–16.* Retrieved from www.justiceinspectorates.gov.uk/hmiprisons/wp-content/uploads/sites/4/2016/07/HMIP-AR_2015-16_web.pdf

Hofstetter, C. R., Hovell, M. F., Macera, C., Sallis, J. F., Spry, V., Barrington, E., . . . Rauh, M. (1991). Illness, injury, and correlates of aerobic exercise and walking: A community study. *Research Quarterly for Exercise and Sport Journals, 62*(1), 1–9.

Independent Monitoring Boards. (2013). *HMP/YOI ISIS: Report of the independent monitoring board.* Retrieved from www.imb.org.uk/wp-content/uploads/2015/01/isis-2013.pdf

Jakab, Z. (2014). Foreword. In S. Enggist, L. Moller, G. Galea et al. (Eds.), *Prisons and health.* Copenhagen: World Health Organization.

Leberman, S. (2007). Voices behind the walls: Female offenders and experiential learning. *Journal of Adventure Education & Outdoor Learning, 7,* 113–120.

Leon, A. S., & Norstrom, J. (1995). Evidence of the role of physical activity and cardiorespiratory fitness in the prevention of coronary heart disease. *Quest, 47,* 311–319.

Lester, C., Hamilton-Kirkwood, L., & Jones, N. K. (2003). Health indicators in a prison population: Asking prisoners. *Health Education Journal, 62,* 341–349. doi:10.1177/001789690306200406

Lowther, M., Mutrie, N., & Scott, E. M. (2002). Promoting physical activity in a socially and economically deprived community: A 12 month randomized control trial of fitness assessment and exercise consultation. *Journal of Sports Sciences, 20*(7), 577–588. doi:10.1080/026404102760000071

McGuire, J. (2008). A review of effective interventions for reducing aggression and violence. *Philosophical Transactions of the Royal Society B: Biological Sciences, 363*(1503), 2577–2597.

Meek, R. (2014). *Sport in prison: Exploring the role of physical activity in correctional settings.* Oxon: Routledge.

Meek, R., & Champion, N. (2012). *Fit for release: How sports-based learning can help prisoners engage in education, gain employment and desist from crime.* Prisoners Education Trust. Retrieved May 26, 2017, from www.prisonerseducation.org.uk/resources/fit-for-release-how-sports-based-learning-can-help-prisoners-engage-in-education-gain-employment-and-desist-from-crime

Meek, R., & Lewis, G. (2012). The role of sport in promoting prisoner health. *International Journal of Prisoner Health, 8*(3–4), 117–130. doi:10.1108/17449201211284996

Meek, R., & Lewis, G. (2014). The impact of a sports initiative for young men in prison: Staff and participant perspectives. *Journal of Sport and Social Issues, 38*(2), 95–123. doi: 10.1177/0193723512472896

Mental Health Act. (2007). *ch. 20.* Retrieved from www.legislation.gov.uk/ukpga/2007/12/pdfs/ukpga_20070012_en.pdf

NASDC. (2016). *Our theory of change: Exploring the role of sport for development in the prevention and desistance from crime.* Retrieved from www.nasdc.org/power-of-sport/theory-of-change/

National Health Service Act. (2006). *ch. 41.* Retrieved from www.legislation.gov.uk/ukpga/2006/41/pdfs/ukpga_20060041_en.pdf

National Offender Management Service. (2011). *Service specification for physical education.*

Ministry of Justice. (2017, November 3). Prison population figures: 2017. *Population bulletin: Weekly.* Retrieved from www.gov.uk/government/statistics/prison-population-figures-2017

Nelson, M., Specian, V. L., Tracy, N. C., & DeMello, J. J. (2006). The effects of moderate physical activity on offenders in rehabilitative program. *Journal of Correctional Education, 57*(4), 276–285.

Pollard, E. L., & Lee, P. D. (2003). Child well-being: A systematic review of the literature. *Social Indicators Research, 61*(1), 59–78.

Power, T. G., Ullrich-French, S. C., Steele, M. M., Daratha, K. B., & Bindler, R. C. (2011). Obesity, cardiovascular fitness, and physically active adolescents' motivations for activity: A self-determination theory approach. *Psychology of Sport and Exercise, 12,* 593–598.

Prison Reform Trust. (2014). *Punishment without purpose: What is the Incentives and Earned Privileges (IEP) scheme?* Prison Reform Trust. London. Retrieved April 12, from www.prisonreformtrust.org.uk/Portals/0/Documents/punishment%20without%20purpose%20FINAL2941007.pdf

Prisons and Probation Ombudsman. (2016). *I. Prisoner mental health.* London: Prisons and Probation Ombudsman. Retrieved from www.ppo.gov.uk/wp-content/uploads/2016/01/PPO-thematic-prisoners-mental-health-web-final.pdf

Prochaska, J., & DiClemente, C. (1983). Stages and processes of self-change of smoking: Toward an integrative model of change. *Journal of Consulting and Clinical Psychology, 51*(3), 390–395.

Reis, H. T., Sheldon, K. M., Gable, S. L., Roscoe, J., & Ryan, R. M. (2000). Daily well-being: The role of autonomy, competence, and relatedness. *Personality and Social Psychology Bulletin, 26,* 419–435.

Sallis, J. F., Hovell, M. F., Hofstetter, C. R., Elder, J. P., Hackley, M., Caspersen, C. J., & Powell, K. E. (1990). Distance between homes and exercise facilities related to frequency of exercise among San Diego residents. *Public Heath Reports, 105*(2), 179–185.

Senior, J., & Shaw, J. (2007). Prison healthcare. In Y. Jewkes (Eds.), *Handbook on prisons*. Cullompton: Willian Publishing.

SEU, Social Exclusion Unit. (2002). *Reducing re-offending by ex-prisoners*. London: Social Exclusion Unit.

Sloan, C., Gough, B., & Conner, M. (2010). Healthy masculinities? How ostensibly healthy men talk about lifestyle, health and gender. *Psychology & Health*, *25*(7), 783–803. doi:10.1080/08870440902883204

Spilner, M., & Robertson, S. (2000). Take 10,000 steps a day! *Prevention 2000*, 90.

Stewart, D. W. (2008). *Problems and needs of newly sentenced prisoners: Results from a national survey*. London: Ministry of Justice.

Ullrich-French, S., & Cox, A. (2009). Using cluster analysis to examine the combinations of motivation regulations of physical education students. *Journal of Sport and Exercise Psychology*, *31*, 358–379.

Vlachopoulos, S. P., & Michailidou, S. (2006). Development and initial validation of a measure of autonomy, competence, and relatedness in exercise: The basic psychological needs in exercise scale. *Measurement in Physical Education and Exercise Science*, *10*, 179–201.

Wang, C. K. J., Chatzisarantis, N. L. D., Spray, C. M., & Biddle, S. J. H. (2002). Achievement goal profiles in school physical education: Differences in self-determination, sport ability beliefs, and physical activity. *British Journal of Educational Psychology*, *72*, 433–445.

Ware, J. E., & Sherbourne, C. D. (1992). The MOS 36-item short-form health survey (SF-36). I. Conceptual framework and item selection. *Medical Care*, *30*(6), 473–483.

Watson, R., Stimpson, A., & Hostick, T. (2004). Prison health care: A review of the literature. *International Journal of Nursing Studies*, *41*(2), 119–128. doi:10.1016/S0020-7489(03)00128-7

White, R. W. (1963). *Ego and reality in psychoanalytic theory*. New York, NY: International Universities Press.

Woodall, J. (2016). A critical examination of the health promoting prison two decades on. *Critical Public Health*. doi:10.1080/09581596.2016.1156649

Woods, D., Breslin, G., & Hassan, D. (2017). A systematic review of the impact of sport-based interventions on the psychological well-being of people in prison. *Mental Health and Physical Activity*, *12*, 50–61.

World Health Organisation. (1995) Health in prisons. Health promotion in the prison setting. Summary Report on a WHO meeting, London, 15–17, October 1995. Copenhagen: Author.

Further reading

Meek, R. (2014). *Sport in prison: Exploring the role of physical activity in correctional settings*. Oxon: Routledge.

This book is the first of its kind to explore the role of sport in prisons and its subsequent impact on rehabilitation and behavioural change.

Woods, D., Breslin, G., & Hassan, D. (2017). A systematic review of the impact of sport-based interventions on the psychological well-being of people in prison. *Mental Health and Physical Activity*, *12*, 50–61.

This article presents a contemporary overview of sports-based interventions in prisons with a comprehensive set of guidelines that future interventions should adhere to when targeting prisoners' well-being.

9

REFLECTIONS ON IMPLEMENTING THE ACTIVE CHOICES RUGBY PROGRAMME TO ENHANCE MENTAL HEALTH AND WELL-BEING OF YOUNG MEN IN PRISON

David Woods and Gavin Breslin

Learning objectives

After reading this chapter you should be able to:

1   Understand the risks to the mental well-being of young men within prisons.
2   Critically examine the potential for sport to be incorporated into mental well-being interventions in prison.
3   Critically examine the benefits of sport interventions on hedonic and eudaimonic well-being.
4   Critically examine the need for the inclusion of behaviour change theory in intervention design.
5   Appreciate the role of reflexive practice for researcher development and intervention programme improvement in prisons.

Introduction to the theme

The Active Choices Rugby Programme aimed at enhancing mental well-being of prisoners will be described in this chapter. The aims of the chapter are: to provide an insight into the specific challenges to mental well-being faced by young men in prison; to outline how sporting interventions can be used to help tackle these challenges; to present a reflexive account of implementing and evaluating a sporting intervention within the unique prison environment; and to provide researchers and practitioners alike with lessons learned to help shape future research, theory and practice in this field.

The Active Choices Rugby Programme targeted both the hedonic and eudaimonic aspects of mental well-being of young men in prison. Hedonic well-being is concerned with experiencing positive affect, carefreeness and subjective life satisfaction, and eudaimonic well-being is concerned with feelings of meaning, value, accomplishment, self-realisation and good relationships (Huta, 2016; Stewart-Brown & Janmohamed, 2008). Steger and Shin (2012), succinctly surmise that hedonia equates to pleasure and eudaimonia equates to mattering. Specific factors of interest were also improvements in perceived autonomy, competence and relatedness, the three elements of basic psychological needs theory (Ryan & Deci, 2001), and whether participants felt they were engaged through choice or an autonomy supportive environment.

Within the prison population, researchers have reported a myriad of perceived benefits to mental well-being from sporting interventions (Amtmann & Kukay, 2016; Battaglia et al., 2014; Buckaloo, Krug, & Nelson, 2009; Cashin, Potter, & Butler, 2008; Gallant, Sherry, & Nicholson, 2015; Martin et al., 2013; Martos-Garcia, Devis-Devis, & Sparkes, 2009). Positive effects have been shown for life-skill improvement, self-esteem, self-efficacy, confidence, hopelessness, depression, mood and resiliency. Despite these positive reports, there has been a consistent absence of incorporating health behaviour change theories across sporting interventions within prison (Meek & Lewis, 2014a). This view is supported in our recent systematic review where we also highlight the lack of well-designed study protocols (Woods, Hassan, & Breslin, 2017a). In essence, a greater understanding of 'how and why' sporting interventions achieve their outcomes within prison contexts was required. This mirrors a criticism of the broader youth-sport development literature, as Jones, Edwards, Bocarro, Bunds, and Smith (2017, p. 163) comment "while there is a wealth of knowledge on the youth development outcomes sport can influence, there is much less on how or why this development occurs". The Active Choices in Rugby Programme and the associated research conducted aimed to assess whether previous reported benefits in well-being could be achieved within a young men's prison, and if present, whether this could these potentially be attributed to supporting conditions within the sporting intervention related to basic psychological needs theory (Ryan & Deci, 2001).

Describe the client or group being targeted

It is estimated that within the United Kingdom up to 90% of prisoners aged over 16 years are mentally unwell (Durcan, 2016). Fraser, Gatherer, and Hayton (2009) suggest that mental conditions and states such as depression, anxiety and stress-related conditions affect the majority of prisoners, whilst Leigh-Hunt and Perry (2015) present estimates of prisoners suffering from depression and anxiety ranging from 30% to 75%, depending on data collection technique and definitions of mental health and disorders used. Blaauw, Kerkhof and Roesch (2000), following their analysis of mental disorders in European prisoners, suggested the following categorisation: between 6–12% of the prison population would require transfer or urgent psychiatric attention; 40–50% would require assistance from health care services; and 40–60% would benefit most from mental health awareness training. Although definitive figures are difficult to ascertain, the research consistently demonstrates a high prevalence of poor mental health and well-being of prisoners, coupled with an absence of targeted and consistent mental health promotion training (Lewis & Meek, 2012).

The majority of prisoners will suffer from, or have been subjected to, adverse health determinants such as poor educational attainment, illiteracy, substandard housing, high unemployment and childhood abuse or neglect (MacNamara & Mannix-McNamara, 2014; World Health Organization (WHO), 1999). This increased vulnerability of prisoners to mental ill-health is then exacerbated within prisons were conditions are hostile (Fraser et al., 2009; Wildeman & Wang, 2017). Conditions such as over-crowding, interpersonal distrust, bullying, marginalisation, social withdrawal, a decreased sense of self-worth, mental health stigma, discrimination and a lack of purposeful activity and/or privacy can have a detrimental effect (Ferszt, Salgado, DeFedele, & Leveillee, 2009; WHO, 2007; Wildeman & Wang, 2017).

Prisoners with comparatively lower mental health are also at greater risk of suicide, self-harm, violence and victimisation (Fazel, Hayes, Bartellas, Clerici, & Trestman, 2016), and in 2016, the Prisons and Probation Ombudsman found that 70% of prisoners who had committed suicide between 2012 and 2014 had existing mental health needs. In England and Wales, the number of reported self-harm incidents in 2016 (40,161) marked an increase of 73% between 2012 and 2016. There were also 120 self-inflicted deaths reported in prison in 2016, almost twice the number in 2012, and higher than any previous year on record.

Initial needs assessment

Despite being faced with such startling statistics related to the prevalence of mental ill-being and the hostile environmental and social conditions outlined within prisons, there remains scope for optimism in relation to meeting the health needs of prisoners. A unique opportunity exists to implement targeted health promotion activities to those with limited experience of accessing similar activities prior to their incarceration (Wildeman & Wang, 2017; MacNamara & Mannix-McNamara, 2014). Dumont, Brockmann, Dickman, Alexander, and Rich (2012), reported that within the United States of America (USA), contact with prison health care represents the first experience of accessing preventative and chronic medical care for many adults. A targeted example of this was the establishment by the WHO of the Health in Prisons Project (HIPP) in 1995. HIPP advocates the promotion of a whole-prison approach to the successful implementation of health promotion and reforming interventions (WHO, 2007). Regarding mental health and well-being specifically, the Trenčín Statement highlighted that "promoting mental health and well-being should be central to a prison's health care policy" (WHO, 2007, p. 6). While the realisation of health promoting prisons has been criticised for lack of pace and weakening commitment over the last decade (Woodall, 2016), the principle of the policy highlighted in the statement remains critical. Improved mental well-being is of benefit to those imprisoned, and the wider society, given its centrality to successful prisoner rehabilitation and reintegration into the community following release (Hayton, 2007).

A multitude of key services, partnerships and actions exist within the criminal justice system to potentially meet the mental health needs of prisoners and improve their mental well-being (Durcan, 2016). However, many prisoners who stand to benefit from those services do not wish to engage with traditional treatment pathways (Stewart, 2008). Access to sport and exercise facilities are judged to have potential to meet these health needs and positively impact prisoners' mental well-being (WHO, 1999; Woods, Breslin & Hassan, 2017b). Researchers have demonstrated that sport can offer a more acceptable means to engage prisoners in health and well-being activity beyond traditional public health approaches (Meek, Champion, & Klier, 2012; Meek & Lewis, 2014b); based on this no site-specific initial needs assessment was conducted. The Active Choices Rugby Programme was offered within the prison as an intervention designed, in part, to use the context of sport to engage young men within prison to improve their mental well-being. The programme targets young men aged between 18–24 years, serving time at a young men's prison within the United Kingdom (UK). Fourteen men agreed to participate in the research/evaluation, from a total of 20 participating in the programme.

Framework and intervention for delivery

Active Choices in Rugby Programme is a sport-based initiative delivered by a sports governing body in partnership with local councils. The main objective of the initiative is to encourage individuals to be more active through sport more often and in turn benefit from improved physical and mental well-being. The local council delivery team worked in partnership with the young men's prison, located within their council boundary, to facilitate a six-week rugby coaching programme. Each week the sessions would introduce new core ruby skills (e.g., passing, safe tackling, kicking), raise awareness of the rules and etiquette of the game, and facilitate a short match. Alongside the skill improvement aims, additional aims of the programme were to improve teamwork, self-confidence, self-esteem and mental well-being, via the fostering of a positive mental outlook for the future. The coach had extensive experience of coaching rugby across all age groups and levels, and the programme was specifically designed to provide an induction into contact rugby (previously unavailable within the young men's prison), with an aim of holding coaching participants to a sufficient standard whereby they are match ready and can continue to play the sport in the community upon release.

The Active Choices Rugby Programme was not created with a theory of change incorporated. However, the coach felt these additional aims could be achieved informally throughout the progression of the programme as he gained participants' trust. This reflected the assumption of positive impact on mental well-being from sporting interventions, without theoretical foundations or subsequent testing of the supporting conditions, common in many sport-based programmes (Jones et al., 2017; Woods et al., 2017a). We therefore, retrospectively assessed perceived benefit to mental well-being, through one-to-one semi-structured interviews and quantitative measures of well-being, incorporating the Short Warwick Edinburgh Mental Well-being Scale (Stewart-Brown & Janmohamed, 2008) and the Basic Psychological Needs Scale (Deci & Ryan, 2000). The presence of an autonomy supportive environment within the Active Choices Rugby programme, through the Sport's Climate Questionnaire (Deci, 2001), was also assessed for. Autonomy supportive environments have been shown to have a positive impact on mental well-being, basic psychological need satisfaction and self-determined motivation (Amorose, 2007; Gillet, Vallerand, Amoura, & Baldes, 2010; Mageau & Vallerand, 2003; Meek & Lewis, 2014a). Participants were assessed at the start of the programme, after three weeks (the mid-point), six weeks and eight weeks.

Intervention evaluation and lessons learned through self-reflection

Participants' mean SWEMWBS scores (mental well-being) across all time-points remained stable with no large increase or decrease and were relatively positive. This indicated a more positive state of mental well-being within the young men's prison than has been reported across the prison population more generally (Australian Institute of Health and Welfare, 2015; Durcan, 2016; Travis, Western, & Redburn, 2014). An important consideration which may have influenced this finding is the fact that the prison had been very recently rebranded as a "college" rather than a prison, with prisoners referred to as "students" and with a considerable emphasis placed on education and the provision of purposeful learning activities. The positive SWEMWBS scores observed highlighted the dangers of assuming a 'deficit model' (Coalter, 2013), whereby poor mental well-being, and/ or related constructs such as low self-esteem, are assumed within all at-risk populations. However, it is also important to note there were existing high levels of participant involvement in sport and exercise activities, which could also have impacted their baseline scores. All participants reported consistent attendance at the gym up to five times a week, citing the positive impacts on their mental well-being as a key motivation. This view resonates with findings that those who engage with aerobic and gym activities are associated with a lower mental health burden (compared with those not engaging), in particular when they engage for durations of 45 mins and frequencies of three to five times per week (Chekroud et al., 2018).

Qualitative findings showed a short-term perceived benefit to mental well-being, particularly the hedonic perspective of subjective happiness and satisfaction, as a result of the intervention. Short-term positive affect was demonstrated through reported improvements in mood, mental escapism and having an event to look forward to. These findings support previous research within the prison population reporting similar outcomes (Amtmann & Kukay, 2016; Bilderbeck, Farias, Brazil, Jakobowitz, & Wikholm, 2013; Gallant, Sherry, & Nicholson, 2015; Hilyer et al., 1982; Parker, Meek, & Lewis, 2014). Participants also reported a short-term reduction in related deficit measures of mental well-being, specifically, reduced feelings of anger and stress. These results also add to the existing body of research which has reported similar reductions in feelings of stress, anxiety and anger (Battaglia et al., 2014; Bilderbeck et al., 2013; Harner, Hanlon, & Garfinkel, 2010; Martin et al., 2013; Nelson, Specian, Tracy, & DeMello, 2006; Gallant et al., 2015; Meek & Lewis, 2014a; Parker et al., 2014).

In contrast to the short-term positive benefits reported, a theme emerged which centred on a lack of any lasting benefit to mental well-being, in contrast to findings from two previous prison-based studies incorporating intervention follow-up. These studies reported medium to long-term well-being benefits at two months (Leberman, 2007) and up to two years (Meek & Lewis, 2014a). However, intervention contact time was considerably less in the Active Choices Rugby Programme (one hour a week, over six weeks) in comparison to the Leberman study (20-day residential outdoor activity course) and the Meek and Lewis study (12 to15 weeks, 5 days a week intensive contact course). Reflecting these comparative differences in intervention contact time, participants and the coach on the Active Choices Rugby Programme cited course duration and frequency as reasons for the lack of lasting benefit, alongside inconsistent programme attendance by the participants. These findings, relating to programme efficacy and feasibility highlighted the importance of facilitating programmes of sufficient duration and frequency within the prisons if the potential for a lasting benefit to mental well-being is to be realised (Woods et al., 2017b). We examined if basic psychological needs (Ryan & Deci, 2001) mediated the relationship between the sport-based intervention and any resultant perceived benefits to mental well-being. Quantitative results suggested that each of the three fundamental psychological needs of autonomy, competence and relatedness were consistently perceived as being met for those who participated across each of the four time-points, with no large increase or decrease observed throughout participant involvement in Active Choices. However, emergent themes reported from the qualitative analyses demonstrated increased feelings of relatedness within the participants, during the programme and at follow-up, particularly with new or vulnerable prisoners who participated. Increased feelings of competence, through improvements in individual rugby skills were also reported. Increased feelings of relatedness can be directly linked to improved mental well-being (Reis, Sheldon, Gable, Roscoe, & Ryan, 2000), both the hedonic perspective through an immediate positive affect, and the eudaimonic perspective, which partly focuses on developing and maintaining positive relationships. This supports previous researchers who reported improved prisoner relationships, pro-social behaviours and sense of achievement following involvement in SBIs (Leberman, 2007; Meek & Lewis, 2014a; Parker et al., 2014) as well as that sport provides a coping mechanism for new prisoners during their transition into prison life (Gallant et al., 2015). Results demonstrated that perceived improvements in competence were also moderated by the outcome expectancy of participants. That is, those who previously playing sport at a high level (trials for top tier sports teams before being imprisoned) reported only enjoyment rather than a sense of achievement, as they felt they would never comparatively excel at a new sport within six weeks. Results also revealed that the short duration of the Active Choices Rugby Programme and a lack of opportunity to play rugby upon the programme conclusion within the prison prevented any longer-term maintenance of increased feelings of competence. This translated to a short-term perceived benefit to hedonic mental well-being, namely subjective happiness and/or satisfaction, rather than long-term increased psychological flourishing.

In contrast to a perceived increase in the needs satisfaction of relatedness and competence, albeit the latter short-term, qualitative results revealed no perception of increased feelings of autonomy, with the exception of three prisoners indicating that they might choose to continue playing on release. This is not surprising as the programme offered no formal "through the gate" assistance in facilitating this, in contrast to programmes detailed within other studies (Meek & Lewis, 2014a; Parker et al., 2014; Williams, Collingwood, Coles, & Schmeer, 2015). Results also highlighted the potential for the thwarting of autonomy needs satisfaction due to participants being denied access to the course, without notice, on occasions of acute security or staffing issues. In contrast, quantitative results obtained from the Sport Climate Questionnaire (Deci, 2001) indicated the positive facilitation of an autonomy supportive environment during the programme. This would suggest that although participants experienced increased feelings of acting out of choice and having input into decisions during the training sessions, this did not translate to outside of the game environment. Two key points emerge from this observation, it cannot be assumed that mental well-being benefits will transfer beyond the sporting environment within prisons. This mirrors the findings of non-prison-based research into the transferability of human-orientated functions in youth-sport development (Jones et al., 2017; Edwards, 2015), which highlight the importance of intentional design and well managed practices to achieve effective transfer. Leading on from this, the lack of transfer from the programme can potentially be linked to the lack of health behaviour change theory during design and wrap-around non-sporting services and transitional support, contents observed on other sporting interventions based on what is referred to as a "sport-plus" model (Meek & Lewis, 2014a; Parker et al., 2014; Williams et al., 2015).

As well as programme design, the role of contextual factors or assets, such as the influence of the coach, parents, peers and environment, are highly influential in realising the potential for positive developmental impact and mental well-being through sport (Amorose, 2007; Atkins, Johnson, Force, & Petrie, 2015; Gillet et al., 2010; Lerner, Dowling, & Anderson, 2003). The results from the Active Choices Rugby Programme strengthen previous findings and demonstrated both the positive and negative impact that contextual influences can have. The relationship fostered between the coach and participants, which centred around values of positive reinforcement, respect and equality, emerged as a key influence on the positive affect reported by participants. In line with basis needs theory, participants reported that the programme allowed them to relate better to other prisoners, increased their competence and improved their sense of autonomy; they attributed these changes to the supportive coaching sessions. However, the impacts of the prison environment on programme efficacy and feasibility were consistent sources of frustration for participants and the coach, with programme duration, frequency and attendance all acting as limiters to the potential for longer-term perceived benefit to mental well-being that could have been accrued.

Negative impacts of low commitment, irregular attendance and poor scheduling on programme success, of which the latter two are under greater control of the prison, have been reported in previous studies (Harner et al., 2010; Gallant et al., 2015). Our findings expand on these, by highlighting the negative impact these factors can also have on programme efficacy, as fluctuating attendance led to an unachieved programme goal – to coach a team to a standard sufficient enough to compete against a visiting team, which the coach believed would have facilitated increased benefit to mental well-being. Therefore, if similar team-orientated sporting interventions within prison, dependent on attendance numbers, are to realise greater potential to benefit mental well-being, they must actively seek to maximise prisoner engagement and aspirations in areas under their control. Flexibility in timetabling is one area, alongside continued facilitation of greater access to the new sporting activities introduced, albeit dependent on sport specific expertise available and resource implications.

Programme feasibility and efficacy also had a direct impact on the fidelity of the research model, with the impact of fluctuating attendance numbers and lack of consistent participants from baseline to follow-up negatively impacting the scope for longitudinal quantitative analysis. As one participant [P1] who declined to be involved at time-point three commented, "*there's no point, nothing's changed*". Although such a comment in itself represents a telling qualitative insight, the temporary withdrawal (he participated at time-point 4), alongside the broader changeable make-up of programme participants, was of detriment to the planned quantitative analysis. As a result, there was only limited realisation of one of the research aims, to provide a robust longitudinal measure of perceived benefit to mental well-being rather than ill-being, with the latter over-represented in sport-based intervention studies, both in prisons (Woods et al., 2017a) and in non-prison youth development studies (Jones et al., 2017). This therefore remains a requirement for future research in the area.

Challenges of conducting sport-based research programmes in prison

Becker (2007, p. 90) notes there is a tendency for impersonal, passive writing that is commonly regarded as "scientific" to hide the bits that most readers of prison research want to know. However, the potential for being more open and revealing needs to be balanced with the criticisms of "prison tourism" (Piché & Walby, 2010), and the author who adopts an 'I-was-there' tell-all persona in their writing. With this balance in mind, the following insights are examples of challenges of conducting prison research, whilst remaining respectful of the privileged access granted and openness of those who participated in the programme.

The reflexive approach adopted and outlined by Edge (2011), is comprised of interacting elements, prospective and retrospective reflexivity. The former is focused on the effect of the researcher on the research, whilst the latter calls for an honest reflection of the effect of the research on the researcher. Mann (2016, p. 28) argues that a strength of this approach is the recognition of the "mutual shaping, reciprocality and bi-directionality, and that interaction is context-dependant". This was an appropriate approach to take therefore, given the unique environmental context of conducting research in prison.

Jewkes (2012) comments that despite prisons' prominent place in popular culture, they remain shrouded in myth and mystique. Upon reflection, how such myths and mystiques may cause a reaction upon being granted access and entering a prison for the first time were not considered. This was brought into sharp focus however during the first prison visit, which was to meet with a Prison Officer in charge of the Physical Education Department. The unfamiliar and mythical environment brought to the fore a sudden and unexpected mix of insecurity and confusion. In turn, these feelings led to somatic reactions usually associated with stress or anxiety (e.g., sweaty palms, slight tightening of the chest). Although these reactions were relatively short-lived experiences, which dissipated following a meet and greet with prison staff and a tour of the prison, they were present on each occasion a new and unfamiliar prison was entered to conduct research. Sparks, Bottoms, and Hay (1996) commented that prisons are special places, as there are few other institutional settings where the extremes of social life are so starkly represented and enacted. Despite learning to anticipate the spike in somatic anxiety upon entering a prison for the first time, there was a consistent acute awareness of the unique environment and an appreciation of being granted access to it.

Previously, prison researchers have described the difficulty in navigating 'insider' and 'outsider' boundaries, the juxtaposition of wanting to be both visible and invisible and whether positioning oneself in the field disturbs and contaminates it (Rowe, 2014). The research within the young men's prison required interviews to be conducted between the hours of 10:00–12:00 or 14:00–16:00, with the onus on the researcher, having been granted open access, to locate and conduct interviews with each individual participant, rather than this being organised by the prison management. The reason being, if interviews were formally scheduled into a prisoner's daily timetable by prison management (insiders) and subsequently not attended, it would negatively impact their privileges. Although this afforded the participants welcomed autonomy with regard to their participation, the outcome of this was that participants did not always want to participate as agreed (with an outsider), which led to difficulty at times securing consistent participation throughout the research.

Another outcome of no fixed time being set for the interviews by prison management, was that considerable time was spent locating participants in various scheduled workshops that were spread over a large geographical area within the prison. There was also an unexpected period of learning to adapt to the short-term focus of the participants. Despite going into the prison a week in advance of the interviews in order to arrange the meetings face-to-face for the following week, participants would often commit but then forget. This approach was therefore altered to facilitate a brief visit to each participant the day before their scheduled interviews to confirm. Therefore, although the number of interviews secured within each time-point might normally have taken only a matter of days to achieve, securing a sufficient number of interviews and rescheduling with participants usually required daily visits to the prison for up to three weeks.

The experiences of navigating the prison grounds to locate participants also resonated with the mixed feelings of wanting to be both invisible and visible. Wanting to be invisible, as being a clearly identifiable 'outsider' often attracted unsolicited attention from other prisoners with questions on many topics that were not the focus of the research; whilst also needing to be visible to ask questions regarding the whereabouts of participants and the directions to different workshops, particularly at the outset of the research.

The question of whether positioning oneself in the field disturbs and contaminates it as highlighted by Rowe (2014) was brought into sharp focus on two occasions. The first occurred during one of the Active Choices Rugby Programme sessions. The first author would attend the start of each rugby session to record who was there and then leave shortly after. However, on one occasion, two minutes into the session, one of the participants sustained an injury and had to be carried off. As a result, one of the participants shouted towards the first author, "*Hey mister, can you play, c'mon, otherwise we have uneven teams?!*" The chosen research methods were focused on the semi-structured interviews and questionnaires, not on observation of the rugby training sessions, and certainly not on participating in the sessions. However, whilst it was clear that remaining at the prison and participating in the rugby training session that evening was not an option, on a personal level it resulted in the first author feeling compromised and guilty. Compromised in that the refusal to play highlighted the clear research boundaries; and guilty, as many of those participating in the session had volunteered to contribute to the research and yet this was not reciprocated when they asked for assistance. After politely declining, the coach of the session explained researcher participation was not possible due to health and safety reasons and they continued playing with their uneven teams, albeit briefly disappointed.

The second occasion when a research presence acutely disrupted the environment was during qualitative data collection within the prison. Throughout the first two data collection time-points, many of the interviews were conducted in the onsite prison café, with the prison officers granting permission for participants to leave their workshop and return following the interview. On this particular occasion, having approached the workshop gate, the scheduled interview participant was visible, sitting just inside. Having exchanged greetings, he confirmed he was happy to participate in the interview and suggested to conduct the interview in coffee shop. This was agreed on the assumption it would be acceptable, just as it had been on previous occasions. However, the prison officer in the workshop explained that if the participant wanted to be interviewed it would have to take place in a small office space within the workshop, as there were tighter restrictions around the amount of time prisoners could spend in the cafe. This refusal quickly escalated into an angry and heated exchange between the participant and the prison officer about why the interview could not be held in the café, and the prison officer asking the participant to apologise for putting the researcher in an awkward position. The immediate outcome was the participant becoming very frustrated, adopting a verbally aggressive attitude toward the interview, and ultimately declining to participate.

Aware of how difficult it was to secure access and complete interviews, this was a very frustrating scenario and one where the 'outsider' researcher was completely powerless to intervene. It was also directly relatable to the question posed by Earle (2013), that is, how does one resolve the inevitable tensions that arise from positioning oneself in the field, or from being positioned by others on one side or another? With no previous experience to draw on, the approach adopted was to leave and return to the workshop after a short period of time and ask again if the participant would like to do the interview as scheduled. Thankfully, the tension had dissipated and the participant was now calmer and willing to conduct the interview within the workshop office. However, it was observed that the participant was noticeably more negative about his environment and the impact it had on his well-being, than he had been during previous interviews. This experience highlighted the micro-relations researchers must enter into in order to negotiate the access to participants within prisons (Drake & Harvey, 2014), and to never assume one had 'mastered' the workings of the prison as they could change at any time depending on security concerns, regime structures or pressing staff/ prisoner concerns.

Prison often requires men to adopt and project hegemonic prison masculinities (De Viggiani, 2012), and previous reflexive accounts of prison studies have detailed how the role of the researcher can be drawn into stereotypical displays of macho-culture (Ugelvik, 2014). This scenario was experienced when on one occasion, following the completion of a one-to-one interview in a private office, the first author and the participant returned to a group of five young men sitting within a workshop. A cup of tea was offered, and being respectful of the time they had afforded to participate in the research, the offer was accepted. Following a string of questions posed in relation to sport (not unexpected given the research topic), they proceeded to ask a string of personal questions about experience(s) of sex, whilst bragging about their own. Perhaps because of the age difference, (they were 18–24 and the researcher closer to 40), this was not perceived as a threatening 'test' of masculinity, albeit mildly uncomfortable. The researcher politely replied he was happily married man and would not be answering such questions. They laughed and continued the line of questioning and bragging amongst themselves.

Upon reflection, during each prison visit the approach adopted aligned with Goffman's view of impression management (Goffman, 1959). He argued that people engage in 'front stage' and 'back stage' performances in different spheres of life, and when an audience is present, we as social actors behave differently than when there is no audience present. When conducting interviews and focus groups, the researcher's front stage performance was always one of being the empathetic listener – open, accommodating, empathising and non-judgmental. At times, depending on the personal story being told or the category of prisoner being interviewed, this proved challenging. This proved challenging because 1) the experiences which the researchers were empathising with were so far removed from their own reality; and 2) due to an awareness of the nature of offence committed (although this information was never proactively sought), which the back-stage performer might have been actively critical of under different circumstances. To deal with these challenges, the approach was always to be very clear about the role of the researcher – to objectively focus on and enquire about the participant's views of their mental well-being and their perceived benefits from sport-based interventions. The prevailing view of the prison governors met throughout the research was also called to mind often, that the removal of liberties was the punishment for crimes committed, and following that, that every individual had equitable rights to a positive quality of life, both mentally and physically.

Overall, when reflecting on the experiences of conducting prison research, it was considered a privilege to have been granted relatively unique access to these secured institutions. The openness of the participants was always of note, who following relatively short periods of time became familiar with the research; they were candid and up-front regarding their mental well-being. Therefore, although prison research presents a number of unique challenges for intervention design and implementation, and for the broader research process, it is also a unique opportunity to learn and develop research skills whilst adding to a critical knowledge base for improving the mental well-being of those at great risk in our communities.

Conclusion

The Active Choices Rugby Programme for prisoners led to a reported benefit on short-term hedonic mental well-being, through increased positive affect and reduced stress and anger. However, quantitative results did not demonstrate a similar perceived benefit to mental well-being, and overall results did not evidence lasting benefits. Short-term perceived benefits to the basic psychological needs of relatedness and competence during participation were also reported in participant interviews, suggesting a link between these benefits and observed improvements in hedonic well-being. However, direction of causality could not be confirmed. The perceived benefit of the coach-participant relationship, and his role in creating an autonomy supportive environment as measured by the Sport Climate Questionnaire (Deci, 2001) was also a critical contextual factor in facilitating short-term mental well-being.

Quantitative results did not reveal any substantial change in participant satisfaction of basic psychological needs within daily prison environment over the duration of the Active Choices Rugby Programme. This demonstrates that benefits experienced within sporting interventions will not automatically transfer outside of the sporting environment to living in prison, and highlights the need for deliberate programme design and explicit facilitation in order to encourage wider positive benefits.

Programme duration, frequency and participant commitment were all cited as limitations to realising longer-term benefits to mental well-being, as well as sources of participant frustration. Providers of similar programmes and prison management therefore need to work collaboratively to ensure that similar sporting interventions are afforded appropriate time and space alongside other purposeful activities to increase the realisation of positive benefits. Where appropriate time and space are not available to implement multi-week interventions, sport may still be used as a forum through which innovative programmes can seek to provide more direct benefits to mental well-being within a shorter timeframe.

References

Amorose, A. J. (2007). Coaching effectiveness. In M. S. Hagger & N. L. D. Chatzisarantis (Eds.), *Intrinsic motivation and self-determination in exercise and sport* (pp. 209–227). Leeds: Human Kinetics.

Amtmann, J., & Kukay, J. (2016). Fitness changes after an 8-week fitness coaching program at a regional youth detention facility. *Journal of Correctional Health Care, 22*(1), 75–83.

Atkins, M. R., Johnson, D. M., Force, E. C., & Petrie, T. A. (2015). Peers, parents, and coaches, oh my! The relation of the motivational climate to boys' intention to continue in sport. *Psychology of Sport and Exercise, 16*, 170–180.

Australian Institute of Health and Welfare. (2015). *The health of Australia's prisoners 2015*. Canberra, ACT: Australian Institute of Health and Welfare.

Battaglia, C., di Cagno, A., Fiorilli, G., Giombini, A., Borrione, P., Baralla, F., . . . Pigozzi, F. (2014). Participation in a 9-month selected physical exercise programme enhances psychological well-being in a prison population. *Criminal Behaviour and Mental Health, 25*(5), 343–354.

Becker, H. S. (2007), *Writing for social scientists: How to start and finish your thesis, book, or article* (2nd ed.). Chicago, IL: University of Chicago Press.

Bilderbeck, A. C., Farias, M., Brazil, I. A., Jakobowitz, S., & Wikholm, C. (2013). Participation in a 10-week course of yoga improves behavioural control and decreases psychological distress in a prison population. *Journal of Psychiatric Research, 47*(10), 1438–1445.

Blaauw, E., Kerkhof, A. J. F. M., & Roesch, R. (2000). Mental disorders in European Prison Systems. *International Journal of Law and Psychiatry, 23*, 649–663.

Buckaloo, B. J., Krug, K. S., & Nelson, K. B. (2009). Exercise and the low-security inmate changes in depression, stress, and anxiety. *The Prison Journal, 89*(3), 328–343.

Cashin, A., Potter, E., & Butler, T. (2008). The relationship between exercise and hopelessness in prison. *Journal of Psychiatric and Mental Health Nursing, 15*, 66–71.

Chekroud, S. R., Gueorguieva, R., Zheutlin, A. B., Paulus, M., Krumholz, H. M., Krystal, J. H., & Chekroud, A. M. (2018). Association between physical exercise and mental health in 1·2 million individuals in the USA between 2011 and 2015: A cross-sectional study. *The Lancet, 5*, 739–746. https://doi.org/10.1016/S2215-0366(18)30227-X

Coalter, F. (2013). *Sport for development: What game are we playing?* London: Routledge.

DeViggiani, N. (2012). Trying to be something you are not: Masculine performances within a prison setting. *Men and Masculinities, 15*(3), 271–291.

Deci, E. L. (2001). *The sport climate questionnaire*. Retrieved January 2, 2016, from SelfDeterminationTheory.org website http://selfdeterminationtheory.org/pas-sport-climate/

Deci, E. L., & Ryan, R. M. (2000). The "what" and "why" of goal pursuits: Human needs and the self-determination of behavior. *Psychological Inquiry, 11*, 227–268.

Drake, D. H., & Harvey, J. (2014). Performing the role of ethnographer: Processing and managing the emotional dimensions of prison research. *International Journal of Social Research Methodology, 17*(5), 489–501.

Dumont, D. M., Brockmann, B., Dickman, S., Alexander, N., & Rich, J. D. (2012). Public health and the epidemic of incarceration. *Annual Review of Public Health, 33*(1), 325–339.

Durcan, G. (2016). *Mental health and criminal justice: Views from consultations across England & Wales*. Centre for Mental Health.

Earle, R. (2013). What do ethnographers do in prison? *Criminal Justice Matters, 91*(1), 18–19.

Edge, J. (2011). *The reflexive teacher educator: Roots and wings*. New York, NY: Routledge.

Edwards, M. B. (2015). The role of sport in community capacity building: An examination of sport for development research and practice. *Sport Management Review, 18*(1), 6–19.

Fazel, S., Hayes, A. J., Bartellas, K., Clerici, M., & Trestman, R. (2016). Mental health of prisoners: Prevalence, adverse outcomes, and interventions. *The Lancet Psychiatry, 3*(9), 871–881.

Ferszt, G. G., Salgado, D., DeFedele, S., & Leveillee, M. (2009). Houses of healing: A group intervention for grieving women in prison. *The Prison Journal, 89*(1), 46–64.

Fraser, A., Gatherer, A., & Hayton, P. (2009). Mental health in prison: Great difficulties but are there opportunities? *Public Health, 123*, 410–414.

Gallant, D., Sherry, E., & Nicholson, M. (2015). Recreation or rehabilitation? Managing sport for development programs with prison populations. *Sport Management Review, 18*(1), 45–56.

Gillet, N., Vallerand, R. J., Amoura, S., & Baldes, B. (2010). Influence of coaches' autonomy support on athletes' motivation and sport performance: A test of the hierarchical model of intrinsic and extrinsic motivation. *Psychology of Sport and Exercise, 11*, 155–156.

Goffman, E. (1959). *The presentation of self in everyday life*. London: Penguin.

Harner, H., Hanlon, A. L., & Garfinkel, M. (2010). Effect of Iyengar yoga on mental health of incarcerated women: A feasibility study. *Nursing Research, 59*(6), 389–399.

Hayton, P. (2007). Protecting and promoting health in prisons: A settings approach. In L. Møller, H. Stöver, R. Jürgens, A. Gatherer, & H. Nikogosian (Eds.), *Health in prisons: A WHO guide to the essentials in prison health* (pp. 15–20). Copenhagen: WHO Regional Office for Europe.

Hilyer, J. C., Wilson, D. G., Dillon, C., Caro, L., Jenkins, C., Spencer, W. A., . . . Booker, W. (1982). Physical fitness training and counselling as treatment for youthful offenders. *Journal of Counselling Psychology, 29*(3), 292–303.

Huta, V. (2016). Eudaimonic and hedonic orientations: Theoretical considerations and research findings. In *Handbook of eudaimonic well-being* (pp. 215–231). New York: Springer International Publishing.

Jewkes, Y. (2012). Autoethnography and emotion as intellectual resources: Doing prison research differently. *Qualitative Inquiry, 18*(1), 63–75.

Jones, G. J., Edwards, M. B., Bocarro, J. N., Bunds, K. S., & Smith, J. W. (2017). An integrative review of sport-based youth development literature. *Sport in Society, 20*(1), 161–179.

Leberman, S. (2007). Voices behind the walls: Female offenders and experiential learning. *Journal of Adventure Education & Outdoor Learning, 7*, 113–120.

Leigh-Hunt, N., & Perry, A. (2015). A systematic review of interventions for anxiety, depression, and PTSD in adult offenders. *International Journal of Offender Therapy and Comparative Criminology, 59*(7), 701–725.

Lerner, R. M., Dowling, E. M., & Anderson, P. M. (2003). Positive youth development: Thriving as the basis of personhood and civil society. *Applied Developmental Science, 7*(3), 172–180.

Lewis, G., & Meek, R. (2012). Sport and physical education across the secure estate: An exploration of policy and practice. *Criminal Justice Matters, 90*(1), 32–34.

MacNamara, C., & Mannix-McNamara, P. (2014). Placing the promotion of health and well-being on the Irish prison agenda – the complexity of health promotion in Irish prisons. *Irish Journal of Applied Social Studies, 14*(1), 49–59.

Mageau, G. A., & Vallerand, R. J. (2003). The coach-athlete relationship: A motivational model. *Journal of Sports Sciences, 21*, 883–904.

Mann, S. (2016). *The research interview: Reflective practice and reflexivity in research processes*. London: Palgrave Macmillan.

Martin, R. E., Adamson, S., Korchinski, M., Granger-Brown, A., Ramsden, V. R., Buxton, J. A., . . . Hislop, T. G. (2013). Incarcerated women develop a nutrition and fitness program: Participatory research. *International Journal of Prisoner Health, 9*(3), 142–150.

Martos-García, D., Devís-Devís, J., & Sparkes, A. C. (2009). Sport and physical activity in a high security Spanish prison: An ethnographic study of multiple meanings. *Sport, Education and Society, 14*, 77–96.

Meek, R., Champion, N., & Klier, S. (2012). *Fit for release: How sports based learning can help prisoners engage in education, gain employment and desist from crime*. London: Prisoners Education Trust.

Meek, R., & Lewis, G. E. (2014a). The impact of a sports initiative for young men in prison: Staff and participant perspectives. *Journal of Sport & Social Issues, 38*(2), 95–123.

Meek, R., & Lewis, G. E. (2014b). Promoting well-being and desistance through sport and physical activity: The opportunities and barriers experienced by women in English prisons. *Women & Criminal Justice, 24*(2), 151–172.

Nelson, M., Specian, V. L., Tracy, N. C., & DeMello, J. J. (2006). The effects of moderate physical activity on offenders in a rehabilitative program. *Journal of Correctional Education, 57*(4), 276–285.

Parker, A., Meek, R., & Lewis, G. (2014). Sport in a youth prison: Male young offenders' experiences of a sporting intervention. *Journal of Youth Studies, 17*(3), 381–396.

Piché, J., & Walby, K. (2010). Problematizing carceral tours. *The British Journal of Criminology, 50*(3), 570–581.

Reis, H. T., Sheldon, K. M., Gable, S. L., Roscoe, J., & Ryan, R. M. (2000). Daily well-being: The role of autonomy, competence and relatedness. *Personality and Social Psychology Bulletin, 26*, 419–435.

Rowe, A. (2014). Situating the self in prison research: Power, identity, and epistemology. *Qualitative Inquiry, 20*(4), 404–416.

Ryan, R. M., & Deci, E. L. (2001). On happiness and human potentials: A review of research on hedonic and eudaimonic well-being. *Annual Review of Psychology, 52*(1), 141–166.

Sparks, R., Bottoms, A. E., & Hay, W. (1996). *Prisons and the problem of order*. Oxford: Clarendon Press.

Steger, M. F., & Shin, J. Y. (2012). Happiness and meaning in a technological age: A psychological approach. In P. Brey, A. Briggle, & E. Spence (Eds.), *The good life in a technological age* (pp. 92–108). New York, NY: Routledge.

Stewart, D. (2008). *The problems and needs of newly sentenced prisoners: Results from a national survey*. London: Ministry of Justice.

Stewart-Brown, S., & Janmohamed, K. (2008). *Warwick-Edinburgh mental well-being scale*. User guide. Version 1. Retrieved from www.healthscotland.com/documents/2702.aspx

Travis, J., Western, B., & Redburn, F. S. (2014). *The growth of incarceration in the United States: Exploring causes and consequences*. Washington, DC: National Academies Press.

Ugelvik, T. (2014). *Power and resistance in prison: Doing time, doing freedom.* Palgrave Macmillan UK.

Wildeman, C., & Wang, E. A. (2017). Mass incarceration, public health, and widening inequality in the USA. *The Lancet, 389*(10077), 1464–1474.

Williams, D., Collingwood, L., Coles, J., & Schmeer, S. (2015). Evaluating a rugby sport intervention programme for young offenders. *Journal of Criminal Psychology, 5*(1), 51–64.

Woodall, J. (2016). A critical examination of the health promoting prison two decades on. *Critical Public Health, 26*(5), 615–621.

Woods, D., Breslin, G., & Hassan, D. (2017a). A systematic review of the impact of SBIs on the psychological well-being of people in prison. *Mental Health and Physical Activity, 12,* 50–61.

Woods, D., Breslin, G., & Hassan, D. (2017b). Positive collateral damage or purposeful design: How sport-based interventions impact the psychological well-being of people in prison. *Mental Health and Physical Activity, 13,* 152–162.

World Health Organisation. (1999). *Mental health promotion in prison: Report on a WHO meeting.* Copenhagen: World Health Organisation, Regional Office for Europe.

World Health Organisation. (2007). *Health in prisons: A WHO guide to the essential in prison health.* Copenhagen: World Health Organisation.

World Health Organisation. (2007). *Trenčín statement on prisons and mental health.* Copenhagen: World Health Organisation, Regional Office for Europe.

Further reading

Woods, D., Breslin, G., & Hassan, D. (2017). Positive collateral damage or purposeful design: How sport-based interventions impact the psychological well-being of people in prison. *Mental Health and Physical Activity, 13,* 152–162.
(For a more detailed exploration of the role of behavior change theory in prison based sporting interventions aimed at improving mental well-being)

Jones, G. J., Edwards, M. B., Bocarro, J. N., Bunds, K. S., & Smith, J. W. (2017). An integrative review of sport-based youth development literature. *Sport in Society, 20*(1), 161–179.
(This article provides an interesting discussion around the broader topic of sport-based youth development and the need for well-designed strengths based interventions)

Brosens, D., Dury, S., Vertonghen, J., Verté, D., & De Donder, L. (2017). Understanding the barriers to prisoners' participation in sport activities. *The Prison Journal, 97*(2), 181–201.
(This article discusses the barriers to sports participation in prison, despite the potential for benefits to well-being, thus highlighting the challenges to be addressed by all stakeholders)

10

CRITICAL REFLECTION AND THE WAY FORWARD FOR MENTAL HEALTH IN SPORT

Gavin Breslin and Gerard Leavey

Critical reflections: mental health interventions in sport

Public health has much to gain from well-designed and solidly implemented sports-based interventions to improve mental health and wellbeing. However, such interventions may be among the most complex to deliver and evaluate, having to grapple with highly varied contextual challenges of permissions and access, and ensuring fidelity in the training and delivery of the intervention and the expectations and acceptability of those participating, whether they be young people with addiction problems or people in prison.

Our purpose in bringing together some of the key researchers in the field of sports and mental health was to create an informational resource, based on insights gained from practice and experience upon which fellow academics could draw. Importantly, we wanted to offer useful exemplars of contemporary research, theory and practice in order to better prepare practitioners to intervene and support the mental health and wellbeing of those involved in sport. The goal was particularly important as our recent systematic review of mental health interventions in sport concluded that despite its potential for significant public health gains, this area is strikingly underdeveloped and all too often poorly theorised (Breslin, Shannon, Haughey, Donnelly, & Leavey, 2017). In achieving our goal, we hope to further stimulate critical enquiry of the evidence based reflection on current practice and force precision in future development of programmes to improve mental health and wellbeing of those involved sport.

This is the first book of its kind that explores the detailed plans and approaches of those expert practitioners and researchers in this emerging field. The authors of each chapter have provided detailed accounts of how they conducted a needs assessment, determined a suitable framework for programme delivery (or, as in some cases, not!), how they evaluated their programmes, and finally, how they could have undertaken some steps of programme design differently. The authors' reflections illustrate how intervening to raise awareness or improve mental health presents considerable and complex challenges, and even though we should take caution in programme design and delivery, the demand for intervention is high amongst the sporting community.

As highlighted by the chapters, there is considerable heterogeneity in sports settings, populations covered and problems targeted. Each of the chapters offers insights into the challenges faced by researchers in these settings and provides strong critical first-hand experience about how these should be addressed during the development and implementation of sports-based interventions. Key among these is the need for sound theoretical underpinning for the programmes (Baumer and Meek, Chapter 8), i.e. what are the outcomes to be achieved and what is the logic model or theory of change that will optimally facilitate these? Others point to the need for building community-based participatory approaches, ensuring that all the key stakeholders views and attitudes are understood and accommodated within the programme and therefore minimising the later emergence of problematic assumptions and resistance to various aspects of the intervention. For example, Liddle et al. (Chapter 6) in their Ahead of the Game programme, demonstrated that successful implementation depended on a deep engagement and embedding within the participating clubs' cultures and organisational structures. Importantly too, they show the need for pragmatic flexibility in the roll-out of the programme while still retaining fidelity to the model. Similarly, Jones, O'Keeffe and Smith (Chapter 7) adopt a realist evaluation (Pawson & Tilley, 1997; Pawson, 2006) to understand programme contexts and uncover the often 'hidden' mechanisms that undermine successful implementation. Again, central to achieving the goals of any programme is engagement with diverse stakeholders, understanding relationships, and gaining the confidence and involvement of champions within the target setting.

Galante et al. (Chapter 2) adopt a thoughtful and helpful reflective stance within their case study of Anna and the difficulties, both psychological and social, she and others faced in obtaining the desired family support within the programme and legal and ethical issues related to confidentiality. TOPPS has considerable promise in dealing with mental health problems in a non-stigmatising way, but given the stigma associated with such problems, the authors show the importance of evaluation and the requirement for sensitive adaptation of programmes in all settings. TOPPS has also been implemented in a randomised controlled trial showing improvements in mental health outcomes with American college athletes. It remains to be seen however whether TOPPS could be effective outside America where the student athlete support services and culture around college sport varies. Also with a focus on student athletes, the State of Mind Ireland (Chapter 5) shows potential to destigmatise mental health through a short programme. The SOMI programme continues to be adjusted by the authors, to include self-determination theory in its design and evaluation. The authors are currently adjusting the programme for inclusion in prison settings, and for those with disabilities. Nixdorf et al. (Chapter 3) in their comprehensive and detailed exposition of a CBT programme to reduce burnout and depression among junior elite swimmers indicate the need for simply understanding the competing demands and structures of their participants' lives. If not, one assumes, the intervention itself may become a source of anxiety and stress. Lastly, Woods and Breslin (Chapter 9) brought attention to the benefits of the researcher engaging in reflections on their role in the evaluating mental health in sport programmes in prison settings, and the challenges that extreme or unconventional research environments present.

With the detail provided in each chapter and across various populations, we hope you are aided in how to plan, take cognisance of the environment/setting and select an appropriate programme content, then how to implement and evaluate such interventions. To support you further, we make some suggestions for the way forward in mental health in sport, and we strongly recommend that you download the suggested additional readings highlighted in each of the chapters to further support your learning in advancing this field of research, theory and practice.

The way forward for mental health in sport

There has been a recent flourishing of mental health awareness programmes in sport, as evidenced by the Chapters in this book that have shown variation in programme conception, design, measurement, delivery methods, use of theory and evaluation; however, there appears to be little consensus in so far as being able to compare practice (see also Rice et al., 2016; Breslin et al., 2017). Based on this variation, we have launched the development of the *Psychosocial and Policy-Related Approaches to Mental Health Awareness in Sport- Consensus Statement.* The consensus statement is required to assist programme designers, deliverers and policy makers on: (a) definitions of mental health awareness outcomes, and (b) methods for conducting and reporting interventions with sporting population groups (i.e. coaches, athletes and officials). Since the original idea for this book was conceived, several consensus statements in sport have been published that have focused on elite athletes or elite athlete clinical service provision (Schinke, Stambulova, Si, & Moore, 2017; Moesch et al., 2018), overtraining (Meeusen et al., 2013), or that have been specific to a mental disorder (Mountjoy et al., 2014). The authors of these consensus statements are to be commended as each of these statements have their merits, but may not go far enough in addressing mental health awareness programme design, or evaluation in the broader sport population beyond elite athletes. The statements do not take account of the growing interest to promote mental health messages to the public who do not participate in sport but are a keen audience or make up the sporting fan base. A recent evidenced-based *Wellbeing in Sport Policy Action Plan for Northern Ireland* demonstrates how sport environments can be used to improve mental health for all involved in sport and the surrounding community (Sport Northern Ireland, 2018). One action from the plan of which there are 19 and 49 time bound delivery outputs across five years highlights the need for consensus in evaluating the evidence for mental health awareness in sports clubs. Indeed, in the development of the Action Plan the Working Group in Mental Health and

Wellbeing in and Through Sport highlighted the absence of available research in the form of systematic reviews to guide policy creation. This led to the group commissioning their own research. After the group commissioned their own review (Breslin et al., 2017), the lack of consistency between study methods and measures made drawing conclusions and importantly offering scientific evidence very difficult without being cautious in the absence of evidence. With the lack of evidence and with a growing body of evidence emerging, this is the time to encourage consensus is how we go about promoting mental health and supporting those involved in sport. Some reasons for the development of a consensus statement were shared recently at a symposium in Dublin Ireland, these are represented in Box 10.1 below:

BOX 10.1   SEVEN REASONS WHY A CONSENSUS STATEMENT ON MENTAL HEALTH IN SPORT IS REQUIRED?

1   There has been *increasing recognition* of mental health issues in sport
2   Growth of *sport-based* mental health awareness programmes
3   Variation in programme content, design, theory and evaluation
4   Uncertain what *outcomes* or *impact* programmes are having
5   Variations in *measurement tools* selected- and variation in *validation and reliability* of these tools
6   What is the *minimal training* for sport and exercise psychologists or *club officers* in supporting or guiding programme content development?
7   What recommendations can we provide *policy makers?*

In response to the gap in recommendations to aid policy makers, the proposed consensus statement builds on previous statements, with a specific focus on determining effective reporting of mental health awareness programmes for effective policy design (Breslin et al., under review; Sport Northern Ireland, 2018). The key objectives of the consensus statement are: (1) To define mental health awareness constructs for inclusion in programmes in sport; (2) To identify valid measures for use in intervention studies with the sporting population, and establish standards for data collection, analysis and reporting procedures and; (3) To provide policy makers with guidance for implementing awareness programmes in sport.

In the development of the consensus statement, a two-day meeting of experts was facilitated, comprising international stakeholders representing various groups (e.g. research, policy, sporting organisations, mental health charities, safeguarding, etc). The first was at a satellite symposium at the European College of Sports Science (ECSS) Congress in Dublin, Ireland (July 2018), and the second was at the British Psychological Society's Division of Sport and Exercise Psychology, Annual Conference in Belfast (December 2018). Representatives were from the following groups: (1) Professionals with experience in sports teams; (2) Sports federations and organisations; (3) Researchers in the field of sports; (4) Editorial members of scientific journals, and; (5) Policy makers in sport.

Prior to the first meeting, a series of statements were produced in a draft version of a statement and distributed online to all attendees and other recommended persons who could not attend. The Delphi method was used to determine the adequacy of the statements for inclusion in the final document. A revision was then prepared, and a summary was shared requesting further views from a wider audience during a six-week period. All remarks received were reviewed by two lead authors and, if applicable, were incorporated into revisions of the manuscript, where a suggested change was not incorporated, a written explanation was prepared and distributed to group members. After the final iteration, all members of the group were asked to confirm their agreement with the final consensus statement that was then published. The consensus statement provides evidence and theory-based guidance on awareness definitions, programme content, and methodological approaches for the design, implementation and evaluation of mental health awareness programmes in sport.

Finally, we would like to thank each of the authors for sharing their experiences and contributing to the book. We also wish that as well as developing an appreciation for the endeavours made by the authors in bringing about positive changes to many people's lives, you apply what you have learned into your own practice, and with an open mind reflect on your practice for the improvement of mental health of those involved in sport.

References

Breslin, G., Shannon, S., Haughey, T., Donnelly, P., & Leavey, G. (2017). A systematic review of interventions to increase awareness of mental health and well-being in athletes, coaches and officials. *Systematic Reviews 31*, 6(1), 177. doi: 10.1186/s13643-017-0568-6

Breslin, G., Smith, A., Cotterill, S., Donnelly, P., & Donohue, B. (under review). Psychosocial and policy-related approaches to mental health awareness in sport: Charting the path towards a consensus statement. *Frontiers in Public Health*.

Meeusen, R., Duclos, M., Foster, C., Fry, A., Gleeson, M., Nieman, D., Raglin, J., Rietjens, G., Steinacker, J., & Urhausen, A. (2013). Prevention, diagnosis and treatment of the overtraining syndrome: Joint consensus statement of the European College of Sport Science (ECSS) and the American College of Sports Medicine (ACSM). *European Journal of Sport Science, 13*(1), 1–24. doi: 10.1080/17461391.2012.730061

Moesch, K., Kenttä, G., Kleinert, J., Quignon-Fleuret, C., Cecil, S., & Bertollo, M. (2018). FEPSAC position statement: Mental health disorders in elite athletes and models of service provision. *Psychology of Sport and Exercise, 38*, 61–71.

Mountjoy, M., Sundgot-Borgen, J., Burke, L., et al. (2014). The IOC consensus statement: Beyond the female athlete triad—Relative Energy Deficiency in Sport (RED-S). *British Journal Sports Med, 48*, 491–497.

Pawson, R. (2006). *Evidence-based policy: A realist perspective*. London: Sage Publications.

Pawson, R., & Tilley, N. (1997). *Realistic evaluation*. London: Sage Publications.

Rice, S, M., Purcell R., De Silva S., et al. (2016). The mental health of elite athletes: A narrative systematic review. *Sports Medicine, 46*, 1333–1353.

Schinke, R. J., Stambulova, N. B., Si, G., & Moore, Z. (2017). International society of sport psychology position stand: Athletes' mental health, performance, and development. *International Journal of Sport and Exercise Psychology*. doi:10.1080/1612197X.2017.1295557

Sport Northern Ireland (2018). *Wellbeing in sport action plan 2018-2023*. Retrieved October 16, 2018, from www.communities-ni.gov.uk/publications/wellbeing-sport-action-plan-2018-2023

INDEX

Note: Page numbers in *italics* indicate figures and page numbers in **bold** indicate tables on the corresponding pages.